Financial Cooperatives and Local Development

This book examines the opportunities opened up for financial cooperatives by the recent financial crisis, and explores the role of these institutions in promoting and sustaining local development. The global financial crisis has not only shown the limits of the mainstream theory of markets and rational expectations, but has also generated a great deal of disillusionment with the banking system and underlined the importance of a healthy society for the welfare of the individual. Consequently, new and innovative ways of providing finance are needed, especially for strengthening the development of local societies.

The international contributors to this volume combine theoretical insights with empirical investigations of the relationship between financial cooperative models and local development. The authors revisit the finance and development literature to situate the key characteristics of cooperative credit in a dynamic and demanding context, and then outline the critical path that financial cooperatives should follow to provide banking services and products that are both efficient and vital for local development. They argue that the current context provides ample opportunities for meaningful and innovative financial intermediation, and they explain why cooperative banks' strategic development should reinforce their original values and strengthen their links with local societies in order to be successful.

Researchers, policymakers, and practitioners will find in this book:

- the necessary tools and approaches to reassess and compare the philosophy and performance of stakeholder-oriented banks with profit-maximizing banks;
- case studies of the proactive role played by cooperative banks in promoting and supporting the interests and development of local societies;
- insights into the functions of cooperative banking that surpass the supply of savings and the selection of efficient investments;
- a critical approach to microfinance institutions that sheds light not only on their benefits, but also on the shortcomings that arise in addressing poverty and financial inclusion in highly deprived communities.

Silvio Goglio is Associate Professor of Political Economy at the University of Trento, Italy, and Coordinator of the Research Area in Cooperatives and Development at Euricse, Trento, Italy.

Yiorgos Alexopoulos is Researcher at the Agricultural University of Athens, Greece, and a Research Fellow at Euricse, Trento, Italy. He is also head of the Scientific Committee of the Greek Institute of Cooperation and is an advisor to the Greek Association of Cooperative Banks on institutional and development issues.

Routledge studies in development economics

1 **Economic Development in the Middle East**
Rodney Wilson

2 **Monetary and Financial Policies in Developing Countries**
Growth and stabilization
Akhtar Hossain and Anis Chowdhury

3 **New Directions in Development Economics**
Growth, environmental concerns and government in the 1990s
Edited by Mats Lundahl and Benno J. Ndulu

4 **Financial Liberalization and Investment**
Kanhaya L. Gupta and Robert Lensink

5 **Liberalization in the Developing World**
Institutional and economic changes in Latin America, Africa and Asia
Edited by Alex E. Fernández Jilberto and André Mommen

6 **Financial Development and Economic Growth**
Theory and experiences from developing countries
Edited by Niels Hermes and Robert Lensink

7 **The South African Economy**
Macroeconomic prospects for the medium term
Finn Tarp and Peter Brixen

8 **Public Sector Pay and Adjustment**
Lessons from five countries
Edited by Christopher Colclough

9 **Europe and Economic Reform in Africa**
Structural adjustment and economic diplomacy
Obed O. Mailafia

10 **Post-apartheid Southern Africa**
Economic challenges and policies for the future
Edited by Lennart Petersson

11 **Financial Integration and Development**
Liberalization and reform in sub-Saharan Africa
Ernest Aryeetey and Machiko Nissanke

12 **Regionalization and Globalization in the Modern World Economy**
Perspectives on the Third World and transitional economies
Edited by Alex E. Fernández Jilberto and André Mommen

13 **The African Economy**
Policy, institutions and the future
Steve Kayizzi-Mugerwa

14 **Recovery from Armed Conflict in Developing Countries**
Edited by Geoff Harris

15 **Small Enterprises and Economic Development**
The dynamics of micro and small enterprises
Carl Liedholm and Donald C. Mead

16 **The World Bank**
New agendas in a changing world
Michelle Miller-Adams

17 **Development Policy in the Twenty-First Century**
Beyond the post-Washington consensus
Edited by Ben Fine, Costas Lapavitsas and Jonathan Pincus

18 **State-Owned Enterprises in the Middle East and North Africa**
Privatization, performance and reform
Edited by Merih Celasun

19 **Finance and Competitiveness in Developing Countries**
Edited by José María Fanelli and Rohinton Medhora

20 **Contemporary Issues in Development Economics**
Edited by B.N. Ghosh

21 **Mexico Beyond NAFTA**
Edited by Martín Puchet Anyul and Lionello F. Punzo

22 **Economies in Transition**
A guide to China, Cuba, Mongolia, North Korea and Vietnam at the turn of the twenty-first century
Ian Jeffries

23 **Population, Economic Growth and Agriculture in Less Developed Countries**
Nadia Cuffaro

24 **From Crisis to Growth in Africa?**
Edited by Mats Lundal

25 **The Macroeconomics of Monetary Union**
An analysis of the CFA franc zone
David Fielding

26 **Endogenous Development**
Networking, innovation, institutions and cities
Antonio Vasquez-Barquero

27 **Labour Relations in Development**
Edited by Alex E. Fernández Jilberto and Marieke Riethof

28 **Globalization, Marginalization and Development**
Edited by S. Mansoob Murshed

29 **Programme Aid and Development**
Beyond conditionality
Howard White and Geske Dijkstra

30 **Competitiveness Strategy in Developing Countries**
A manual for policy analysis
Edited by Ganeshan Wignaraja

31 **The African Manufacturing Firm**
An analysis based on firm surveys in sub-Saharan Africa
Dipak Mazumdar and Ata Mazaheri

32 **Trade Policy, Growth and Poverty in Asian Developing Countries**
Edited by Kishor Sharma

33 **International Competitiveness, Investment and Finance**
A case study of India
Edited by A. Ganesh Kumar, Kunal Sen and Rajendra R. Vaidya

34 **The Pattern of Aid Giving**
The impact of good governance on development assistance
Eric Neumayer

35 **New International Poverty Reduction Strategies**
Edited by Jean-Pierre Cling, Mireille Razafindrakoto and François Roubaud

36 **Targeting Development**
Critical perspectives on the millennium development goals
Edited by Richard Black and Howard White

37 **Essays on Balance of Payments Constrained Growth**
Theory and evidence
Edited by J.S.L. McCombie and A.P. Thirlwall

38 **The Private Sector After Communism**
New entrepreneurial firms in transition economies
Jan Winiecki, Vladimir Benacek and Mihaly Laki

39 **Information Technology and Development**
A new paradigm for delivering the internet to rural areas in developing countries
Jeffrey James

40 **The Economics of Palestine**
Economic policy and institutional reform for a viable Palestine state
Edited by David Cobham and Nu'man Kanafani

41 **Development Dilemmas**
The methods and political ethics of growth policy
Melvin Ayogu and Don Ross

42 **Rural Livelihoods and Poverty Reduction Policies**
Edited by Frank Ellis and H. Ade Freeman

43 **Beyond Market-Driven Development**
Drawing on the experience of Asia and Latin America
Edited by Makoto Noguchi and Costas Lapavitsas

44 **The Political Economy of Reform Failure**
Edited by Mats Lundahl and Michael L. Wyzan

45 Overcoming Inequality in Latin America
Issues and challenges for the twenty-first century
Edited by Ricardo Gottschalk and Patricia Justino

46 Trade, Growth and Inequality in the Era of Globalization
Edited by Kishor Sharma and Oliver Morrissey

47 Microfinance
Perils and prospects
Edited by Jude L. Fernando

48 The IMF, World Bank and Policy Reform
Edited by Alberto Paloni and Maurizio Zanardi

49 Managing Development
Globalization, economic restructuring and social policy
Edited by Junji Nakagawa

50 Who Gains from Free Trade?
Export-led growth, inequality and poverty in Latin America
Edited by Rob Vos, Enrique Ganuza, Samuel Morley, and Sherman Robinson

51 Evolution of Markets and Institutions
A study of an emerging economy
Murali Patibandla

52 The New Famines
Why famines exist in an era of globalization
Edited by Stephen Devereux

53 Development Ethics at work
Explorations – 1960–2002
Denis Goulet

54 Law Reform in Developing and Transitional States
Edited by Tim Lindsey

55 The Assymetries of Globalization
Edited by Pan A. Yotopoulos and Donato Romano

56 Ideas, Policies and Economic Development in the Americas
Edited by Esteban Pérez-Caldentey and Matias Vernengo

57 European Union Trade Politics and Development
Everything but arms unravelled
Edited by Gerrit Faber and Jan Orbie

58 Membership Based Organizations of the Poor
Edited by Martha Chen, Renana Jhabvala, Ravi Kanbur and Carol Richards

59 The Politics of Aid Selectivity
Good governance criteria in World Bank, U.S. and Dutch development assistance
Wil Hout

60 Economic Development, Education and Transnational Corporations
Mark Hanson

61 **Achieving Economic Development in the Era of Globalization**
Shalendra Sharma

62 **Sustainable Development and Free Trade**
Shawkat Alam

63 **The Impact of International Debt Relief**
Geske Dijkstra

64 **Europe's Troubled Region**
Economic development, institutional reform and social welfare in the Western Balkans
William Bartlett

65 **Work, Female Empowerment and Economic Development**
Sara Horrell, Hazel Johnson and Paul Mosley

66 **The Chronically Poor in Rural Bangladesh**
Livelihood constraints and capabilities
Pk. Md. Motiur Rahman, Noriatsu Matsui and Yukio Ikemoto

67 **Public-Private Partnerships in Health Care in India**
Lessons for developing countries
A. Venkat Raman and James Warner Björkman

68 **Rural Poverty and Income Dynamics in Asia and Africa**
Edited by Keijiro Otsuka, Jonna P. Estudillo and Yasuyuki Sawada

69 **Microfinance: A Reader**
David Hulme and Thankom Arun

70 **Aid and International NGOs**
Dirk-Jan Koch

71 **Development Macroeconomics**
Essays in memory of Anita Ghatak
Edited by Subrata Ghatak and Paul Levine

72 **Taxation in a Low Income Economy**
The case of Mozambique
Channing Arndt and Finn Tarp

73 **Labour Markets and Economic Development**
Edited by Ravi Kanbur and Jan Svejnar

74 **Economic Transitions to Neoliberalism in Middle-Income Countries**
Policy dilemmas, crises, mass resistance
Edited by Alfedo Saad-Filho and Galip L. Yalman

75 **Latecomer Development**
Innovation and knowledge for economic growth
Banji Oyelaran-Oyeyinka and Padmashree Gehl Sampath

76 **Trade Relations between the EU and Africa**
Development, challenges and options beyond the Cotonou Agreement
Edited by Yenkong Ngangjoh-Hodu and Francis A.S.T. Matambalya

77 **The Comparative Political Economy of Development**
Africa and South Asia
Edited by Barbara Harriss-White and Judith Heyer

78 **Credit Cooperatives in India**
Past, present and future
Biswa Swarup Misra

79 **Development Economics in Action (2nd edition)**
A study of economic policies in Ghana
Tony Killick

80 **The Multinational Enterprise in Developing Countries**
Local versus global logic
Edited by Rick Molz, Cătălin Ratiu and Ali Taleb

81 **Monetary and Financial Integration in West Africa**
Temitope W. Oshikoya

82 **Reform and Development in China**
What can China offer the developing world?
Edited by Ho-Mou Wu and Yang L. Yao

83 **Towards New Developmentalism**
Market as means rather than master
Edited by Shahrukh Rafi Khan and Jens Christiansen

84 **Culture, Institutions, and Development**
New insights into an old debate
Edited by Jean-Philippe Platteau and Robert Peccoud

85 **Assessing Prospective Trade Policy**
Methods applied to EU-ACP economic partnership agreements
Edited by Oliver Morrissey

86 **Social Protection for Africa's Children**
Edited by Sudhanshu Handa, Stephen Devereux and Douglas Webb

87 **Energy, Bio Fuels and Development**
Comparing Brazil and the United States
Edited by Edmund Amann, Werner Baer and Don Coes

88 **Value Chains, Social Inclusion and Economic Development**
Contrasting theories and realities
Edited by A.H.J. (Bert) Helmsing and Sietze Vellema

89 **Market Liberalism, Growth, and Economic Development in Latin America**
Edited by Gerardo Angeles Castro, Ignacio Perrotini-Hernández and Humberto Ríos-Bolivar

90 **South-South Globalization**
Challenges and opportunities for development
Edited by S. Mansoob Murshed, Pedro Goulart and Leandro A. Serino

91 **Trade Infrastructure and Economic Development**
Edited by Olu Ajakaiye and T. Ademola Oyejide

92 **Microcredit and International Development**
Contexts, achievements and challenges
Edited by Farhad Hossain, Christopher Rees and Tonya Knight-Millar

93 Business Regulation and Non-State Actors
Whose standards? Whose development?
Edited by Darryl Reed and Peter Utting and Ananya Mukherjee Reed

94 Public Expenditures for Agricultural and Rural Development in Africa
Edited by Tewodaj Mogues and Samuel Benin

95 The Global Economic Crisis and the Developing World
Implications and prospects for recovery and growth
Edited by Ashwini Deshpande and Keith Nurse

96 The Microfinance Impact
Ranjula Bali Swain

97 Gendered Insecurities, Health and Development in Africa
Edited by Howard Stein and Amal Hassan Fadlalla

98 Financial Cooperatives and Local Development
Edited by Silvio Goglio and Yiorgos Alexopoulos

Financial Cooperatives and Local Development

Edited by Silvio Goglio and
Yiorgos Alexopoulos

Routledge
Taylor & Francis Group
LONDON AND NEW YORK

First published 2013
by Routledge
2 Park Square, Milton Park, Abingdon, Oxon OX14 4RN

Simultaneously published in the USA and Canada
by Routledge
711 Third Avenue, New York, NY 10017

Routledge is an imprint of the Taylor & Francis Group, an informa business

British Library Cataloguing in Publication Data
A catalogue record for this book is available from the British Library

Library of Congress Cataloging in Publication Data
Financial cooperatives and local development / edited by Silvio Goglio and Yiorgos Alexopoulos.
p. cm.
Includes bibliographical references and index.
1. Financial institutions. 2. Banks and banking. 3. Sustainable development. I. Goglio, Silvio, 1948– II. Alexopoulos, Yiorgos.
HG173.F4893 2012
334'.2–dc23 2012003733

ISBN: 978-0-415-69837-5 (hbk)
ISBN: 978-0-203-10534-4 (ebk)

Typeset in Times New Roman
by Wearset Ltd, Boldon, Tyne and Wear

MIX
Paper from responsible sources
FSC® C004839
FSC www.fsc.org

Printed and bound in Great Britain by
TJ International Ltd, Padstow, Cornwall

Contents

Figures and tables

Figures

Tables

Contributors

Mokbul Morshed Ahmad is Associate Professor of Regional and Rural Development Planning at the School of Environment, Resources and Development, Asian Institute of Technology, Thailand. His research interests include rural development, non-governmental organizations, and community development.

Yiorgos Alexopoulos is Researcher at the Agricultural University of Athens and a Research Fellow at Euricse, Trento, Italy. He is head of the Scientific Committee of the Greek Institute of Cooperation, and is an advisor to the Greek Association of Cooperative Banks on institutional and development issues. His research interests include rural and local development, social economy, and local and cooperative credit.

Amélie Artis is a researcher at Sciences PO Grenoble, France. She has a PhD in Economics from Pierre-Mendès-France University, and her current research focuses on social banking and financial regulation, and on cooperatives and non-profit organizations.

Miriam Del Rocío Arredondo Barrera is an MSc student in Public Administration at the Monterrey Institute of Technology and Higher Education, Mexico. She has a BSc in International Finance from the University of Monterrey, and her interests include microfinance, community development, and social responsibility.

Holger Blisse is a research assistant in the Department of Business Administration/Cooperative Studies at the University of Vienna. His research interests include cooperatives, foundations, and social banking and finance.

Elisabetta De Antoni is Associate Professor of Political Economy at the University of Trento, Italy. Her main research fields are macroeconomics, monetary theory, and the history of economic thought. Currently, she is working on heterodox monetary theories after Keynes.

Stefano Di Colli is Economist at the Research Department of Italian Federation of Co-operative Credit Banks (Federcasse) and Adjunct Professor of Financial Economics at the University of Teramo, Italy. He has a PhD in Money, Banking, and Finance and an MA in Economics from the University of Rome 'Tor Vergata'.

David Eduardo De la Cerda Garza is a graduate student in International Finance in the Department of Business at the University of Monterrey, Mexico. His research focuses on microfinance as a model for development in the poverty zones, specifically in the north of Mexico.

Giovanni Ferri is Professor of Political Economy at the University of Bari, Italy, and a member of the Banking Stakeholder Group at the European Banking Authority. He has worked at the Bank of Italy and the World Bank, consulted for several governments, and published extensively on financial instability and the finance-development nexus.

Cynthia Giagnocavo is Research Fellow at the University of Almería, Spain, in the Faculty of Economics and Business Studies and works in the field of financial cooperatives, agricultural cooperatives, and the social economy. A former banking and finance lawyer with a background in environmental studies, her work is interdisciplinary with a focus on sustainable economies and business structures.

Silvio Goglio is Associate Professor of Political Economy at the University of Trento, Italy, and Coordinator of the Research Area in Cooperatives and Development at Euricse, Trento. His research interests include collective efficiency and local governance, institutional changes and economic performance, local and cooperative credit, and regional development.

Morayma Lizbeth Martin González has a BSc in International Finance and has worked on several community development projects in Mexico. Her interests include finance and social development.

Paul A. Jones is Senior Lecturer and head of the Research Unit for Financial Inclusion at Liverpool John Moores University, UK. His research interests are mainly in the fields of financial services for people on low incomes, money and advice, and the development of cooperatives and credit unions.

Panu Kalmi is Professor of Economics at the University of Vaasa, Finland. His research interests include financial markets and institutions, and comparative ownership structures in banking.

Theodoros A. Katerinakis is Adjunct Faculty and a PhD candidate in the Department of Culture and Communication at Drexel University, USA, and he has had a career in cooperatives. His research interests include cooperative banking, social network analysis and ethics, regional and island economics and development, and aviation communication.

Eeva Kerola is Researcher and a PhD student at the Aalto University School of Economics, Finland. Her research interests are in the fields of banking, financial economics, and monetary policy.

Rosario Laratta is Associate Professor of Community Policy and Management at Meiji University, Japan. He has a PhD in Sociology from Warwick University, UK, and widely published comparative research on non-profit organizations.

Juan S. Lopez is head of the Research Department of the Italian Federation of Co-operative Credit Banks (Federcasse). He has an MPhil from the Social Policy Research Unit of the University of Sussex, UK.

Anita Marchesini has an MA in Economy and Management of Cooperative Enterprises and Non-Profit Organizations. She currently works in the fiscal division of a consumer cooperative.

Sachiko Nakagawa is Associate Professor of Social Economy in the Faculty of Policy Management, Keio University, Japan. She has a PhD in Management of Social Enterprises and Nonprofit Organizations from Keio University and has done research on social enterprises and social inclusion, focusing on work integration social enterprises for the disabled.

Luis Fernández-Revuelta Pérez is Professor of Finance and Accounting at the University of Almería, Spain. He has held the University of Almería Chair in Agribusiness of the Financial Cooperative Cajamar. His main research interests are management accounting in different types of organizational forms.

Alan J. Robb is Adjunct Professor in the Master of Management—Co-operatives and Credit Unions programme at the Sobey School of Business, Saint Mary's University, Canada. He is also an independent financial commentator and consultant to cooperatives on accounting, ethics, and governance issues based in Christchurch, New Zealand.

María de la Luz Bravo Santillán has a PhD in Administration from the Autonomous University of Aguascalientes, México. Her research focuses on management control systems, and she designed a Balanced Scorecard for small- and medium-sized enterprises.

James H. Smith is a lecturer in the Master of Management—Co-operatives and Credit Unions programme at the Sobey School of Business, Saint Mary's University, Canada. He teaches Advanced Co-operative Financial Analysis and Management and is a CPA whose specialty and research interests are in the taxation of cooperatives and the cost of equity capital to cooperatives.

David Uclés Aguilera is an economist and Director of Studies at the Fundación Cajamar in Almería, Spain.

J. Tom Webb is Program Manager of the international Master of Management—Co-operatives and Credit Unions programme at the Sobey School of Business, Saint Mary's University, Canada. His research areas include cooperative economics, cooperative accounting, regulation of cooperatives, cooperative business solutions, and demutualization.

Abbreviations and acronyms

ABCD	asset-based community development
ABCUL	Association of British Credit Unions Limited
ADIE	Association pour le Droit à l'Initiative Économique
ASA	Association for Social Advancement (Bangladesh)
BRAC	Bangladesh Rehabilitation Assistance Committee
CBC	Co-operative Bank of Chania (Hellas)
CESYF	Centro para la Solidaridad y Filantropía (Mexico)
CUCA	Credit Union Current Account
Euricse	European Institute on Cooperative and Social Enterprises
FCP	Fonds Commun de Placement
Fed	Federal Reserve System of the United States
FINCA	Foundation for International Community Assistance
FSCS	Financial Services Compensation Scheme (UK)
GDP	gross domestic product
HHI	Herfindahl–Hirschman Index
ICA	International Co-operative Alliance
IPA	Inclusive Partnership Approach
KYC	know your customer
M&As	mergers and acquisitions
MFI	microfinance institution
MRRU	Microfinance Research and Reference Unit (Bangladesh)
NGO	non-governmental organization
OECD	Organisation for Economic Co-operation and Development
SCP	Structure-Conduct-Performance
SIP	System of Institutional Protection
SME	small- and medium-sized enterprises

Introduction

Cooperative finance and sustainable local development

Yiorgos Alexopoulos and Silvio Goglio

Nowadays economies are increasingly characterized by a growing proportion of intangible assets, not only of products, but also of—and in some cases in—productive factors. This new reality has profound consequences for the definition of capital and necessitates a reconsideration of how intangible factors, such as knowledge, social capital, and entrepreneurship, interact in the production process and influence the systemic mechanisms that affect collective efficiency. Consequently, there is a pressing need for a broad rethinking of the tools of local policy and development strategies.

Although such views are gaining ground among theorists and practitioners, a great number of those who attempt to design and undertake development programmes and evaluations still seem most comfortable dealing with tangible outcomes. This approach is linked to the fact that in most cases they have been trained to think in terms of top-down models: the style and skill requirements for a more qualitative and process-oriented approach are very different and more likely to be held by people trained in disciplines other than accounting and economics. However, the dominance of power structures created by individuals who share common academic and professional backgrounds is a potentially powerful force for maintaining the status quo in how development should be pursued. In sum, we believe that a radical interpretation of participatory development and evaluation is in conflict with the prevailing ethos of developmental managerialism.

This book builds on the premise that development should be regarded as a cultural as well as an economic phenomenon since the objectives, productive forces, and the impact of development must also be considered. A sustainable development process should take into account positive and negative externalities that affect the overall objectives of development. This process involves not only the conservation of resources, but also an understanding of their valorization, especially of those factors of production such as social and human capital and the environment. This objective, however, might prove difficult to achieve if local actors do not assume direct responsibility for the projects and the risk of selecting investments and stimulating innovations in a given local system. Following the principle of vertical subsidiarity, local actors should delegate as little as possible of these tasks to higher levels. A virtuous relation between the local governance of development and its sustainability needs active local actors responsible for their decisions. Pivotal in this regard is the growing importance of local *governance*, which challenges the conventional—but increasingly obsolete—emphasis on local *government*.

The growing importance of intangible assets is closely related to the evolution of production and competition, which is increasingly characterized by the pursuit of flexibility and quality. These goals require a continuous process of innovation and production of knowledge that, in turn, solicits cooperative capacity, not only inside and among firms, but also between public and private actors. In this dialectical environment, a new entrepreneurial philosophy is needed. Since competition increasingly challenges territorial systems, a region's efficiency depends on its ability to improve the interaction of its social, cultural, political, and economic components. Hence, the role of public and collective actions that aim to produce external positive economies and minimize the production of negative economies becomes critical (Goglio 1999). Following this approach, the task of any expression of collective action, and not only of public administration, entails both stimulating the commitment to patterns of cooperation that are considered strategic for development and systemic efficiency on the one hand, and preventing behaviours that deplete or dissipate local physical, human, and social resources on the other.

It is essential that local development should not be considered a homogeneous phenomenon in terms of either the patterns or policies that facilitate it. Obviously, there are common features in different patterns of development, but they are combined in different proportions and coexist with a territorially defined array of factors. Economic actions, outcomes, and institutions are affected by the personal relations among actors and their networks. Trust, social relationships, and social control through norms and values as well as the common experiences of agents are important factors for explaining economic activity, which is specific for every case considered (Granovetter 1990).

Since national and regional development is an interaction, an amalgam, and not a summing up of different patterns of local development, many supposed homogeneities disappear under analytic scrutiny. Hence, it is useful to speak of biodiversity in the patterns of development that stem from the biodiversity of territories, resource endowments, and the availability of critical factors, such as knowledge and social capital, whose appropriateness and functional efficiency determine the final outcome.

Credit is one such critical factor and can be supplied through several different channels. Nevertheless, it is important to underline that finance and banking play an instrumental role, and when financial profit does not stem from the promotion of real development and does not represent net product, it should not be considered proper profit; it is merely a form of redistribution that seldom benefits the weakest participants in an economic system or marginal areas and activities. Moreover, since the diversified supply of credit is important for any economic system, its actors should be encouraged and supported by appropriate normative frames. In order to understand the role of banking and finance in the biodiversity of local systems, two issues need to be addressed: the role of credit and finance in development and the role of banks in the development agenda of every territory.

Financial systems and development

A number of authors have investigated the relationship between financial development and economic growth, dealing with different aspects of this relationship at both the theoretical and empirical levels (Gurley and Shaw 1955; Patrick 1966; Goldsmith 1969; McKinnon 1973; and Shaw 1973).[1] Some studies have attempted to determine whether financial development leads to higher rates of growth and analyse the strength of this relationship. Others have focused on identifying the channels of transmission from financial intermediation to growth. What emerges from this research is that 'finance contributes to growth to the extent that it increases the volume of development or improves its allocation' (De la Fuente and Marin 1996, 272). The original contributions to this literature agree that there is a strong positive correlation between the extent of financial development and economic growth. However, they emphasize different channels of transmission. Goldsmith (1969) focuses mainly on the relationship between financial development and the efficiency of investment, while McKinnon (1973) and Shaw (1973) emphasize the role played by financial liberalization in increasing savings and, hence, investment.

Research on the relationship between financial development and growth has been inspired by the rapidly expanding endogenous growth literature (e.g. Williamson 1986; Bernanke and Gertler 1989). By focusing on cases where the marginal product of capital always remains positive, this literature provides a framework of analysis in which financial markets affect long-run, and not just transitional, growth. Models along these lines by Bencivenga and Smith (1991) and Greenwood and Jovanovic (1990) emphasize how the creation and growth of financial institutions lead to a positive relationship between financial intermediation and economic growth. Most of these studies emphasize the role of financial intermediation in improving the efficiency—rather than the volume—of investment (Bencivenga and Smith 1991; De Gregorio and Guidotti 1995; Levine 1997).

In other words, credit may affect development in two ways. The so-called Hicksian channel involves the intermediation of saving performed by the financial system through the diversification of risks and the reduction of transaction costs. This intermediation provokes an increase in the saving rate and of the fraction of savings channelled into investment, directing investments to alternatives with greater returns. The so-called Schumpeterian channel operates by screening entrepreneurs and certifying their quality, thereby promoting specialization and the development of entrepreneurship, as well as the adoption of new technologies. Theoretical and empirical studies suggest that the best allocation of credit among alternative projects and careful selection of investments according to their marginal productivity—i.e. the Schumpeterian channel—prevails over the push effect on capital accumulation exerted by the greater supply of liquidity—i.e. the Hicksian channel.[2] However, these objectives are more easily achieved if the financial system can establish continuous relationships with its clients.

More specifically, De Gregorio and Guidotti (1995) examined whether financial development positively affects economic growth via increases in the volume of investment, in the efficiency of investments, or in both. Their contribution is important since for the first time it provided evidence on the direction of the relationship between financial development and investment. Some of their main results were as follows (De Gregorio and Guidotti 1995, 443):

- They found a positive effect of financial development on the long-run growth of real per capita GDP, and it was particularly strong in middle and low-income countries.
- They suggest that the effect of financial intermediation on growth 'is due mainly to impact on the efficiency of investment rather than its volume ... and the relative importance of improved efficiency of investment is higher in low and middle income countries than in high income countries'.
- They stress the importance of the quality of intermediation as a critical factor along with the magnitude of the level of financial intermediation.

These findings are consistent with Levine's observation that 'the development of financial markets and institutions is a critical and inextricable part of the growth process' and adequate comprehension of long-period development is not possible until the evolution and functioning of financial systems have been understood. This conclusion, however, must be drawn 'hesitantly and with ample qualifications' (Levine 1997, 688–9). In our opinion there are four reasons for this.

First, financial systems and their functions should not be regarded independently of the ongoing pattern of development and the socio-political and economic context in which they operate. As long as one does not have the opportunity to study innovative approaches searching for the most appropriate, territorially determined developmental course, the mechanism of that reciprocal interaction will remain ambivalent and it will be difficult to identify in any paradigm the precise direction of the causal connections. Financial development does not seem to have the same impact on every sector and firm, and consequently does not on all territories. Since markets and financial institutions reduce the cost of credit, their development will facilitate the development of those firms and sectors which depend most on external financing—namely, those that have greater investment commitments, are more capital intensive, and/or are more innovative.[3]

Second, along the same lines, it can be argued that the functionality of a financial structure depends on its capacity to reduce the information and incentive problems posed by firms to financiers. Since financial structures of different kinds perform different roles and obtain different results, it is evident that, depending on the features of the economic system and its informational frictions, certain solutions will be more functional than others. As Boot and Thakor (1997) predict in their theoretical analysis of financial system architecture, an optimal financial system will be skewed toward bank financing if borrowers have relatively poor credit reputations. On the other hand, capital market financing will prevail if borrowers have relatively good credit reputations, and if they can respond to the signals conveyed by market prices. Thus, Boot and Thakor appear to regard market finance as superior to bank finance, since informational asymmetries in the former are weaker than in the latter.[4]

In particular, as the evolutionary theory of the firm shows, the youngest and smallest firms have the most serious problems of information asymmetry, mainly because they do not have long examinable records and/or have not yet established structured relations with the financial system.[5] Such firms are also unable to sustain the fixed costs necessary to access the financial market and the stock exchange. Berger and Udell (1998) report that the main financial sources for small firms—approximately 70 per cent of total financing—are the principal owner, commercial banks, and commercial credit; this percentage diminishes, but not significantly, with the growth in the size and age of the firm. If despite informational opacity young firms are able to achieve a balance between internal and external financing, this is because a significant proportion of external financing is in reality of internal origin since it is guaranteed by personal assets, mainly those of the owners.[6] A small firm's debt composition also depends on the sector in which it operates, with a greater likelihood of external equity investments such as angel finance and venture capital in sectors with high growth potential but also with high risk, and of external indebtedness with banks and other financial institutions in sectors with stable returns (Berger and Udell 1998, 619, 622–4, and 626).[7]

The third reason that explains why the relationship between financial markets and growth must be qualified is that when the analysis shifts to the level of territories, we see that most developing economies have bank-based financial systems and financial markets play a relatively minor role. Various explanations have been given for this pattern. For example, when accounting rules and more generally regulatory enforcement institutions are weak, banks are better placed to protect creditor rights. Small investors are deterred from investing in the stock market for fear of being exploited by stock price manipulators and insider traders (Studart 1995, 55–6). They feel that their savings are better protected in deposit or saving accounts at banks, which are generally subject to some form of supervision by the state (Berglof and Bolton 2002, 92).

On the corporate side, as Stiglitz (1991) suggests, less developed countries must expect that firms within their economies will need to rely heavily on bank lending rather than securities markets as sources of funds. Stiglitz views this pattern as advantageous because he sees banks as providers of short-term loans based on careful screening of borrowers and as having the power to monitor firms' bond repayments.[8] Since banks are generally well acquainted with their borrowers' businesses, they can avoid some of the informational asymmetry problems of capital markets, and hence banks enjoy both better selection and better enforcement powers than would be available through the capital markets. This explains why bank credit is of particular importance not only for this type of firm but also, in general, for a region or country in its early phases of development, when small firms requiring specific financial services predominate and financial and stock markets are neither liquid nor able to meet the demands of a large part of the production system. By contrast, bank credit diminishes in importance as firm size increases and with sectoral and territorial growth.

The fourth and final reason to qualify the relationship between financial markets and growth is that the existence of a developed financial system is not a sufficient condition for local development. Setting aside the presence of opportunities and the propensity to invest, financial intermediaries and banks may play in a given territory roles that range from passive, or even parasitic, to positive and proactive. In their proactive role as true agents of development, they must be able to reconcile two, sometimes conflicting, exigencies: the pursuit of managerial efficiency and the pursuit of territorial efficiency. Since the features that define territorial efficiency are typical factors of externality, it is necessary to determine which types of financial institutions boost these externalities, and then to introduce policies that induce business strategies to concur with territorial efficiency. Reconciliation between the two different efficiencies differs according to the context. Consequently, it is necessary to consider differences among potential financial solutions, but it is equally important to appraise the weight of the institutional and corporate nature of banks, as well as their governance.

To sum up, our argument is that banks do matter in regional growth not simply because they are responsible for credit provision. Amos and Wingender (1993) suggest that financial institutions can be either demand driven or supply leading. Those institutions that are demand driven are characterized by financial activities that passively respond to development stimulated by other factors, such as increases in investment and consumption, while those that are supply leading are characterized by development that is directly stimulated through the financial sector. If financial activity plays an active role in economic development and is regionally differentiated, then it can also contribute to unbalanced regional growth or locally focused development initiatives. Hence, banks are not simply intermediaries that allocate a predetermined amount of savings among alternative uses, but they can be active agents that direct resources to finance investments in place, thereby fostering development of the economy (Minsky 1993, 82). The potential importance of regionally differentiated financial activity to local growth lies at the heart of the regional aspects of banking intermediation analysis.

Small banks and local development

The specific role of banks is to assure finance in situations where information asymmetries and incentivization problems obstruct a direct relationship between savers and firms. The financial circumstances of firms differ according to the magnitude of information asymmetry and the need to prevent opportunistic behaviour. The financial theory of intermediation and practical experience suggest that peripheral regions and small- and medium-sized firms (SMEs) have financial exigencies different from those of core regions and large firms, and that banks may differ in their readiness to aid their development. Research reveals not only the greater dependence on bank credit by local small firms, but also the weaker commitment of large banks to small firms. There are several reasons why large banks tend to ration credit to smaller firms: greater portfolio diversification, which makes it more costly for them to select and control smaller clients; organizational diseconomies, which may induce them to forgo certain market segments; the standardization of local-level client relations adopted to remedy information and agency problems; the centralization to company headquarters of final decisions; and prudential behaviour by often transitory branch managements (Alessandrini *et al.* 2003; Alexopoulos and Goglio 2011). Relationships between large banks and smaller firms consequently tend to privilege high-quality credit, which can be evaluated with the standard financial analysis procedures used for large firms. This procedure of evaluation, in turn, explains why large banks can apply significantly lower prices in these cases (see Berger and Udell 1998, 658). One may therefore hypothesize a distinctive role for small banks, which, *ceteris paribus*, are better able to interpret the needs of, and place trust in, nascent entrepreneurship.

The weight of local banks—defined as banks of small size operating in a circumscribed territorial setting and run by local managements (Ferri 1997)—in the 'quantitative financing' of small firms is well documented in the literature. However, 'the evidence on the efficiency of local banks in selecting clients and on their ability to stimulate the growth of local economies is rather meagre'—or, at least, ambiguous (Alessandrini and Zazzaro 2001, 85–6; Alessandrini *et al.* 2003, 21). In particular, the mechanisms that may facilitate the financing of small firms and influence local development in general seem to be more complex than those mechanisms that involve the role of local banks in terms of their specific operation in the territory and their influence on commercial and personal credit. These mechanisms also comprise the characteristics of the social and economic system as a whole and their impact on the financial system.

Consequently, local banks' deep roots in the territory and their participation in the life of local communities may offset disadvantages of scale and generate 'relationships of various kinds, not necessarily economic, whereby each member acquires information about the others which an external operator cannot have, or can only have by sustaining substantial costs' (Angelini *et al.* 1997, 298). Thus, small banks may be better positioned to ascertain the debt class of borrowers, verify the extent of their opportunistic behaviour, and ensure that debts are repaid by imposing or inducing social sanctions (Hoff and Stiglitz 1990; Stiglitz 1990; Varian 1990). These advantages may be even greater in the case of cooperative credit banks, if one considers their advanced efficiency of peer monitoring, and may be further strengthened by their ability to recover economies of scale at the level of consortia and by the tax concessions granted to such banks

(Ferri 1997). Focusing on the ability of local banking systems to establish closer and more flexible relationships with SMEs and to monitor their profitability, three points should be stressed.

First, the appropriateness of local banks does not necessarily refer to an allocation of credit best suited to the territory's development. The duration and intensity of any local credit relationship may also foster phenomena that could undermine allocative efficiency. Firms that have larger concentrations of credit with a bank may face decreased financial leverage because as the concentration increases and the cost of the investment necessary to assess the firm's creditworthiness grows, the bank acquires greater bargaining power, which enables it to benefit from its dominant position and impose more onerous conditions on rates and services and, thus, appropriate an increased part of the firm's profits (Sharpe 1990; Rajan 1992). For firms, this may neutralize their potential advantages accruing from the mitigation of information problems through their enduring client relations, inducing them to reduce the bank's informational control by resorting to multiple lines of credit and/or relying on short-term loans to manage their long-term financing. Inevitably, such reactions lead to an aggressive consolidation of the insurance approach of banks that stems from their disinclination—and even inability—to direct and control firms already unwilling to subject themselves to their scrutiny. Consequently, banks penalize the financing of new and smaller-scale business initiatives that have greater information asymmetry problems.

Second, continuous and exclusive client relations may foster collusion between a bank's officials and local vested interests, a problem that large banks normally seek to prevent by rotating personnel. Alternatively, they may induce local banks to adopt conservative low-risk strategies that prioritize exclusive financial relationships with known firms undertaking activities already present in the area, and to the detriment of new business initiatives and new production lines.

Third, the deep territorial roots of a local banking system may exert two negative influences on a territory's development: the amplification of exogenous economic shocks through regional credit channels and/or the intensification of endogenous crises. The functions of the banking system foster this instability, while credit expansion during economic upturns fuels expansion as well as recession when credit is destroyed (Dow 1987, 22–3; Samolyk 1994, 260–1). This process depends not only on the informational segmentation of local credit markets but also on the geographical segmentation of banking systems. On the other hand, banks operating in several geographical areas may be more able to offset difficulties in crisis zones with the better results they have obtained in their other operational zones. This multiplier effect, however, may be partly dampened by the greatest propensity of local banks to financially sustain their clients if it is easier for them to internalize the future benefits of their financial support (Beretta *et al.* 2000).

The financial scenario before and after the crisis

In the last two decades, the banking system has undergone radical changes in size and organizational structure. These changes have affected the modus operandi of banks and their specialization and mutual equilibrium, sometimes stressing and at other times reducing diversities. The leading causes of these changes can be traced to rapid progress in information and communication technology, financial innovations, deregulation and the decreasing role of states, growing international openness, and changes in demand for banking and financial services. These factors have all led to increased competition and prompted a far-reaching process of concentration among banking institutions and a rationalization of their productive structures.

The long trend of mergers and acquisitions (M&As), which has involved every type and dimension of banking, has led to an increase in the average size of banks, more complex and structured forms of group organization, and a diversification of customer relation policies and methods. M&As can be considered, first of all, as a necessary reaction to changes in market structure: for big banks, a possible solution to needs of repositioning, and for smaller banks, to needs of scale economies and as a preventive defence against takeovers (European Central Bank 2000; Belaisch *et al.* 2001; Corvoisier and Gropp 2001). However, due to their larger scale, the new banks created by M&As may be less likely to approach smaller lenders and borrowers, who are more dependent on personal relationships: SMEs, families, unskilled workers, unemployed, women, young people, and the elderly (Leyshon and Thrift 1993, 1995; Berger *et al.* 2001).

Conventional banking institutions either lack the spatial configuration to serve local markets or withdraw from local markets as a result of a re-engineering process that their restructuring-for-profit, cost-rationalization strategies compel. Consequently, the risk of demarketing their retail branches from certain segments of the population and from peripheral areas and activities becomes evident. These strategies include minimum loan sizes, tiered interest rates that yield little interest on savings/deposit accounts with low balances, account maintenance charges on low balance deposit accounts, and the use of credit-scoring systems that lead to outright refusals to grant loans or to open some types of accounts.

Even when operative at local level, however, conventional banks are most likely to apply more secure loan policies based on standardized credit policies, screening and monitoring, and a focus on market segments that offer them advanced opportunities for profits under a 'less risky' lending policy. Cost considerations again prevent them from 'investing' in the relationship-based transactions that are necessary to address the needs of informationally opaque borrowers. Relationship lending might be considered as contrary to their standardized credit policies, which are based on easily observed, verifiable, and transmittable data—i.e. pure transaction lending. Thus, because of physical or 'informational' distance, conventional banks are not efficient in generating borrower-specific information, which due to its 'soft' characteristics may be difficult to transmit through the 'rigid' communication channels of large institutions. Many potential borrowers are therefore denied loans because they lack adequate credit records or collateral, or they apply for loans that are too small to be profitable for large banks.

The financial market crisis that erupted during the summer of 2007 and worsened after September 2008 cannot be separated from this structural change since it is also a consequence of the bad governance of this change or of the inability—in some cases even unwillingness—to institute new forms of governance adapted to the new context. In broad terms, the origins of the crisis can be located in global trade and financial unbalances, past USA monetary policy and the subsequent excess of liquidity, the increased appetite for risk by investors, the bulging expectations about real estate and stocks values, and the speculative bubbles that followed.

If we focus solely on the financial sector, the crisis seems to be articulated around a number of financial innovations and reckless forms of behaviour that gave rise to an unreasonably elastic credit system, to the detriment of transparency: securitization of loans, financial disintermediation, structuring of credit claims, risk reduction of financial institutions, the incautious granting of bank loans, poor information about debtors' conditions, huge increases in out-of-budget activities by banks, reckless behaviour and conflict of interests by rating agencies, and the emergence of many financial operators not liable to regulatory control. All these innovations and forms of misbehaviour have introduced growing uncertainty that has damaged trust in—and within—the banking system, increasing the cost of capital and depressing the economy (International Monetary Fund 2007; Bank of Italy 2008). Five aspects should be stressed:

- The development of 'innovative' complex products has nothing to do with usual and simple banking activities.
- The crisis has shown the limits of the dominant theory of complete markets and perfect information that hypothesises the emergence of an effective 'self-regulation' capacity of the financial system. It is worth noting that under the influence of this theory, the state and the regulatory authorities have reduced their control over financial markets.
- As a consequence, the role of governance arrangements and risk management systems for the stability of individual institutions and the financial system as a whole has become critical. The reforms that legislators and authorities have been called upon to carry out at various supranational and national levels have to be based on 'common rules' and a greater role for 'organisational and corporate governance' variables (Ferri 2008).
- Even after channelling billions of euros into the banking circuit, the problem remains, as it seems that funding has difficulties in reaching the real economy. Banks are still rationing credit, in particular to SMEs, because of their opacity and lack of collateral, but also because of the banks' incapacity to evaluate projects and screen firms (Stiglitz and Weiss 1981).
- Conventional banks do not seem to have learned from the crisis: banks'

budgets are still opaque and highly risky behaviour has restarted, as is shown by the prompt revival of junk bonds, hedge funds, futures, and the bonus culture.

Cooperative credit

The theoretical and research literatures indicate that the allocative efficiency of a financial system—as well as its consequent contribution to economic growth at the territorial level—depends to a large extent on its interaction with the local economy's pattern of development, and on the social context in which firms operate. This hypothesis leads to a thorough assessment of cooperative credit, the activity of which is largely directed toward their members—i.e. mainly SMEs, households, and farmers. Cooperative banks can achieve the minimum efficient size for these purposes, while their pyramidal structure compensates for their small size. Moreover, through their structure and operative philosophy, cooperative banks can usually avert the typical dangers of mergers taking place outside the cooperative system.

Indeed, as data from the European Association of Co-operative Banks for the period from 2004 to 2009 demonstrate, although cooperative banks were actively involved in M&As and the number of these banks decreased by 14.5 per cent, total cooperative banking outlets increased during the same period by 11.4 per cent (European Association of Cooperative Banks 2010; Alexopoulos and Goglio 2011, 36). This finding is indicative of a rather different post-merger behaviour, which results in stronger organic development, consistent with the cooperative banks' orientation to retaining strong links to, and reinforcing their proximity advantages within local areas (Alexopoulos and Goglio 2009, 2011). Hence, as reported by Cannari and Signorini (1997), for the Italian Banche di Credito Cooperativo (Cooperative Credit Banks) the share of credit lines extended to family-run and artisan firms is above the average, while that allocated to financial enterprises is around half of that of other banks. The observable characteristics of clients remaining equal, these banks have less risky portfolios, as shown by the default/loan ratio, and they make less frequent recourse to credit rationing, with particularly high drawing ratios—i.e. the ratio of credit drawn to credit lines granted, including overdrafts.

Thus, the competitive advantage of cooperative banks seems to have increased recently due to their ability to reinforce and better exploit the capacities that distinguish them from conventional banks. Their strong roots in their territories and good knowledge of the entrepreneurial environment may reduce information asymmetries, enable them to assess individual creditworthiness more efficiently, decrease monitoring costs, and reduce adverse selection and moral hazard. Moreover, research points to the likelihood that cooperative banks establish a sort of implicit contract with their member-customers whereby the bank undertakes to stabilize the availability and cost of money for businesses, while the member-customers undertake not to abandon the bank at times of abundant and cheap credit (Ferri and Pittaluga 1997). In this way, the cooperative banks' intrinsic ethical dimension and greater propensity for territorial efficiency is reinforced by their members' cooperative ethos.

At the same time, however, small cooperative banks face diseconomies of scale and inadequate international openness, which are not always remediable through the financial institutions at the apex of the network in which they are generally organized. Furthermore, they may also experience various drawbacks such as conflicts of interest in addressing local operators and members, and excessive reliance on informal practices due *inter alia* to the limited mobility of personnel. Whether 'these potential negative factors actually become disadvantages depends both on the organizational structure of each individual bank and on the characteristics of the environment in which it operates' (Cannari and Signorini 1997, 238–9). What should be kept in mind is that whilst in some areas and market segments the competitive advantages of cooperative credit banks may prevail over those of other banks, in other cases their disadvantages may prevail.

Before the recent crisis, several studies highlighted the importance of cooperative banks for financial stability in the regions they serve, suggesting that cooperative banks have generally lower incentives to take on risks and, consequently, they tend to adopt less risky strategies (Fonteyne 2007; Hesse and Čihák 2007; Groeneveld and de Vries 2009). In addition, these studies conclude that cooperative banks seem to be more stable due to the much lower volatility of their returns, which more than offset their apparently lower profitability. The reason behind the observed lower variability of returns can be found in the fact that cooperative banks in normal times pass on most of their returns to members and customers, but are able to withhold this surplus in weaker periods. To some extent, this finding reflects the mutual support mechanisms that many cooperative banks have created.

This last remark highlights the special features of the cooperative organizational model. Historically, cooperative banks' small size has been balanced by their network organization and the formation of higher order institutions. Their structure as *networks of banks* and not as *bank networks* has made it possible to exploit the advantages deriving from their small size. In addition, mutual help and solidarity among the autonomous cooperative banks has lessened the negative impacts of their small size (Alexopoulos 2004; Oliver Wyman 2008).

The onset of the crisis has served to shed light on issues that are strongly connected to the philosophy of the financial cooperatives, in terms of their everyday business. Thus, some scholars have stressed that cooperative banks defend consumer interests, and their presence and mode of operation maximize consumer surplus (Fonteyne 2007; Ferri 2008). Cooperative banks utilize their ability to offer simple and transparent products that are priced fairly, designed to meet local needs, and marketed in a manner that ensures that risks are well understood and communicated. Moreover, Fonteyne (2007) and Ferri (2008) indicate the ways in which credit cooperatives—compared to commercial banks—may be helpful during periods of credit crunch:

- they may be less inclined to ration credit to customers;
- they may be less prone to raise the loan rate during periods of financial stress;

- thanks to better capitalization and more prudent lending, credit cooperatives may be less likely to be distressed themselves and, therefore, may be more able to continue assisting their customers in times of financial stress.

These three potential beneficial effects of cooperative banks stem from their governance, business model, and specialization—all of which derive from relationship-based retail banking.[9]

Since in most cases the economics of a small business is indistinct from the household economy of the entrepreneur, the fruits of the mutually beneficial cooperation between the member and his/her cooperative bank diffuse into the household and affect its prosperity. Hence, the positive effects of the operation of cooperative institutions are not constrained to the entrepreneurial sphere, but rather involve and influence almost spontaneously more dimensions of the local socio-economic reality (Alexopoulos 2004).

The book's objectives

Does this new banking environment offer new opportunities for growth in cooperative banking? In general, the answer is that it does. Increases in levels of concentration and banking market shares, new expansionary strategies, and processes of rationalization that aim to strengthen competition abandon and leave exposed financial areas and economic activities that may become prey to local non-institutional and uncontrolled lenders. Research has shown that M&As involving big banks lead to loan reductions to SMEs, while M&As involving small banks lead to increases (Ahrendsen *et al.* 1999; Berger *et al.* 2001). Thus, M&As and the consequent repositioning by new post-merger banks have important side effects, which include opening new spaces and opportunities for additional entries or small banks already present in the market. Historically, financial cooperatives expand in banking markets that are socially and/or spatially segmented. The mix of community bonds, shared responsibility, and the capacity to mobilize local savings not only reduces information asymmetry and solves scale diseconomies due to small loans, but also re-establishes and strengthens trust in the banking system.

Both structural changes and the financial crisis have created a context where, at least at the local level, the model of financial intermediation that credit cooperatives follow is encouraged to flourish: there are certain sections of the population that face increased difficulties accessing the financial system, while some peripheral communities and sectors are confronted with an increasingly restricted set of options. This context is indicative of the role that credit cooperatives can play in 'plugging the gap' between local needs and the mainstream services. But important questions remain: How is this advanced role to be achieved? What are the competitive advantages of cooperative banks in the current context? And how can they reinforce and capitalize on them?

In order to provide answers to these questions, the book aims to deepen understanding of cooperative banking through a diverse set of approaches. The reader is invited to identify the different functions of the cooperative banking model, and thus the different levels on which it is articulated. At the same time, the volume provides the tools and the necessary background for an assessment of the model's operational and organizational dimensions. Thus, even though each chapter can be read independently, the aim of the volume is to provide a coherent, albeit multifaceted, interpretation of the model and its contribution to sustainable local development.

The book is organized into three parts. First, it reconsiders the philosophy and performance of stakeholder-oriented banks compared to that of profit-maximizing banks. Second, it offers a series of case studies that investigate the proactive roles that cooperative banks play in promoting and supporting local development, not only in the case of strong pre-existing community bonds, but also for that of weak communities as well, where the creation of new social capital is still a challenge. Finally, it provides an appraisal of cooperative-based microfinance, in order to situate this alternative micro-level intermediary in the local development context.

Notes

1 For surveys, see Chapter 2 of Alexopoulos (2004) and Goglio (2009).
2 Following De Gregorio (1997, 70), 'financial intermediation affects growth mainly by increasing the marginal productivity of capital' at a ratio of three to one. The Hicksian channel is more explicitly considered by the neoclassical theories of growth, while the Schumpeterian channel has been examined by, among others, Fama (1985), Minsky (1986), Moore (1988), Stiglitz and Weiss (1988), King and Levine (1993), Galetovic (1994), and Levine (1999).
3 Following Rajan and Zingales (1998, 584), opportunities to expand or reduce the potential for new firms and technological and innovative sectors are an important factor 'in determining the size composition of an industry as well as its concentration'. In general, such opportunities are an important channel of influence on patterns of economic development at national, regional, and sub-regional levels.
4 However, as Beck and Levine (2002, 147) note, financial economists have debated the relative merits of bank-based and market-based financial systems for over a century. In their literature review, they provide a plethora of information about the advantages and the disadvantages of the two architectures (Beck and Levine 2002, 148–9). In their results, however, they argue that distinguishing countries by their overall financial development and legal system efficiency is more useful than distinguishing countries by whether they are relatively bank-based or market-based (Beck and Levine 2002, 175). Therefore, research should focus on the quality of the financial services that the intermediaries are offering, and consequently their efficiency as intermediaries, regardless of the financial system's architecture, in order to stress their importance in development.
5 'Perhaps the most important characteristics defining small business finance is informational opacity ... small firms do not enter into contracts that are publicly visible or widely reported ... do not issue traded securities ... do not have audited financial statements that can be shared with any provider of outside finance. As a result, small firms often cannot credibly convey their quality ... may have difficulty building reputations to signal high quality or nonexploitive behaviour to overcome informational opacity' (Berger and Udell 1998, 616).
6 According to Berger and Udell (1998, 638), '91.94 per cent of all small business debt

to financial institutions is secured, backed by collateral; 51.63 per cent is guaranteed by the owners of the firm'.

7 The diversity of funding among similar firms may also be due to the fact that 'different sources of funding may be substitutes or complements ... angel finance and venture capital are often complementary sources ... venture capital and public equity are also complements' (Berger and Udell 1998, 627).

8 This argument should be examined in conjunction with the role of government interventions, either directly as credit providers or indirectly as regulators, in the less developed economies. See Stiglitz (1994) for a wider discussion of government interventions and Cole and Slade (1994) for a more specific example.

9 On relationship banking, see Petersen and Rajan (1994), Berger and Udell (1995), Harhoff and Körtring (1998), and Di Salvo *et al.* (2004).

References

Ahrendsen, B.L., Dixon, B.L., and LaDerrek, T.L. (1999) 'Independent commercial bank mergers and agricultural lending concentration', *Journal of Agricultural and Applied Economics*, 31(2): 215–27.

Alessandrini, P. and Zazzaro, A. (2001) 'L'evoluzione dei sistemi finanziari locali: i nodi da sciogliere', in P. Alessandrini (ed.) *Il sistema finanziario italiano tra globalizzazione e localismo*, Bologna: Il Mulino, pp. 77–93.

Alessandrini, P., Papi, L., and Zazzaro, A. (2003) 'Banche, territorio e sviluppo', *Moneta e credito*, no. 221: 1–43.

Alexopoulos, Y. (2004) *Financial Co-operatives and Rural Development in Greece*, PhD Thesis, University of Leicester.

Alexopoulos, Y. and Goglio, S. (2009) 'Financial deregulation and economic distress: is there a future for financial co-operatives?', Euricse Working Paper no. 001/09, Trento, Italy: European Research Institute on Cooperative and Social Enterprises.

Alexopoulos, Y. and Goglio, S. (2011) 'Financial cooperatives: problems and challenges in the post-crisis era', *Journal of Rural Cooperation*, 39(1): 34–47.

Amos, O. and Wingender, J. (1993) 'A model of the interaction between regional financial markets and regional growth', *Regional Science and Urban Economics*, 23(1): 85–110.

Angelini, P., Di Salvo, R., and Ferri, G. (1997) 'Disponibilità e costo del credito per le piccole imprese: relazioni di clientela e banche cooperative', in F. Cesarini, G. Ferri, and M. Giardino (eds) *Credito e sviluppo: banche locali co-operative e imprese minori*, Bologna: Il Mulino, pp. 293–333.

Bank of Italy (2008) 'Economic Bulletin', no. 51, January, Rome: Bank of Italy.

Beck, T. and Levine, R. (2002) 'Industry growth and capital allocation: does having a market- or bank-based system matter?', *Journal of Financial Economics*, 64(2): 147–80.

Belaisch, A., Kodres, L., Levy, J., and Ubide, A. (2001) 'Euro-area banking at the crossroads', IMF Working Paper no. WP/01/28, Washington, DC: International Monetary Fund.

Bencivenga, V.R. and Smith, B.D. (1991) 'Financial Intermediation and Endogenous Growth', *Review of Economic Studies*, 58(2): 195–209.

Beretta, E., Omiccioli, M., and Torrini, R. (2000) 'Banche locali e amplificazione degli shock economici attraverso il canale creditizio', in L.F. Signorini (ed.) *Lo sviluppo locale: un'indagine della Banca d'Italia sui distretti industriali*, Corigliano Calabro, Italy: Meridiana Libri, pp. 271–85.

Berger, A.N. and Udell, G.F. (1995) 'Relationship lending and lines of credit in small firm finance', *Journal of Business*, 68(3): 351–81.

Berger, A.N. and Udell, G.F. (1998) 'The economics of small business finance: the roles of private equity and debt markets in the financial growth cycle', *Journal of Banking and Finance*, 22(6–8): 613–73.

Berger, A., Goldberg, A., and White, L. (2001) 'The effects of dynamic changes in bank competition on the supply of small business credit', *European Finance Review*, vol. 5: 115–39.

Berglof, E. and Bolton, P. (2002) 'The great divide and beyond: financial architecture in transition', *Journal of Economic Perspectives*, 16(1): 77–100.

Bernanke, B. and Gertler, M. (1989) 'Agency costs, net worth, and business fluctuations', *American Economic Review*, 79(1): 14–31.

Boot, A.W.A. and Thakor, A.V. (1997) 'Financial system architecture', *Review of Financial Studies*, 10(3): 693–733.

Cannari, L. and Signorini, L.F. (1997) 'Rischiosità e razionamento: un'analisi dell'efficienza allocativa delle banche di credito cooperativo e dei divari Nord-Sud', in F. Cesarini, G. Ferri, and M. Giardino (eds) *Credito e sviluppo: banche locali cooperative e imprese minori*, Bologna: Il Mulino, pp. 335–82.

Cole, D. and Slade, B. (1994) 'How bank lending practices influence resource allocation and monetary policy in Indonesia', Development Discussion Paper no. 444, Cambridge, MA: Harvard Institute for International Development.

Corvoisier, S. and Gropp, R. (2001) 'Bank concentration and retail interest rates', Working Paper no. 72, Frankfurt am Main: European Central Bank.

De Gregorio, J. (1997) 'Il ruolo della banca locale: un confronto internazionale', in F. Cesarini, G. Ferri, and M. Giardino (eds) *Credito e sviluppo: banche locali cooperative e imprese minori*, Bologna: Il Mulino, pp. 59–87.

De Gregorio, J. and Guidotti, P.E. (1995) 'Financial development and economic growth', *World Development*, 23(3): 433–48.

De la Fuente, A. and Marin, J.M. (1996) 'Innovation, bank monitoring and endogenous financial development', *Journal of Monetary Economics* 38(2): 269–301.

Di Salvo, R., Lopez, J.S., and Pezzotta, A. (2004) 'L'evoluzione del relationship banking nei mercati locali: il ruolo delle Banche di Credito Co-operativo. Un'analisi degli spostamenti di clientela', *Cooperazione di Credito*, 183(4): 81–113.

Dow, S. (1987) 'The treatment of money in regional economics', *Journal of Regional Science*, 27(1): 13–24.

European Association of Cooperative Banks (2010) 'Key Financial Statistics 2009'. Online. Available at: www.eurocoopbanks.coop/?id=403 (accessed 29 July 2011).

European Central Bank (2000) 'Mergers and Acquisitions Involving the EU Banking Industry: facts and implications', Frankfurt am Main: European Central Bank. Online. Available at: www.ecb.int/pub/pdf/other/eubkmergersen.pdf (accessed 14 October 2010).

Fama, E. (1985) 'What's different about banks?', *Journal of Monetary Economics*, 15(1): 29–39.

Ferri, G. (1997) 'Introduzione', in F. Cesarini, G. Ferri, and M. Giardino (eds) *Credito e sviluppo: banche locali co-operative e imprese minori*, Bologna: Il Mulino, pp. 383–414.

Ferri, G. (2008) 'Why co-operative banks are particularly important at a time of credit crunch', mimeographed, University of Bari, Italy.

Ferri, G. and Pittaluga, G.B. (1997) 'Il finanziamento delle imprese nelle fasi di restrizione monetaria. Il caso del credito cooperativo', in F. Cesarini, G. Ferri, and M. Giardino (eds) *Credito e sviluppo: banche locali co-operative e imprese minori*, Bologna: Il Mulino, pp. 383–414.

Fonteyne, W. (2007) 'Cooperative banks in Europe: policy issues', IMF Working Paper 07/159, Washington, DC: International Monetary Fund.

Galetovic, A. (1994) 'Credit market structure, firm quality, and long-run growth', Discussion Papers in Economics no. 171, Princeton, NJ: Woodrow Wilson School of Public and International Affairs, Princeton University.

Goglio, S. (1999) 'Local public goods: productive and redistributive aspects', *Economic Analysis*, 2(1): 5–21.

Goglio, S. (2009) 'Local credit and territorial development: general aspects and the Italian experience', in A. Bonoldi and A. Leonardi (eds) *Recovery and Development in the European Periphery (1945–1960)*, Bologna: Il Mulino, pp. 241–80.

Goldsmith, R.W. (1969) *Financial Structure and Development*, New Haven, CT: Yale University Press.

Granovetter, M. (1990) 'Economic action and social structure: a history and an agenda', in R. Friedland and A.F. Robertson (eds) *Beyond the Marketplace: rethinking economy and society*, New York: Aldine de Gruyter, pp. 89–107.

Greenwood, J. and Jovanovic, J. (1990) 'Financial development, growth, and the distribution of income', *Journal of Political Economy*, 98(5): 1076–107.

Groeneveld, H. and de Vries, B. (2009) 'European co-operative banks: first lessons of the subprime crisis', *International Journal of Co-operative Management*, 4(2): 8–21.

Gurley, J. and Shaw, E. (1955) 'Financial aspects of economic development', *American Economic Review*, 45(4): 515–38.

Harhoff, D. and Körtring, T. (1998) 'Lending relationship in Germany: empirical results from survey data', *Journal of Banking and Finance*, 22(10–11): 1317–52.

Hesse, H. and Čihák, M. (2007) 'Co-operative banks and financial stability', IMF Working Paper 07/2, Washington, DC: International Monetary Fund.

Hoff, K. and Stiglitz, J.E. (1990) 'Introduction: imperfect information and rural credit markets—puzzles and policy perspectives', *World Bank Economic Review*, 4(3): 235–50.

International Monetary Fund (2007) *Global Financial Stability Report: financial market turbulence—causes, consequences, and policies*, October, Washington DC: International Monetary Fund.

King, R.G. and Levine, R. (1993) 'Finance, entrepreneurship and growth: theory and evidence', *Journal of Monetary Economics*, 32(3): 513–42.

Levine, R. (1997) 'Financial development and economic growth: views and agenda', *Journal of Economic Literature*, 35(2): 688–726.

Levine, R. (1999) 'Law, finance, and economic growth', *Journal of Financial Intermediation*, 8(1–2): 8–35.

Leyshon, A. and Thrift, N. (1993) 'The restructuring of the UK financial services industry in the 1990s: a reversal of fortune?', *Journal of Rural Studies*, 9(3): 223–41.

Leyshon, A. and Thrift, N. (1995) 'Geographies of financial exclusion-financial abandonment in Britain and the United States', *Transactions of the Institute of British Geographers*, 20(3): 312–41.

McKinnon, R.I. (1973) *Money and Capital in Economic Development*, Washington DC: Brookings Institute.

Minsky, H.P. (1986) *Stabilizing an Unstable Economy*, New Haven, CT: Yale University Press.

Minsky, H.P. (1993) 'On the non-neutrality of money', *Quarterly Review Federal Reserve Bank of New York*, 18(1): 77–82.

Moore, B.J. (1988) *Horizontalists and Verticalists: the macroeconomics of credit money*, Cambridge: Cambridge University Press.

Oliver Wyman (2008) 'Co-operative Bank: Customer Champion', prepared for the European Association for Cooperative Banks. Online. Available at: www.eurocoopbanks.coop/GetDocument.aspx?id=b64bf803-bb4e-4f4d-b7d9-e72c34f92b19 (accessed 18 August 2011).

Patrick, H.T. (1966) 'Financial development and economic growth in underdeveloped countries', *Economic Development and Cultural Change*, 14(2): 174–89.

Petersen, M. and Rajan, R. (1994) 'The benefits of lending relationship: evidence from small business data', *Journal of Finance*, 49(1): 3–37.

Rajan, R.J. (1992) 'Insiders and outsiders: the class choice between informal and armslength debt', *Journal of Finance*, 47(4): 1367–400.

Rajan, R.G. and Zingales, L. (1998) 'Financial dependence and growth', *American Economic Review*, 88(3): 559–86.

Samolyk, K. (1994) 'Banking conditions and regional economic performance: evidence of a regional credit channel', *Journal of Monetary Economics*, 34(2): 259–78.

Sharpe, S.A. (1990) 'Asymmetric information, bank lending, and implicit contracts: a stylized model of customer relationships', *Journal of Finance*, 45(4): 1069–87.

Shaw, E.S. (1973) *Financial Deepening in Economic Development*, New York: Oxford University Press.

Stiglitz, J.E. (1990) 'Peer monitoring in credit markets', *World Bank Economic Review*, 4(3): 351–66.

Stiglitz, J.E. (1991) 'Government, financial markets, and economic development', NBER Working Papers no. 3669, Cambidge, MA: National Bureau of Economic Research.

Stiglitz, J.E. (1994) 'The Role of the State in Financial Markets', in *Proceedings of the World Bank Annual Conference on Development Economics, 1993*, Washington, DC: World Bank, pp. 19–52. Online. Available at: http://go.worldbank.org/SM7YJE9UG0 (accessed 18 August 2011).

Stiglitz, J.E. and Weiss, A. (1981) 'Credit rationing in markets with imperfect information', *American Economic Review*, 71(3): 393–410.

Stiglitz, J.E. and Weiss, A. (1988) 'Banks as social accountants and screening device for the allocation of credit', NBER Working Papers no. 2710, Cambidge, MA: National Bureau of Economic Research.

Studart, R. (1995) 'Saving, financial markets and economic development: theory and lessons from Brazil', in P. Arestis and V. Chick (eds) *Finance, Development and Structural Change: post-Keynesian perspectives*, London: E. Elgar, pp. 46–70.

Varian, H.R. (1990) 'Monitoring agents with other agents', *Journal of Institutional and Theoretical Economics*, 146(1): 153–74.

Williamson, S.D. (1986) 'Costly monitoring, financial intermediation, and equilibrium credit rationing', *Journal of Monetary Economics* 18(2): 159–79.

Part I

Stakeholder-oriented versus profit-maximizing banks

The contributions in this part reassess and compare the philosophy and performance of stakeholder-oriented banks and profit-maximizing banks. While restraining from referring to any pro-cooperative argument that could skew results in favour of financial cooperatives, this part employs a twofold approach to situate cooperative credit in the financial system. Using a macroeconomic approach, it examines the qualitatively different components of the modern financial arena, the consequent perceived and actual risks introduced in the system, and their contradictory repercussions on critical economic variables. Using a sector-level approach, it then conducts benchmarking evaluations of the available financial intermediaries based on *conventional* and *commonly accepted methods* in order to assess differences in performance among banks with different ownership and organizational regimes. Finally, this part draws the reader's attention to the significant institutional and organizational features of credit cooperatives that call for a careful application of any assessment procedure or regulatory intervention.

In Chapter 1, Elisabetta De Antoni extends Minsky's views on the financial evolution of capitalism and his financial instability hypothesis to the recent crisis. She concludes that the speculative short-sighted mentality of the trader is replacing the prudent far-sighted mentality of the banker, and while loans have become more liquid and safer for individual lenders, they have become less liquid and riskier for the economy as a whole. As a result, the function of financial institutions as 'ephors' of capitalism, envisaged by Schumpeter, has been jeopardized, but an alternative can be implemented: shared-prosperity capitalism, which De Antoni argues is fertile ground for the development of cooperative banking.

In Chapter 2, Giovanni Ferri, Panu Kalmi, and Eeva Kerola provide a long-term comparison of the performance of European banks across different organizational structures, using performance measures such as profitability, cost efficiency, and loan losses. Their analysis reveals that even before the outbreak of the crisis that necessitated a reassessment of the merits of different ownership structures, there was no convincing evidence supporting the claim that joint-stock ownership was superior to stakeholder ownership in European banking. Therefore, the resilience of the stakeholder model stems from its competitive advantage, rather from alleged regulatory interference. Moreover, by assessing the value of organizational diversity in the banking sector, the chapter provides evidence on the sustainability of different banking business models.

In Chapter 3, Juan S. Lopez and Stefano Di Colli assess the level of competition in the Italian banking system based on a comprehensive panel dataset of Italian commercial, cooperative, and popular banks. Their estimations reveal a hump-shaped profile throughout the time horizon under consideration, suggesting increasing competition in the Italian banking sector. Furthermore, the analysis shows that cooperative banks enjoy a lower degree of market power than commercial banks, in contrast with evidence from most of the recent studies. Thus, their results reject the claim that non-profit maximizing institutions survive in the market because they enjoy some sort of market power provided by complacent regulation.

In Chapter 4, Alan J. Robb, James H. Smith, and J. Tom Webb provide an overview of how capital in cooperative businesses differs from capital in investor-oriented businesses, both conceptually and in terms of behaviour, and consider the implications of 'the cooperative capital difference'. Their analysis focuses on these attributes of capital in cooperatives that call for sensitive treatment in order to avoid adverse consequences in their operation and development. In particular, they examine the characteristics of 'cooperative capital' against 'investor capital', critically comment on policies that are used to attract capital, stress the impact of non-cooperative capital on a cooperative's balanced behaviour, and draw valuable implications for a prudent public policy and regulatory treatment of cooperative capital.

1 Cooperative banking

A Minskyan perspective

Elisabetta De Antoni

In the last decades of the past century, the transactions executed by the financial system—and, above all, the incomes distributed by it—grew faster than the real economy. In the leading industrialized country, households, the government, and the economy as a whole accumulated unprecedented levels of indebtedness. With the tidal wave of liberalization, financial techniques and innovations became increasingly unscrupulous and opaque. At the beginning of the new century, financial fragility reached dangerous levels: the symptoms of a 'disaster foretold' were before everybody's eyes.

This situation, however, clashed with the dogmas of dominant economic theory: the free market was intrinsically stable and financial markets were perfectly efficient. Consequently, there was no reason to worry. We had even entered the Great Moderation, a new era in which the trade cycle and inflation had been definitively bridled. While admitting the key role of imperfections in macroeconomics, Olivier Blanchard (2000) inaugurated the new century by pondering: 'What do we know about macroeconomics that Fisher and Wicksell did not?' With hindsight, we must have forgotten something even more important than what we have learnt! In the twenty-first century, the world economy has been swept by one of the biggest financial crises within human memory, a crisis that has had devastating effects on the real economy.

Opposing dominant theory throughout his life, Hyman P. Minsky (1974, 267) repeatedly warned that 'the capitalist market mechanism is flawed, in the sense that it does not lead to a stable-price–full-employment equilibrium' and that 'the basis of the flaw resides in the financial system'. In his view, the economy follows a cyclical path that involves recurrent financial crises. The historical evidence, he argued, confirms that financial crises are systemic and not idiosyncratic (Minsky 1991), and he thus posed the question: 'Can "it" happen again?' (Minsky 1982a). 'It' was the Great Depression and Minsky's answer was affirmative. In the twentieth century, post-war big government prevented the worst: 'the most significant economic event of the era since World War II is something that has not happened: there has not been a deep and long-lasting depression' (Minsky 1982a, xi). If this is true, however, the return to laissez-faire actively promoted by the mainstream of the profession in recent decades represents 'a prescription for economic disaster' (Minsky and Whalen 1996–7, 161). That disaster is now before our eyes.

Given Minsky's prescience, it is now more important than ever to understand his approach. Specifically, we shall see how the analysis of the functioning of the system and of capitalism's financial evolution led Minsky to propose the creation of a nationwide network of *community development banks*, which are in many ways similar to cooperative banks. The first section of this chapter examines Minsky's 'financial instability hypothesis', the second analyses his re-reading of the financial evolution of capitalism, the third extends his analysis to the recent financial crisis, and the fourth highlights the importance of community banking—the community development banks advocated by Minsky plus cooperative banks.

The 'financial instability hypothesis'

Minsky (1975) presented his 'financial instability hypothesis' as an authentic interpretation of Keynes's (1936) thought. Indeed, the two authors should be considered as two sides of the same coin that gaze in opposite directions:[1] Keynes towards a depressed economy that tends to chronic underinvestment and thus high and long-lasting unemployment, and Minsky towards a vibrant economy naturally inclined to over-investment and over-indebtedness.[2] Minsky's point of departure is that 'stability—or tranquillity—is destabilising' (Minsky 1975, 127; 1978, 37) and that 'the fundamental instability is upward' (Minsky 1974, 272; 1975, 165).[3] A period of tranquillity—in which the financial system is robust and there are no relevant shocks, so that profits are systematically greater than debt commitments—increases confidence in the future, giving rise to wealth re-allocation from money to non-monetary assets that stimulates credit and capital accumulation. The result is an increase in investment financed by indebtedness. Thus, stability gives rise to a debt-financed expansion (Minsky 1986, 183).

Expansion, in turn, triggers an impulse-amplifying mechanism primarily based on the links between investments, profits, and investments. An initial rise in investment provokes an income expansion, and thereby implies a rise in profits. Besides validating past investment decisions, this rise improves profit expectations and confidence. This improvement in turn gives rise to a further increase in the volume of investment financed by indebtedness. The impulse-amplifying mechanism is strengthened by the money and financial markets. With growing optimism, the speculative demand for money shrinks. As a consequence, the demand for non-monetary assets increases, thereby strengthening the expansion of credit and investments. The money supply increases associated with income expansion also lead to the same results. Through its wealth effects, the rise in asset prices further stimulates both the availability of credit and the propensity to borrow in order to invest. Moreover, expectations and confidence perform an impulse-amplifying role. As a consequence of these processes, expansion turns into a debt-financed investment boom.

Minsky (1975, 1978, 1982a, 1982b, 1986) highlights two drawbacks of such a boom. The first concerns firms' indebtedness. In the increasing euphoria, external financing grows proportionally more than internal financing and, eventually, debt commitments become greater than profits. Given the expectation of a future bonanza, firms start financing the principal by indebtedness—i.e. speculative financing—and interest payments—i.e. ultra-speculative or Ponzi financing. Consequently, the fulfilment of debt commitments is no longer provided by profits but by the rolling over or the automatic increase of indebtedness. The initially robust financial system thus becomes fragile.[4] The second drawback is that the persistence of the boom inevitably ends up creating either bottlenecks in the financial system or inflationary pressures in the goods market that push the central bank in a deflationary direction. In both cases, the result is an increase in the rate of interest.[5]

The rise in interest rates ends the boom, thereby throwing the investments-profits-investments chain into a downward spiral. The unexpected increase in the cost of funds is thus associated with an equally unexpected fall in (the still insufficient) profits. Given the situation of financial fragility, the fulfilment of inherited debt commitments would require an increase in (the already high) indebtedness. This solution, however, is neither desirable nor even possible since the confidence underlying the indebtedness will have faded away. We thus come to the financial crisis, which Minsky (1982b) defined as a situation in which firms' debt commitments can no longer be fulfilled in the 'ordinary' way—i.e. by profits (hedge finance) or by indebtedness (speculative and Ponzi finance).

Under the new circumstances, the only solution is the sale of assets, which after the boom are mainly illiquid assets. The fall in the asset prices reduces the net wealth of financial intermediaries and firms, further decreasing the propensity to lend and to borrow. This reinforces the need to squeeze indebtedness by selling assets, and asset prices fall precipitously. The fall of capital asset prices strengthens the fall of investments and profits, and vice versa.[6] The cumulative fall in assets prices ends by leading many firms to insolvency. The consequence is a wave of bankruptcies, which in its turn culminates in a deep depression.

Destruction, however, also has a cathartic role: only hedge units—those able to meet their debt commitments from profits—survive. Under these circumstances, a new phase of tranquillity will suffice to increase confidence and to reactivate the entire sequence:

> A relatively low-income, high-unemployment, stagnant recession of uncertain depth and duration will follow a debt-deflation process. As the subjective repercussions of the debt-deflation wear off, as disinvestment occurs, and as financial positions are rebuilt during the stagnant phase, a recovery and expansion begins.[7]
>
> (Minsky 1975, 126–7)

The endogenous approach to the trade cycle characterizing the 'financial instability hypothesis' leads us to the core of Minsky's vision of capitalism: 'instability is determined by mechanisms within the system, not outside it; our economy is not unstable because it is shocked by oil, wars or monetary surprises, but because of its nature' (1986, 172).

Turning to the real world, Minsky (1982a, 1986) finds empirical support for his analysis. The financial instability of the American economy, which he had previously denounced (Minsky, 1963), surfaced during the middle of the 1960s and gave rise to the crises of 1966, 1970, 1974–5, 1979, and 1982. Financial instability, however, had also characterized the period before the First World War and between the World Wars. Historical evidence thus confirms that financial crises are systemic and not idiosyncratic (Minsky 1991). The spectre of a new Great Depression always lies around the corner. Starting from these presuppositions, Minsky (1986, 295) assigns a crucial role to economic policy institutions: 'even though all capitalisms are flawed, we can develop a capitalism in which the flaws are less evident than they have been since 1967'.[8]

As far as the stabilization of the economy is concerned, Minsky does not place much faith in monetary policy. Given that a great part of the money supply is endogenously created by banks and given the innovative capacity of the financial system, the central bank has only a limited control over the supply of money. In any case, its intervention may turn out to be harmful as well as ineffective:

> Monetary policy to constrain undue expansion and inflation operates by way of disrupting financing markets and asset values. Monetary policy to induce expansion operates by interest rates and the availability of credit, which do not yield increased investment if current and anticipated profits are low.
>
> (Minsky 1986, 303–4)

Instead of trying to stabilize the economy through the money supply, the central bank should thus focus on its function as a lender of last resort. By enabling the funding of financial institutions and by sustaining asset prices, it might prevent or reabsorb financial crises, so removing the threat of debt deflations and deep depressions. 'Fiscal policies', Minsky argues, 'are more powerful economic control weapons than monetary manipulations' (1986, 304). Consequently, the task of stabilizing the economy falls mainly on the government. Moreover, the financial system has to be carefully regulated since 'finance cannot be left to free markets' (Minsky 1986, 292). This is the main message of Minsky's (1986) well-known book *Stabilizing an Unstable Economy*.

Setting aside the relative importance assigned to monetary or fiscal manoeuvres, Minsky (1975, 1986) proposes a more general rethinking of the overall aim of economic policy. Specifically, he questions the orthodox mirage of sustainable investment-led growth. Being a determinant of markup and profit, investment increases the price level and income concentration. In addition, it represents a highly unstable component of domestic aggregate demand. Above all, it may turn out to be a failure and compromise financial stability and growth.[9] It follows that

> an economy that aims at accelerating growth through devices that induce capital-intensive private investment not only may not grow, but may be

increasingly inequitable in its income distribution, inefficient in its choices of techniques, and unstable in its overall performance

(Minsky 1986, 292)

The alternative advocated by Minsky is a full-employment economy led by private consumption and coordinated by a 'big government' that has the task to promote and to regulate economic activity in an efficient way.

Minsky's analysis of the financial evolution of capitalism

According to Minsky and Whalen (1996–7, 156), 'Capitalism is a dynamic, evolving system that comes in many forms. Nowhere is this dynamism more evident than in its financial structure'. Focusing on the US financial system, Minsky and Whalen (1996–7) identify four phases of capitalist development.[10]

Commercial capitalism

This phase preceded the Industrial Revolution. At the time, investments were purchased by individual entrepreneurs out of their past savings. External finance essentially satisfied the transaction requirements associated with manufacturing and trade. As Wray (2010) argues, the financial system was characterized by commercial banks that granted short-run credit and issued short-run liabilities (mainly, demand and savings deposits). Short-run bank credit in turn financed advance payments for wage bills, raw materials, and intermediate and final goods, and it was paid back as soon as borrowers (firms or traders) sold their products.

Three aspects of this phase are noteworthy. Given the possible time synchronization between assets and liabilities, commercial banking did not necessarily imply refinancing. In Minsky's terms, this activity was not necessarily speculative. In addition, insofar as they financed the production of capital goods, commercial banks actually performed their main function: promoting the capital development of the economy. Moreover, the success of the banker depended upon the fulfilment of debt commitments by borrowers. The close connection of credit with manufacturing and trade implied cautious underwriting.

Industrial and financial capitalism

The Industrial Revolution inaugurated the first era of capitalism requiring large, long-term capital assets. Investment thus became too expensive for individual entrepreneurs. The ownership of capital assets increasingly required issues of shares and bonds. As a result, the corporate form emerged bringing with it the distinction between the management and ownership of capital assets. Capital accumulation also implied increases in borrowed capital. Indebtedness, however, is a source of financial fragility as well as of growth. An internally financed bad investment impoverishes its owners without necessarily jeopardizing their existence. An externally financed bad investment may threaten not only the investors' existence but also the viability of their financiers. Following Wray (2010), firms' recourse to the issue of shares and bonds was associated with the increasing importance of investment banks. These banks issued liabilities in order to purchase corporate equities and bonds. Insofar as the maturity of their liabilities was shorter than the maturity of their assets, their activities required refinancing. To put it in Minsky's words, they had a speculative nature.

Wray (2010) distinguishes between two kinds of investment banking. According to the 'banks model', the investment bank holds the corporate shares and bonds purchased from firms in its portfolio. In this case, the banker's success depends on the borrowers' success and underwriting continues to be a fundamental activity. According to the 'markets model', on the other hand, the investment bank places the equities and shares purchased from firms into wealth-holders' portfolios. In this case, the quality of the assets evaluated over their entire lives may stop being important for the bank that purchases them. It may be possible to make greater profits by selling these assets at higher prices before they reach maturity. In this case, the prudent and far-sighted mentality of the banker gives way to the speculative and short-sighted mentality of the trader. The generalized growth in firms' external financing and in banks' speculative behaviour progressively eroded the robustness of the financial system. The result was the Great Crash of 1929–33, which brought this second phase to an end.

Paternalistic and managerial capitalism

The New Deal restructuring ushered in the paternalistic era based on countercyclical government budgets, low interest rates due to a Fed unconstrained by gold-standard considerations, and public intervention in financial markets (such as deposit insurance for banks and thrifts and the Glass–Steagall Act's separation of investment from commercial banks).[11] During this period, the government budget assumed responsibility for the support of income and profits. As a result, firms' internal cash flows could finance investments; put otherwise, firms, rather than bankers, were the masters of the private economy. As we have seen, however, in Minsky's view stability is destabilizing. The adequacy and reliability of profits spread optimism and boosted speculative behaviours by firms and their financiers. The sound performance of the economy strengthened the faith in the market and thereby encouraged a process of financial deregulation that gradually subverted the New Deal constraints.

Money-manager capitalism

This current phase of financial capitalism is characterized by three main features. The first concerns the development of trade-oriented investment banks. Traders that are sufficiently large to affect assets prices may increase their profit opportunities. More generally, the existence of scale economies paved the way for public holding companies, in which the bank holding company owns various types of highly leveraged financial firms (Wray 2010). In the tidal wave of liberalization and deregulation characterizing the transition to the twenty-first century, dimensional growth was associated with the assemblage of financial activities. Specifically, with the 1999 repeal of the Glass–Steagall Act, 'investment banking, commercial banking, and all manner of financial services were consolidated in a single financial "big box" superstore with explicit government guarantees over a portion of the liabilities' (Wray 2010, 12) and with an implicit government safety net since these superstores were too big and interconnected to fail. The second feature is represented by the development of a new layer of financial intermediaries between traditional banks and ultimate savers. These new intermediaries are represented by the money managers (mutual funds, pension funds, money market funds, bank trusts, insurance companies, and so on) that currently dominate the scene. The third feature of the phase under examination is the speculative behaviour of money managers. In line with the interests of fund holders, money managers aim to maximize the total return on their assets and, especially, prospective capital gains.[12] From this perspective, the quality of the assets considered over their entire lives is a side issue for the money managers that buy them; what matters most is the opportunity of selling assets at a higher price.

Taken as a whole, Minsky's analysis of the financial evolution of capitalism highlights the eclipsing of the prudent and far-sighted mentality of the banker by the speculative and short-sighted mentality of the trader. The result is a financial system that does not conform to Schumpeter's (1934) vision of financial institutions as the 'ephors of capitalism' that carefully select what can be financed with a view to promoting the capital development of the economy.[13] According to Minsky's analysis, the current financial system is more akin to Keynes's (1936, 159) characterization of advanced financial capitalism as a casino in which speculative behaviours prevail.

A Minskyan analysis of recent financial turmoil

As we have seen, his analysis of the evolution of financial capitalism led Minsky to converge with Keynes. Specifically, the concept of casino capitalism can be found in Chapter 12 of *The General Theory*, where Keynes brings the stock exchange into the analysis. In his view, the main function of the stock market consists in enabling entrepreneurs to sell investment goods to others instead of holding them for their full duration. This shortening of entrepreneurs' time horizons decreases uncertainty in investment decisions and thereby stimulates capital accumulation.[14] However, it also entails a worrying contraindication. When a stock market exists, the return on capital assets over their whole lives may stop being the key issue for the entrepreneurs who buy them. They might expect to make higher profits by selling these assets at higher prices before maturity. If this is the case, the short-run forecasts of share prices—the 'mass psychology of the market' (Keynes 1936, 155)—replace long-term prospective yields. As Keynes (1936, 155) puts it, 'to outwit the crowd, and to pass the bad, or depreciating, half-crown to the other fellow' becomes more important than 'to defeat the dark forces of time and ignorance which envelop our future'. Insofar as speculation replaces entrepreneurship, the selection of investment projects is subject to being misguided. Keynes's (1936, 159) well-known conclusion is that 'when the capital development of a country becomes a by-product of the activities of a casino, the job is likely to be ill-done'.

Keynes's analysis might be re-read in the light of a sort of 'fallacy of decomposition' in decision-making. The 'decomposition' refers to the distinction between the decision to buy and the decision to hold investment goods. When the stock exchange exists, these two types of decision no longer necessarily coincide; managers and owners of capital assets become two separate agents. The fallacy consists in the fact that investment turns out to be more liquid and safer for its individual owner, despite remaining illiquid and risky (and becoming even more illiquid and riskier) for the economy as a whole. To quote Keynes (1936, 155), 'Of the maxims of orthodox finance none, surely, is more antisocial than the fetish of liquidity. ... It forgets that there is no such thing as liquidity of investment for the community as a whole'.

The financial evolution of the capitalism outlined by Minsky implies an increasing decomposition in decision-making. Firms' recourse to external financing introduces the distinction between the purchase of investment goods and their financing: a new figure comes on stage, the financier. Financial intermediation introduces a further distinction between lenders/creditors and ultimate financiers (i.e. savers). So far, however, Minsky's evaluation remains positive: both direct and indirect external financing do not seem to imply any 'fallacy'. The targets and the evaluations of investors and of their financiers end by converging.[15] Insofar as savers and/or financial intermediaries contribute to the assessment of investment profitability, finance renders the evaluation process even more accurate, thus performing the Schumpeterian function of an 'ephor of capitalism'. The 'fallacy of decomposition' reappears, however, with the increasing recourse to secondary financial markets characterizing the 'market oriented' investment banks and today's money managers. When securities are bought with the intention of selling them at higher prices shortly afterwards, the short-run forecasts of these prices—the 'mass psychology of the market'—replace the evaluations of prospective yields over their entire lives. Securities turn out to be more liquid and safer for their individual owners, thereby becoming more illiquid and riskier for the economy as a whole.

These considerations can be extended to the recent evolution of credit markets. The securitization process that started in the 1980s, and expanded rapidly thereafter, created a sort of secondary credit market, introducing the distinction between the lenders (the originators of the loan) and the ultimate creditors (to whom debt commitments are due). When the financial institution that originates the loan can transform it into securities and sell it to others, the short-term forecasts of the prices of these securities—the 'mass psychology of the market'—replaces the evaluation of the long-term prospective yields of the loan (interest payments and reimbursement of the principal). Credit turns out to be more liquid and safer for individual lenders, thereby becoming less liquid and riskier for the economy as a whole. Thanks to securitization, the lenders' function as 'ephors of capitalism' has been further undermined. To put it in Minsky's (1992, 23) words, 'the selection and supervisory function of the lenders and underwriters are not as well done as they might be when the fortunes of the originators are at hazard over the longer term'.

To sum up, the growth of the financial sector in recent decades has been accompanied by an increasing decomposition in decision-making. Insofar as this decomposition has involved the participants in the evaluations and the results, it may have increased the accuracy of decisions by improving the functioning of the financial system. Following Minsky, this seems to have been the case for direct and indirect external financing. More often, however, decomposition seems to have brought with it a lower involvement and a shirking of the responsibilities of participants. This holds for the distinction between the decision to buy and the decision to hold assets associated with the progressive development of the secondary markets in which these assets (capital goods, securities, and loans) can be sold before maturity. Thanks to the existence of secondary markets, the short-term forecasts of asset prices replaced long-term perspective yields misleading the evaluation process. Assets turned out to be more liquid and less risky for the individual, becoming less liquid and riskier for the economy as a whole. Thanks to the increasing 'fallacies of decomposition' associated with the recourse to secondary markets, the unregulated growth of the financial system has implied increasing financial instability.[16] Minsky was well aware of this, and he repeatedly insisted on the need for carefully and continuously updating financial regulation.

A brief digression is useful here on the misleading effects of secondary asset markets. Let us consider the purchase of new investment goods that can be resold on the stock market and/or their financing by securities or by loans that can be sold to others. In order that short-run expected capital gains prevail over long-term perspective yields, secondary markets have to experience an expansionary phase. Not by chance, financial crises are generally preceded by upswings. This explains why Minsky's writings on financial instability focus on the expansionary phase of the cycle.[17] The General Theory, by contrast, focuses on a stagnant economy. In this context, however, Keynes's Chapter 12 might perform a special role: it might warn us that, after an initial phase, finance may jeopardize the sustainability of growth fuelling capitalism's tendency towards stagnation. Re-reading the recent financial crisis from this perspective, for example, we might conclude that unregulated finance may erode the robustness of the financial system and lead to long and persistent depressions.

This seems to be precisely what happened in the recent financial turmoil. From a Minskyan perspective, the sub-prime crisis can be easily understood by focusing first on the expansionary stance of US monetary policy. During the Greenspan era, inflation was contained by competition from relatively cheap Chinese imports while the dollar was sustained by high capital inflows. The Fed consequently felt entitled to support asset prices to the extent that the performance of the real economy required it.[18] Following a script adopted in the past (such as during the stock market crisis in 1987 and the Long Term Capital Management Crisis in 1998), the Fed mitigated the negative consequences of the 2000 dot-com crash by means of an unprecedented cut in interest rates (Leijonhufvud 2009).[19] This reassured the public about the Fed's availability to support financial markets and assets prices (the so-called 'Greenspan put').

Another important aspect of the crisis was the unprecedented wave of financial deregulation and innovation that preceded it. According to Krugman (2008), the two main innovations were loan securitization and the associated development of a shadow banking system. The 1999 repeal of the Glass–Steagall Act permitted bank-originated loans to be readily sold by the originators to other financial intermediaries (often affiliates of the parent bank or holding company). The underwriters in turn packaged the loans and sold tranches of them to investors in the form of structured collateralized debt obligations. As we have seen, the possibility of transferring loans (with the corresponding risks) to others induced banks to grant more and riskier loans.

This securitization process was accompanied by the development of a shadow banking system. Through recourse to new and imaginative financial instruments—such as auction rate securities and asset-backed commercial paper—non-bank financial intermediaries started issuing short-run liabilities in order to finance their long-term assets. In a context of rising prices, those assets could be easily and profitably sold. While bank deposits were subject to constraints (such as supervision, reserve and capital requirements, and insurance fees), however, the new financial instruments were not subject to any restrictions whatsoever. The shadow banking system could therefore perform the same role as banks, but without constraints. Its funds could be invested to a greater extent and in riskier assets, and thus offered higher yields.

The overall effect of the Fed's policy and of financial deregulation and innovation was a widespread increase in credit availability and (above all) a generalized relaxation of credit standards. It was mainly the household sector that benefited from credit expansion, and one consequence was an increase in households' demand for durable consumption goods and, consequently, in income. Households' indebtedness, however, also financed households' demand for houses, and it is precisely here that the sub-prime problem arose. In the euphoria of the housing boom, buyers were granted loans requiring little or no down payment and with monthly payments that were beyond their ability to pay. After all, it did not matter whether the borrower could actually make the mortgage payments out of his/her income. Given the rising trend of house prices, troubled borrowers could either refinance or pay off the mortgage by selling the house. Expected capital gains on houses prevailed over long-term perspective yields on the loan (interest payments and principal reimbursement). As suggested by the term *sub-prime*, loans became less liquid and riskier for the economy as a whole, while turning out to be more liquid and safer for individual originators.

During the housing boom, house prices rose to the point where purchasing a home became beyond the reach of many Americans. By the autumn of 2005, sales began to slow down. Some months later house prices also began to fall—slowly at first, and then at an accelerating speed. As prices fell below the value of the mortgages, many borrowers became insolvent, and the resulting wave of failures in the housing market undermined confidence in mortgage-backed assets. The downgrading of these assets by rating agencies exacerbated and spread the tensions. In the second half of 2007, the prices of mortgage-backed assets collapsed. Holding part of the assets they were used to handling, banks experienced heavy losses, and this in turn jeopardized confidence in financial institutions. The result was a credit crunch and a general de-leveraging that drove the US and the world economy into its worst recession since the 1930s. This outcome was the logical consequence of the evolution of modern finance from the 'ephor of capitalism' advocated by Schumpeter to the 'casino capitalism' denounced by Keynes and Minsky.

Minsky's support for community banking

In recent decades, the financial system has experienced an intense process of concentration. The number of financial institutions has decreased while their average size has risen. Minsky (1993) notes that big banks like big deals, and as a result new small businesses and marginal communities (the poor, blacks, Hispanics, immigrant populations, the inner cities, small towns, and rural areas) are often inadequately served and financed. Minksy (1993, 34) argues that 'if we wish small deals to get a fair shake, then we need small banks having financial relations measured in thousands of dollars rather than in millions'. With hindsight, we might add that these banks would not be 'too big to fail'.

Minsky (1992, 1993) proposed the creation of a nationwide set of profit-seeking community development banks, guided by a government-owned federal bank for community development banks that would serve as their promoter, financier, regulator, supervisor, and coordinator. On the liabilities side, the community development banks would offer both insured and non-insured checkable deposits. On the assets side, the community development banks should be limited to riskless activities that would not compromise their ability to redeem deposits. After an initial phase, community development banks should be profitable or else liquidated.

According to Minsky (1993), a community development bank should provide the following services:

- *Operate a payment system (checkable deposits, debit and credit cards, check-cashing services, and so on).* The provision of these services is likely to be a profitable business in under-banked communities and among those whom traditional banks are reluctant to serve.
- *Provide a secure depository for savings and transaction balances.* If the customers who cash checks also generate saving deposits, the average net amount of currency withdrawn for exchanges decreases, lowering the cost of the payment system for banks.

- *Finance housing and consumer debt.* Community development banks should originate mortgages designed to finance the purchase and rehabilitation of the property within their area. Taking advantage of their access to information unavailable to outside analysts, they should also finance consumer debt that is advantageous to the local community.
- *Provide commercial banking services.* Commercial banking has three main aspects: the development and solicitation of business, the structuring of loans and the supervision of credits. Devoted to their local area, the officers of community development banks would develop a greater awareness of the potential successes and failures in their community than would the branch officers of large traditional banks. The officers of community development banks would not only promote and support local development with greater awareness, but also could take advantage of their relationships with their clients to provide more efficient supervision and consultation.
- *Provide investment-banking services.* Community development banks should underwrite and take positions in the equity and bond liabilities of clients, and thereby provide the long-term financing required by their clients' investment activities and support local economic development. In addition, community development banks would help alleviate the difficulties of new, innovative, and small businesses, which notoriously tend to be discriminated against by financial markets.
- *Provide asset management services and advice.* Lower-income people in marginal communities usually are unfamiliar with the investment alternatives available. Community development banks should advise such clients and provide suitable financial instruments.

In opposition to today's unscrupulous money managers, Minsky proposed a finance system 'on a human scale' and 'with a human face' that is deeply rooted in the local territory and aims to improve local property, stimulate local economic activities, and pursue social equity and cohesion in the local community. The community development banks would privilege the banker's over the trader's mentality; their DNA and their system of regulation would not encourage speculation. In addition to promoting local economic activity, their interventions would strengthen the robustness of the overall financial system. Thanks to community development banks, the capital development of the economy would rely on the proliferation of the new, innovative small businesses that finance would otherwise tend to disregard. As Minsky (1992, 26) puts it, 'community banks are at the heart of a financial structure that will be biased towards resource creation'. The reason that this approach should be adopted is that 'the vitality of the American economy and democracy depends on the continual creation of new, small, and novel enterprises' (Minsky 1993, 34).

Minsky's community development banks obviously have much in common with cooperative banks. Thus, the success of cooperative banking might represent a further confirmation of Minsky's analysis. What distinguishes cooperative banks from Minsky's community development banks is their non-profit character.

Opposed to the unscrupulousness and greed of today's money managers, cooperative banks provide support for the 'moral, cultural and economic conditions' of their local communities.[20] This ethical approach to finance excludes speculative activities, thus counteracting the tendency of the system towards financial fragility. In addition, the ethical approach tends to recompose the interests at stake, encouraging banks to widen their responsibilities instead of offloading them onto others. In the case of cooperative banks, profit maximization is not conceived as a target in itself but as a condition to promote the economic and social development of the local community. The interests of banks are not separable from the interests of their customers: they each presuppose the other.

Conclusion

As we have seen, what distinguishes cooperative banks from Minsky's community development banks is their non-profit character. Minsky, however, would have shared the belief that profit maximization has to be considered as an instrument rather than as a target. In his view, individual interests do not spontaneously lead to collective welfare. Money does not necessarily flow towards its more productive uses. Credit allocation tends to discriminate those new, innovative small businesses that often represent the future. Economic growth does not necessarily increase social welfare and equity. If left to itself, the economy would tend towards '*fortress capitalism*, a system with declining fortunes for all but a minority who seek protection behind walled and gated communities'. The alternative advocated by Minsky is '*shared-prosperity capitalism*' (Minsky and Whalen 1996–7, 161; emphasis added). Community banking—Minsky's community development banks plus cooperative banks—should be understood and encouraged precisely from this perspective.

Notes

1 For the comparison of Minsky and Keynes, see De Antoni (2010).

2 This might be why Minsky (1975, 1986) speaks of a *hypothesis* rather than a *theory* of financial instability.

3 Analogously, Minsky (1986, 219) claims 'any transitory tranquillity is transformed into an expansion'; see also Minsky (1980).

4 According to Minsky (1986, 206–7) a robust financial system is dominated by hedge units, which fulfil their debt commitments by profits. A fragile financial system, on the other hand, is dominated by speculative and ultra-speculative (or Ponzi) units, which fulfil their debt commitments by indebtedness. This dependence on credit makes speculative and ultra-speculative units more vulnerable. When confronted by even an ordinary negative shock such as a rise in the interest rate or a fall in profits, these units have insufficient liquidity, profits, and borrowing capacity to meet inherited debt commitments. Their only possibility is to reduce indebtedness by selling non-monetary assets. The consequent fall in the prices of these assets, however, may lead them to insolvency.

5 Minsky (1978, 45) puts it as follows: 'the internal workings of the banking mechanism or Central Bank action to constrain inflation will result in the supply of finance being less than infinitely elastic leading to a rapid increase in short term interest rates'.

6 In Minsky's view, while the fall in the demand price for investment goods depresses investment, income, and profits, the consequent fall in profit expectation reduces the demand price for investment goods (the present value of expected profits). The result is a cumulative fall in investment, income, and profits.

7 According to De Antoni (2010), however, recovery is not as certain as Minsky argues. Following Minsky, let us assume that tranquillity increases confidence, thus decreasing the interest rate used to calculate the demand price for investment goods (the present value of expected profits). What Minsky neglects is that if expected profits are zero, then the demand price will not increase. Alternatively, the stimulus might not be strong enough to drive the demand price above the supply price. In both these cases, tranquillity alone would not be sufficient to trigger recovery, and depression will be persistent.

8 The role that Minsky (1992) assigns to economic policy institutions is anything but easy. Moreover, these institutions must be continuously revised and kept up to date, since the flaws of capitalism are always evolving. It follows that Minsky strongly disagrees with the adoption of fixed rules in economic policy.

9 Bad investments may generate profits lower than debt commitments and thus foster a wave of bankruptcies that in its turn depress expectations, confidence, and economic activity.

10 See also Minsky (1990) and Minsky and Whalen (1996). Wray (2010) usefully integrates and elaborates the analysis of Minsky and Whalen's two texts (1996, 1996–7).

11 In the wake of the Great Depression, the Glass–Steagall Act of 1933 introduced the separation between commercial and investment banks and prohibited commercial banks from handling private securities. The Glass–Steagall Act was repealed by the Gramm–Leach–Bliley Act of 1999.

12 The total return on assets is the combination of dividends and interest received and the appreciation in per share value (Minsky and Whalen 1996–7, 159).

13 In ancient Sparta, the *ephors* were magistrates that constrained the two kings' powers and activities.

14 Keynes's thesis is that as we look further ahead into the future, our knowledge decreases and our forecasts become less reliable.

15 In defining hedge, speculative, and Ponzi financing, for instance, Minsky (1986, 206–7) considers firms and their financiers as a single entity.

16 This phenomenon reached its climax with the spreading of 'sub-prime' loans and 'junk' bonds that preceded the sub-prime crisis.

17 One of the few exceptions is Minsky (1982b). As Minsky (1986, 173) observes, 'the spectacular panics, debt deflations, and deep depressions that historically followed a speculative boom as well as the recovery from depressions are of lesser importance in the analysis of instability than the developments over a period characterized by sustained growth that lead to the emergence of fragile and unstable financial structures'.

18 In line with Minsky's 'two price' theory, the central bank sustained assets—rather than goods—prices.

19 The dot-com speculative bubble reflected the climate of confidence in technological advancements associated with the growth of Internet-based companies. From 1995 to 2000, this bubble led to an extraordinary rise in the NASDAQ. The Fed reacted to the burst of the bubble by reducing interest rates from 6.5 to 3.5 per cent during 2000 and continued to cut these rates through mid-2004.

20 Article 2 of the Statute of Cooperative Banks approved by Italian cooperative banks in the Thirteenth Conference on Cooperative Credit, Parma, December 2005. In Italy, cooperative banks may have even sustained the robustness of the country's banking system, thus mitigating the domestic repercussions of the international financial crisis.

References

Blanchard, O. (2000) 'What do we know about macroeconomics that Fisher and Wicksell did not?', *De Economist*, 148(5): 571–601.

De Antoni, E. (2010) 'Minsky's upward instability: the not-too-Keynesian optimism of a financial Cassandra', in S. Zambelli (ed.) *Computable, Constructive and Behavioural Economic Dynamics: essays in honour of Kumaraswamy (Vela) Velupillai*, London: Routledge, pp. 462–84.

Keynes, J.M. (1936) *The General Theory of Employment, Interest and Money*, London: Macmillan.

Krugman, P.R. (2008) *The Return of Depression Economics and the Crisis of 2008*, London: Penguin Books.

Leijonhufvud, A. (2009) 'Out of the corridor: Keynes and the crisis', *Cambridge Journal of Economics*, 33(4): 741–57.

Minsky, H.P. (1963) 'Can "it" happen again?', in D. Carson (ed.) *Banking and Monetary Studies*, Homewood, Illinois: R.D. Irwin, pp. 101–11.

Minsky, H.P. (1974) 'The modelling of financial instability: an introduction', in W.G. Vogt and M.H. Mickle (eds) *Proceedings of the Fifth Annual Pittsburgh Conference held April 24–26, 1974, Modelling and Simulation*, vol. 5, Pittsburgh, PA: School of Engineering, University of Pittsburgh, pp. 267–72.

Minsky, H.P. (1975) *John Maynard Keynes*, New York: Columbia University Press.

Minsky, H.P. (1978) 'The financial instability hypothesis: a restatement', *Thames Papers in Political Economy*, London: North East London Polytechnic; reprinted in *Can 'It' Happen Again? Essays on Instability and Finance*, Armonk, NY: M.E. Sharpe (1982), pp. 90–116; and also in P. Arestis and T. Skouras (eds) (1985) *Post Keynesian Economic Theory: a challenge to neo-classical Economics*, Armonk, NY: M.E. Sharpe, pp. 24–55.

Minsky, H.P. (1980) 'Capitalist financial processes and the instability of capitalism', *Journal of Economic Issues*, 14(2): 505–23.

Minsky, H.P. (1982a) *Can 'It' Happen Again? Essays on Instability and Finance*, Armonk, NY: M.E. Sharpe.

Minsky, H.P. (1982b) 'Debt deflation processes in today's institutional environment', *Banca Nazionale del Lavoro, Quarterly Review*, 143(4): 375–94.

Minsky, H.P. (1986) *Stabilizing an Unstable Economy*, New Haven, CT: Yale University Press.

Minsky, H.P. (1990) 'Schumpeter e la finanza', in S. Biasco, A. Roncaglia, and M. Salvati (eds) *Istituzioni e Mercato nello Sviluppo Economico: saggi in onore di Paolo Sylos Labini*, Rome: Laterza, pp. 117–33.

Minsky, H.P. (1991) 'Financial crises: systemic or idiosyncratic?', Working Paper no. 51, Amandale-on-Hudson, NY: Levy Economics Institute, Bard College.

Minsky, H.P. (1992) 'The capital development of the economy and the structure of financial institutions', Working Paper no. 72, Amandale-on-Hudson, NY: Levy Economics Institute, Bard College.

Minsky H.P. (1993) 'Community Development Banks: an idea in search of substance', *Challenge*, 36(2): 33–41.

Minsky, H.P. and Whalen, C.J. (1996) 'Economic insecurity and the institutional prerequisites for successful capitalism', Working Papers Series no. 165, Annandale-on-Hudson, NY: Levy Economics Institute, Bard College.

Minsky, H.P. and Whalen, C.J. (1996–7) 'Economic insecurity and the institutional prerequisites for successful capitalism', *Journal of Post Keynesian Economics*, 19(2): 155–71.

Schumpeter, J.A. (1934) *The Theory of Economic Development*, Cambridge, MA: Harvard University Press.

Wray, L.R. (2010) 'What do banks do? What should banks do?', Working Paper no. 612, Amandale-on-Hudson, NY: Levy Economics Institute, Bard College.

2 Governance and performance

Reassessing the pre-crisis situation of European banks[1]

Giovanni Ferri, Panu Kalmi, and Eeva Kerola

The banking literature has generally focused on shareholder banks that aim to maximize profit. This is partly at odds with the fact that many countries' banking systems feature a large—sometimes even dominant—presence of stakeholder banks whose main objective is not profit maximization. As a case in point, most European countries have a substantial sector of customer-owned cooperative banks or non-profit savings banks. The latter are in some countries privately owned while in others are state owned.

We use data from Bankscope to construct a long and wide panel of more than 300 banks for the years from 1994 to 2007 for 19 European countries to compare bank performance across different organizational structures.[2] As performance measures we use profitability, cost efficiency, and loan losses. We also provide a finer than usual classification of the banks' organizational structure by splitting each group into two subgroups: the commercial banks into general versus specialized banking institutions, the cooperative banks into tightly versus loosely federated, and the savings banks into privately versus state owned.

We find little evidence to support the claim that shareholder-owned banks outperform stakeholder-owned banks. In terms of profitability, shareholder-owned banks are somewhat more successful than stakeholder-owned banks; however, even in that measure private savings banks are doing better than shareholder-owned retail banks. In other measures, stakeholder banks mostly outperform shareholder banks. For instance, cooperative banks report lower loan losses than profit-maximizing commercial banks, and loosely federated cooperative banks and private savings banks have higher cost efficiency than commercial retail banks. Thus, our findings provide a nuanced picture of performance differences.

Views about stakeholder banks became somewhat more benevolent as they weathered the Great Crisis of 2007–9 better than commercial banks, requiring less government assistance (*The Economist* 2010). However, our findings suggest that the negative prejudice against stakeholder banks was misplaced even before the crisis.

The first section of this chapter outlines the main views put forward in the theoretical and empirical literature about the effects of various ownership structures in banking; the second section introduces our classification refinements and, after implementing them, describes our large panel of European banks; the third section reports the results of our empirical analysis; and the fourth section presents the conclusions and draws policy implications.

Ownership structure and performance in European banking

The literature recognizes that the organizational form of banks has important implications for their economic behaviour, performance, and business activities (e.g. O'Hara 1981; Fama and Jensen 1983; Rasmusen 1988). While the main objective of commercial banks is to maximize shareholder value (profits), cooperative or savings banks aim to maximize the value for a larger set of stakeholders—that is, to provide the best products and services to their clients. Thus, comparing shareholder banks with stakeholder banks should not be based only on profitability, but performance should also be measured by other indicators, such as cost efficiency and loan quality.

The peculiarity of cooperative banks lies in their control and profit distribution (Rasmusen 1988). While the shareholders of stock companies decide how to distribute profits and are free to sell their stocks, cooperatives are characterized by a distribution of profits that is rather limited and membership that is (generally) not tradable.[3]

Like cooperative banks, savings banks are non-profit-oriented institutions, with a mandate to contribute to the 'general good', and they can belong to larger networks (Ayadi *et al.* 2009; Schmidt 2009). Unlike cooperatives that are customer owned, savings banks are owned either by the state (e.g. *Landesbanken* in Germany) or by private foundations; consequently, the ownership rights of customers of cooperatives are greater than at savings banks.

Several pundits argue that members of cooperative banks do not have adequate incentive to monitor the managers because of their limited individual financial stakes, non-tradable shares, and ownership dispersion. This makes the principal–agent conflict between owners and management more severe in cooperative banks than in joint-stock banks (Cuevas and Fischer 2006), and this problem may be even more severe in savings banks. In view of this inefficiency in ownership structures, stakeholder banks exist only because of protective regulation (O'Hara 1981).

The observation that stakeholder banks not only survive, but also thrive in many countries has led other researchers to investigate factors other than legal restrictions. Indeed, stakeholder banks could dominate in terms of two other principal–agent connections—between the bank and its borrowers and between the bank and its depositors (Coco and Ferri 2010). First, both cooperative and savings banks usually develop a relationship between the bank and its borrowers, which helps to lower the adverse selection problem (Amess 2002). Second, managers of cooperative banks have lower incentives to take excessive risks, which make deposits safer (Rasmusen 1988; Fonteyne 2007). Larger accumulations of reserves can be used to smooth out fluctuations during the business cycle and therefore generate more certain returns for depositors, as well as reduce the bankruptcy risk (Amess 2002; Schmidt 2009). Allen *et al.* (2008) argue that stakeholder owners put more weight on firm survival than shareholder owners, and under certain circumstances this may even lead to higher long-term firm value than pure profit maximization.

The literature has devoted little attention to the role of external economies that stakeholder banks may accrue from belonging to networks. This collaboration is most extensive among cooperative banks that form either strategic or consensual networks (Desrochers and Fischer 2005; Cuevas and Fischer 2006). There are common elements in both types of networks—such as joint development of resources—but strategic networks also include several features typically lacking in consensual networks: a high degree of cross-insurance or joint liability, joint governance structures, strategic guidance, and in some cases direct intervention from the centre in the case of underperformance by primary-level banks. The second-tier entity is often owned by primary-level banks, and its supervisory body consists of representatives of those banks. In this closed system, primary-level banks hold ownership rights on second-tier banks, but the latter also have some well-specified control rights towards primary-level banks (that otherwise are controlled by their member-customers). The integrated structure helps to control the principal–agent problem generated in the primary level due to the dispersed ownership structure (Desrochers and Fischer 2005; Cuevas and Fischer 2006).

Moreover, savings banks in many countries feature multi-level governance structures with an ownership stake by the government. This integration can be regarded as solving the principal–agent problem for savings banks. However, it has often been argued that government ownership leads to further separation of control and financial incentives, and therefore to underperformance (La Porta *et al.* 2002; Sapienza 2004),[4] so the overall effect of an integrated structure in solving governance problems in systems of state savings banks is unclear.

The uncertainties in the theoretical literature have not been resolved by empirical contributions. Indeed, empirical works on the relationship between different ownership types and bank performance is rather inconclusive. The most relevant studies for our purposes are those conducting international comparisons. Iannotta *et al.* (2007) compare 181 large banks in 15 European countries from 1999 to 2004 and find that mutual banks—by which they mean cooperative and private savings banks—and government-owned banks exhibit lower profitability than private banks, in spite of their lower costs. Public sector banks tend to have poorer loan quality and higher insolvency risk while mutuals have better loan quality and lower asset risk than both private and public sector banks. By and large, this divergence in the results indicates that the financial intermediation model differs across the three bank ownership forms.

Goddard *et al.* (2004) focus on six European countries and find little evidence of any systematic relationship between ownership type and profitability outside Germany, where savings and cooperative banks underperform commercial banks. Only in their all-countries cross-sectional estimation are cooperative banks somewhat less profitable than commercial and savings banks. Girardone *et al.* (2009) find that in the EU-15, cooperative banks are significantly more cost efficient than commercial banks. The differences in cost efficiency across bank types can often be explained by the financial system in each economy. Moreover, in their extensive review of cooperative banks throughout Europe, Ayadi *et al.* (2010) conclude that no radical differences exist between cooperative banks and their peers in terms of performance and efficiency. However, Kontolaimou and Tsekouras (2010) reach rather different conclusions utilizing metafrontier analysis. They conclude that there is a significant technology gap for European cooperative banks relative to other ownership types, which they attribute mostly to the level and/or the composition of outputs, rather than inputs.

Even across country-level studies, no consistent patterns emerge in the relationship between ownership and performance. The two most studied cases are Germany and Spain. Altunbas *et al.* (2001) find that state banks and cooperative banks are more cost and profit efficient than their private counterparts in Germany, possibly because of relatively lower funding costs. Consistent with these findings, Brunner *et al.* (2004) report that German cooperative and savings banks are slightly more profitable than commercial banks, while Beck *et al.* (2009) report that German private banks are less stable. Moreover, Hasan and Lozano-Vivas (2002) find that private savings banks are more cost inefficient (regarding non-interest costs) than commercial banks in Spain. However, when they perform a further series of ordinary-least squares (OLS) estimations, they find that despite higher expense preferences, mutual institutions apparently record higher return on assets and increasing market share relative to commercial banks. Crespí *et al.* (2004) find that savings banks are smaller in size, but more profitable than commercial banks, especially when considering profits from regular banking operations. Garcia-Marco and Robles-Fernandez (2008) reveal major differences in the patterns of risk-taking of Spanish commercial and savings banks. In general, commercial banks are more risk-inclined than savings banks, and small-sized institutions appear to assume lower risks.

Summing up, the lack of unanimity in the empirical literature about whether commercial banks outperform their savings or cooperative counterparts in Europe seems at odds with the widely held view that cooperative and savings banks are less efficient than commercial banks.[5] However, studies of these comparisons face important limitations. One shortcoming is the way ownership types are categorized. Most studies employing the Bankscope database utilize the ownership classification provided in the database and compare cooperatives, commercial banks, and savings banks. In this chapter, we aim to provide a more comprehensive classification of ownership structures.

Data and refinements

Our sample is based on the Bankscope database. Specifically, we use data for 19 European countries, including all EU-15 countries (i.e. EU member countries before the 2004 enlargement) plus Cyprus, Iceland, Norway, and Switzerland.

Initially, we adopted Bankscope's classification of ownership types and included all financial intermediaries that were classified as cooperative banks, commercial banks, savings banks, real estate/mortgage banks, bank holding and holding companies, and governmental credit institutions.

We use only consolidated data for the years from 1994 to 2007. Consolidated data take into account the group structure of the banks and report figures for the entire banking group, rather than for individual components. To avoid double counting, we excluded banks owned by other banks and include banks that merged only until the year before the merger.

The sample mostly includes banks that are classified as commercial banks, savings banks, or cooperative banks, although we modified these classifications as explained below. In addition, we included UK and Irish building societies, although we otherwise exclude mortgage banks.[6] Some large commercial banks are not found under the heading 'commercial banks' but under 'bank holdings & holding companies'. This source was used when appropriate. We also included banks from the category 'specialized governmental credit institutions' if these are savings banks.

We excluded banks that are owned by other banks; sometimes these owners may have been banks outside Western Europe. Thus, we focus on comparing the performance of European-owned companies, most of which focus their activities on national markets, but also include a number of Pan-European banks. We also excluded government-owned commercial banks. Finally, we removed all banks that have fewer than five-year observations and, to deal with outliers, we eliminated the observations for any dependent or independent variables that are below the 1 per cent or above the 99 per cent cut-off.[7]

Two types of refinements were made. First, we re-coded some of the banks when the ownership classification in Bankscope seemed inappropriate. Second, we split commercial banks, cooperative banks, and savings banks into further binary categories.

Since cursory evidence left us unsatisfied about Bankscope's classification of some of the banks in terms of ownership, we painstakingly reviewed this issue. Specifically, we consulted each bank's websites and reclassified all banks into three ownership types: commercial banks, cooperative banks, and savings banks.

We made extensive modifications to the ownership classification, particularly with regards to savings banks. Bankscope classifies as savings banks many converted banks that can no longer reasonably be considered savings banks (e.g. Lloyds TSB or Swedbank). We also changed the classification for a number of Belgian and Italian banks where the non-profit foundation is no longer a dominant shareholder.[8] The French Caisse d'Épargne banks are still classified by Bankscope as savings banks, although since the late 1990s their ownership structure has been cooperative; consequently, we reclassified them as cooperative banks.

Generally, cooperative banks are appropriately defined in Bankscope. One feature of the database, however, is that it provides different levels of aggregation. For example, all French cooperative banks are heavily represented by their regional banks. In addition, there is information also at the group level and subsidiaries for all four cooperative bank groups. On the other hand, for the Netherlands and Finland, both of which have important cooperative banks, only group-level data are available. In the cases where regional data is available, we use the regional level. For some cases, like Germany, we have consolidated data on large banks, while for Austria we have regional-level data on some banks (*Raiffeisenbanken*) and bank-level data on others (*Volksbanken*). Thus, we always aim to utilize the lowest level where consolidated data is available. Since group-level banks are ultimately owned by regional and local banks, this is consistent with the principle of including the ultimate owner. In addition, for government-owned savings banks that are regionally operated, we use the regional level data in our analysis where appropriate (for example, the German *Landesbanken*).

Commercial banks are a relatively straightforward category, and they generally needed no additional re-coding.

The original three groups—savings banks, cooperative banks, and commercial banks—were then further subdivided into six groups depending on their ownership type: (1) private savings banks; (2) state-owned savings banks; (3) tightly federated cooperative banks (i.e. those belonging to a strategic network); (4) loosely federated cooperative banks (i.e. those belonging to a consensual network); (5) general (retail) commercial banks; and (6) specialized commercial banks.

Starting with savings banks, an important classification criterion for these banks is that they can be under private or state ownership. The main examples of state-owned savings banks are German, Austrian, and Swiss saving banks, but there are also some Portuguese ones. Private savings banks exist mostly in Spain (Hasan and Lozano-Vivas 2002; García-Marco and Roblez-Fernandez 2008) and Norway (Bøhren and Josefsen 2008). They are also present in smaller numbers in Denmark, Iceland, and Sweden, although in these countries a substantial number of savings banks have converted into joint-stock companies.

Admittedly, the dichotomization of saving banks is somewhat problematic since the savings banks sector is rather heterogeneous across countries and has been substantially transformed within the past two decades (Ayadi *et al.* 2009). However, distinguishing private from state-owned savings banks is important as their corporate governance set-ups may differ in two important ways. On the one hand, state ownership might negatively impinge on performance as it could lead to inefficiencies due to political interference (La Porta *et al.* 2002; Sapienza 2004). On the other hand, state ownership of savings banks may be beneficial if it leads to more concentrated monitoring.[9]

For cooperative banks, we distinguish between tightly federated and loosely federated or independent cooperative banks. Our division is based on the work of Desrochers and Fischer (2005), who differentiate between atomized, consensual, and strategic networks. The last category corresponds to our 'tightly federated' cooperative banks. Note that the governance set-up of tightly federated cooperative banks may differ markedly: their governance is conditioned to a much larger extent by the directives issued by the central body of the federation vis-à-vis what is experienced by the loosely federated coops. Thus, tightly federated units can benefit from stronger group-level monitoring, but this may be achieved at the cost of less flexibility in their business choices. As such, there might be a trade-off between the two effects.

Finally, we divide commercial banks into general banks and specialized banks that serve niche groups of clients by providing such services as investment banking and asset management. This distinction was drawn by examining each bank's website and judging how the bank describes its own activities. Schure *et al.* (2004) found significant heterogeneity among banks that are classified by Bankscope as commercial banks and conjecture that this might be due to the different business models of banks within this category. Therefore, we expected that there are significant differences between general and specialized commercial banks in terms of such factors as profitability, capitalization, and revenue composition. In contrast, all of the savings banks and cooperative banks in our sample have a retail focus.[10]

Our sample consists of 359 banks or banking groups (see Table 2.1). The largest national groups come from France (62 banks) and Spain (60) followed at

Table 2.1 Number of banks with different ownership types, by country

	Coop1	*Coop2*	*SavPriv*	*SavPubl*	*ComRet*	*ComSpec*	*Sum*
Austria	6	0	0	5	5	2	18
Belgium	0	0	0	0	1	4	5
Cyprus	0	0	0	0	5	0	5
Denmark	0	2	4	0	13	0	19
Finland	1	0	0	0	1	1	3
France	44	0	0	0	4	14	62
Germany	8	1	0	8	3	6	26
Greece	0	0	0	0	7	0	7
Iceland	0	0	3	0	2	0	5
Ireland	0	2	0	0	3	1	6
Italy	2	13	0	0	16	3	34
Luxembourg	1	0	0	0	0	3	4
Netherlands	1	0	0	0	7	6	14
Norway	0	0	18	0	1	0	19
Portugal	1	0	0	2	2	2	7
Spain	0	3	43	0	12	2	60
Sweden	0	1	1	0	5	0	7
Switzerland	1	0	0	10	1	8	20
United Kingdom	0	25	0	0	6	7	38
Sum	65	47	69	25	94	59	359

Source: Elaborated from Bankscope data (see text).

Notes

Code to ownership classifications: Coop1, tightly federated cooperative banks; Coop2, other cooperative banks; SavPriv, private savings banks; SavPubl, public savings banks; ComRet, commercial retail banks; ComSpec, specialized commercial banks.

a considerable distance by the UK (38), Italy (34), and Germany (26). Five countries—Austria, Denmark, Norway, Switzerland, and the Netherlands—have between ten and 20 banks each, while the other nine countries have fewer than ten banks each, with Finland the least at only three. In the sample, 31 per cent are cooperative banks—18 per cent tightly federated and 13 per cent loosely federated; 26 per cent are savings banks—19 per cent privately owned and 7 per cent state owned; 43 per cent are commercial banks—26 per cent general and 17 per cent specialized. Two-thirds of the tightly federated cooperatives are French, and about half of the loosely federated cooperatives are British and 28 per cent are Italian. More than 60 per cent of the private savings banks are Spanish, followed by 26 per cent that are Norwegian. The state-owned savings banks are concentrated in Switzerland (40 per cent of the total), Germany (32 per cent) and Austria (20 per cent). General and specialized commercial banks in the sample are more uniformly distributed across the 19 European countries.

Empirical results

Our key performance variables have been widely utilized in banking research: profitability (measured by return on assets), loan quality (measured by loan losses, an inverse measure), and cost efficiency (cost-to-income ratio, an inverse measure). Profitability is probably the most widely used performance measure. It is appropriate to use return on assets rather than return on equity in a sample that includes banks with different ownership structures and equity valuation. A fundamental issue is whether it is appropriate to evaluate non-profit-maximizing banks based on profitability. Thus, we also included two alternative performance measures: loan losses (percentage of non-performing loans of total loans) and cost efficiency (the ratio of operating costs to operating income).

Our analysis relied solely on descriptive statistics and t-tests for difference in means.[11] Table 2.2 reports the average value of return on assets for each of the six categories for the 19 countries, and the associated test for the differences in means. The difference always refers to the difference between the particular category (ownership class or country) and all the other categories. Profitability is generally lower for stakeholder banks vis-à-vis shareholder banks. In the overall average—across all countries and all years—the return on assets is 0.97 per cent. However, only specialized shareholder banks clearly outperform the others (1.29 per cent), while the value for retail commercial banks lies just slightly above the average (1.02 per cent). The underperformance of stakeholder banks seems obvious only for government-owned savings banks (0.55 per cent) and non-trivial for both tightly federated cooperative banks (0.87 per cent) and loosely federated cooperative banks (0.83 per cent). However, private savings banks have a slightly higher profitability than retail commercial banks (1.08 per cent).

The t-test for difference in means across the ownership categories validates these differences. However, a closer examination of the data reveals that these results reflect country-level heterogeneity rather than ownership-level heterogeneity.

Considering that some of the stakeholder bank classes are over or under-represented in some countries, it might be the case that the overall results suffer from an aggregation bias. Indeed, considering the individual countries, cases in which some types of stakeholder banks outperform shareholder banks do exist. For instance, tightly federated cooperatives outperform retail commercial banks in Finland, France, Germany, Italy, Portugal, and Switzerland; loosely federated cooperatives outperform retail commercial banks in Ireland and Italy; and most strikingly, government savings banks outperform retail commercial banks in Austria, Germany, Portugal, and Switzerland—that is, in all countries where they exist. Thus, the lower levels of profitability in government-owned savings banks seem to be entirely due to their location in countries where the banking profitability is at a low level, and especially in Germany and Austria.

Probably the only big and robust difference between retail commercial banks and stakeholder banks is that between the UK building societies and UK commercial banks. The profitability of building societies is lower than that of commercial banks by about 0.6 per cent. The relatively low profitability of building societies is also a major reason why the UK banking industry in our analysis is identified as less profitable than average, and not more profitable as in some other analyses (e.g. Llewellyn 2005). Indeed, using this database but controlling for country and year effects with multivariate regression, Ferri *et al.* (2010) show that the profitability outperformance of retail commercial banks compared to any stakeholder-owned banking classes is no longer significant.

Table 2.3 shows the average value of loan losses for each of the six categories by country. The extent of ex post credit risk borne is typically lower for stakeholder banks as opposed to shareholder banks. The overall average ratio of loan losses to total loans is 0.50 for all countries and years. Both tightly federated cooperative banks (0.46) and particularly loosely federated cooperatives (0.32) clearly outperform retail commercial banks (0.63), whereas both types of savings banks and specialized commercial banks (0.52) are not statistically different from the average. Nevertheless, the overall results may reflect country-level heterogeneity rather than ownership-level heterogeneity. Considering the individual countries, cases in which some types of stakeholder banks underperform shareholder banks do exist. For example, all types of stakeholder banks underperform retail commercial banks in Austria, Finland, Iceland, Ireland, Portugal, and Sweden. Moreover, tightly federated cooperatives underperform retail commercial banks in Germany and loosely federated cooperatives underperform retail commercial banks in Italy. The most significant differences appear again in the case of the UK, where building societies record very low levels of loan losses (0.08) that compare favourably to the losses of commercial banks (0.32), even though the latter figure is fairly moderate. Thus, recalling that some stakeholder bank classes are over-represented or under-represented in some countries, it may be that again in this case the overall results suffer from an aggregation bias. Ferri *et al.* (2010), however, show that the lower level of loan losses is significant at least for loosely federated cooperative banks, although this result may be driven largely by the UK.

Table 2.2 Country-level summaries of profitability (return on assets, %), 1994–2007

	Coop1	*Coop2*	*Sav1*	*Sav2*	*Com1*	*Com2*	*All*	*Difference (t-stat)*
Austria	0.48 (0.21) (64)			0.60 (0.26) (53)	0.57 (0.38) (56)	2.96 (1.05) (9)	0.67 (0.64) (182)	–0.32 (–6.41**)
Belgium						1.75 (0.71) (34)	1.75 (0.71) (34)	0.79 (5.90**)
Cyprus					0.94 (0.84) (46)		0.94 (0.84) (46)	–0.03 (–0.31)
Denmark		0.38 (0.26) (13)	1.87 (0.67) (39)		1.66 (1.01) (156)		1.62 (0.98) (208)	0.69 (14.90**)
Finland	1.50 (0.63) (9)				1.00 (0.31) (17)		1.10 (0.60) (26)	0.13 (1.02)
France	1.02 (0.43) (357)				0.49 (0.40) (39)	1.10 (0.82) (71)	0.99 (0.53) (467)	0.02 (0.66)
Germany	0.48 (0.34) (63)			0.25 (0.27) (65)	0.17 (0.42) (34)	0.83 (0.59) (39)	0.42 (0.46) (201)	–0.58 (–12.39**)
Greece					1.21 (0.94) (79)		1.21 (0.94) (79)	0.24 (3.14**)
Iceland			1.54 (1.10) (15)		0.91 (0.72) (13)		1.25 (0.98) (28)	0.27 (2.20**)
Ireland		1.08 (0.69) (21)			1.07 (0.48) (45)		1.08 (0.57) (66)	0.11 (1.61)
Italy	0.91 (0.27) (25)	0.99 (0.46) (141)			0.87 (0.59) (147)	2.15 (0.28) (5)	0.95 (0.53) (318)	–0.03 (–0.71)
Luxembourg	0.42 (0.06) (14)					0.56 (0.51) (7)	0.47 (0.29) (21)	–0.51 (–3.47**)
Netherlands	0.54 (0.15) (14)				0.65 (0.39) (71)	0.94 (0.88) (39)	0.73 (0.59) (124)	–0.25 (–4.18**)
Norway			1.13 (0.37) (148)		0.43 (0.59) (12)		1.08 (0.43) (160)	0.11 (2.10*)
Portugal	1.18 (0.25) (9)			0.88 (0.37) (18)	0.61 (0.23) (8)	1.15 (0.77) (10)	0.95 (0.49) (45)	–0.02 (–0.21)
Spain		1.23 (0.55) (29)	0.99 (0.47) (449)		1.23 (0.70) (129)	1.27 (0.82) (8)	1.06 (0.54) (615)	0.10 (3.46**)
Sweden			0.24 (0.77) (8)		0.74 (0.30) (55)		0.67 (0.42) (63)	0.30 (3.56**)
Switzerland	0.60 (0.09) (12)			0.68 (0.41) (88)	0.53 (0.34) (6)	1.61 (1.25) (41)	0.93 (0.85) (147)	–0.05 (–0.88)
UK		0.70 (0.26) (271)			1.29 (0.58) (68)	1.40 (1.04) (46)	0.89 (0.56) (385)	–0.10 (–2.47)
All	0.87 (0.46) (567)	0.83 (0.42) (475)	1.08 (0.54) (659)	0.55 (0.39) (224)	1.02 (0.78) (984)	1.29 (0.99) (312)	0.97 (0.67) (3221)	
Difference (*t*-stat)	–0.12 (–3.96**)	–0.17 (–5.00**)	0.13 (4.59**)	–0.45 (–9.96**)	0.07 (2.80*)	0.35 (9.00**)		

Notes
1 For ownership categories, see Table 2.1.
2 T-tests refer to the differences between the particular category and all the remaining categories.
3 Significance levels: ** 1%; * 5%.

Table 2.3 Country-level summaries of loan quality (loan losses, % of total loans), 1994–2007

	Coop1	*Coop2*	*Sav1*	*Sav2*	*Com1*	*Com2*	*All*	*Difference (t-stat)*
Austria	0.85 (0.47) (64)			0.80 (0.34) (53)	0.73 (0.41) (56)	0.16 (0.19) (9)	0.77 (0.43) (182)	0.28 (7.67**)
Belgium						0.52 (0.59) (34)	0.52 (0.59) (34)	0.02 (0.29)
Cyprus					0.96 (0.64) (46)		0.96 (0.64) (46)	0.47 (6.54**)
Denmark		0.19 (0.21) (13)	0.81 (0.44) (39)		0.92 (0.72) (156)		0.86 (0.67) (208)	0.38 (11.14**)
Finland	.48 (0.70) (9)				.13 (0.30) (17)		0.30 (0.54) (27)	–0.21 (–2.24*)
France	0.37 (0.32) (357)				0.54 (0.31) (39)	0.55 (0.59) (71)	0.41 (0.38) (467)	–0.11 (4.56**)
Germany	0.62 (0.44) (63)			0.51 (0.47) (65)	0.61 (0.55) (34)	0.70 (0.57) (39)	0.60 (0.50) (201)	0.10 (2.81**)
Greece					0.93 (0.54) (79)		0.93 (0.54) (79)	0.43 (7.98**)
Iceland			1.13 (0.72) (15)		0.80 (0.49) (13)		0.98 (0.63) (28)	0.48 (5.24**)
Ireland		0.20 (0.29) (21)			0.17 (0.11) (45)		0.18 (0.19) (68)	–0.33 (–5.63**)
Italy	0.57 (0.35) (25)	0.78 (0.54) (141)			0.71 (0.44) (147)	0.77 (0.55) (5)	0.73 (0.48) (318)	0.25 (8.96**)
Luxembourg	0.32 (0.16) (14)				.	0.60 (0.70) (7)	0.41 (0.43) (21)	–0.08 (–0.84)
Netherlands	0.24 (0.11) (14)				0.32 (0.31) (71)	0.41 (0.44) (39)	0.34 (0.34) (124)	–0.16 (–3.83**)
Norway			0.25 (0.26) (148)		0.50 (0.71) (12)	.	0.27 (0.32) (160)	–0.25 (–6.35**)
Portugal	0.98 (0.28) (9)			0.58 (0.22) (18)	0.46 (0.22) (8)	0.67 (0.77) (10)	0.66 (0.44) (45)	0.16 (2.16*)
Spain		0.38 (0.21) (29)	0.51 (0.34) (449)		0.63 (0.44) (129)	0.72 (0.78) (8)	0.53 (0.37) (615)	0.04 (1.77)
Sweden			0.25 (0.27) (8)		0.24 (0.43) (55)	.	0.24 (0.41) (63)	–0.27 (–4.36**)
Switzerland	0.10 (0.08) (12)			0.24 (0.29) (95)	0.61 (0.67) (6)	0.45 (0.57) (41)	0.30 (0.41)	–0.21 (–5.18**)
UK		0.08 (0.16) (271)			0.32 (0.23) (68)	0.44 (0.50) (46)	0.17 (0.27) (385)	–0.38 (–14.96**)
All	0.46 (0.40) (567)	0.32 (0.45) (475)	0.48 (0.38) (659)	0.48 (0.42) (224)	0.63 (0.55) (984)	0.52 (0.57) (312)	0.50 (0.48) (3221)	
Difference (t-stat)	–0.05 (–2.32*)	–0.21 (–9.22**)	–0.03 (–1.26)	–0.03 (–0.81)	0.19 (10.23**)	0.02 (0.63)		

Notes

1 For ownership categories, see Table 2.1.

2 T-tests refer to the differences between the particular category and all the remaining categories.

3 Significance levels: ** 1%; * 5%.

Table 2.4 reports the average value of cost–income ratios for each of the six bank classes by country. For all countries and years, the overall average of the cost–income ratio is 0.72, and differences across ownership classes are moderate. Loosely federated cooperative banks (0.68) and private savings banks (0.70) slightly outperform the average, and these differences from the average are statistically significant. Specialized commercial banks are about average (0.73), whereas tightly federated cooperatives and retail commercial banks (0.74) are above average, and state-owned savings banks more clearly so (0.77). However, it is again a source of concern that the overall results reflect country-level rather than ownership-level heterogeneity. Examining the individual countries, we find that tightly federated cooperatives underperform retail commercial banks in Austria and the Netherlands and loosely federated cooperatives underperform retail banks in the UK. Private savings banks underperform retail commercial banks in Spain and Sweden. In comparison to retail commercial banks, state-owned savings banks show slightly worse performance in Austria but better performance in Germany, Portugal, and Switzerland. This finding indicates that state-owned savings banks are not doing worse than their competitors in particular countries, but rather happen to be located in countries with particularly high cost-to-income ratios (confirmed by country averages). Thus, recalling that some types of stakeholder banks are over or under-represented in some countries, it may be suspected that also in this case the overall results suffer from an aggregation bias. Indeed, controlling for country specificities via multivariate regressions, Ferri *et al.* (2010) show that both tightly and loosely federated cooperative banks and state savings banks prevail in terms of cost efficiency.

Conclusions

During the two decades prior to the Great Crisis of 2007–10, the European banking industry underwent a major transformation. Initially a heavily regulated industry that offered stable but low returns and was little prone to competition, deregulated banking became quite competitive and one of the most profitable sectors in the economy. Banks that successfully navigated this transition thrived by streamlining their internal production processes and, even more importantly, by linking up increasingly with financial markets. The transformation of their business model from originate-to-hold—the granting of loans and keeping them to maturity—to originate-to-distribute—granting loans and selling immediately via securitization on the financial markets—allowed many banks to become profit powerhouses.

At the same time, the company model of the joint stock commercial bank—once one among several forms, all of them respectable—increasingly became the norm. Savings and cooperative banks were considered odd relics of the past, supported by regulatory framework safeguards rather than by their own efficiency merits, and thus destined to disappear during the next phase of financial liberalization. State ownership was accused of introducing distortions into the savings bank system as reflected, for example, by discussions of the role of

Table 2.4 Country-level summaries of cost efficiency (total operating costs/total operating income, %), 1994–2007

	Coop1	*Coop2*	*Sav1*	*Sav2*	*Com1*	*Com2*	*All*	*Difference (t-stat)*
Austria	0.83 (0.08) (64)			0.81 (0.09) (53)	0.80 (0.14) (56)	0.57 (0.07) (9)	0.81 (0.12) (182)	0.08 (–7.86**)
Belgium						0.62 (0.14) (34)	0.62 (0.14) (34)	–0.08 (–3.49**)
Cyprus					0.77 (0.16) (46)		0.77 (0.16) (46)	0.05 (2.46*)
Denmark		0.70 (0.17) (13)	0.69 (0.12) (39)		0.70 (0.11) (156)		0.70 (0.12) (208)	–0.03 (–2.97**)
Finland	0.65 (0.12) (9)				0.66 (0.06) (17)		0.67 (0.11) (27)	–0.05 (–1.94)
France	0.71 (0.11) (357)				0.79 (0.15) (39)	0.78 (0.16) (71)	0.73 (0.13) (467)	0.01 (1.00)
Germany	0.82 (0.12) (63)			0.82 (0.15) (65)	0.91 (0.15) (34)	0.81 (0.11) (39)	0.83 (0.14) (201)	0.12 (11.87**)
Greece					0.76 (0.15) (79)		0.76 (0.15) (79)	0.04 (2.45*)
Iceland			0.70 (0.13) (15)		0.75 (0.21) (13)		0.73 (0.17) (28)	0.00 (0.14)
Ireland		0.55 (0.09) (21)			0.68 (0.11) (45)		0.63 (0.12) (68)	–0.10 (–5.79)
Italy	0.80 (0.06) (25)	0.77 (0.10) (141)			0.80 (0.11) (147)	0.53 (07) (5)	0.78 (0.11) (318)	0.07 (8.16**)
Luxembourg	0.78 (0.03) (14)					0.77 (0.23) (7)	0.78 (0.13) (21)	0.06 (1.85)
Netherlands	0.77 (0.03) (14)				0.75 (0.10) (71)	0.77 (0.27) (39)	0.76 (0.17) (124)	0.03 (2.76**)
Norway			0.67 (0.10) (148)		0.80 (0.27) (12)		0.68 (0.13) (160)	–0.04 (–3.93**)
Portugal	0.76 (0.05) (9)		.	0.72 (0.09) (18)	0.80 (0.09) (8)	0.63 (0.23) (10)	0.73 (0.14) (45)	–0.00 (0.10)
Spain		0.65 (0.10) (29)	0.71 (0.10) (449)		0.69 (0.12) (129)	0.59 (0.21) (8)	0.70 (0.11) (615)	–0.03 (–4.58**)
Sweden			0.96 (0.16) (8)		0.67 (0.16) (55)		0.71 (0.19) (63)	–0.01 (–0.80)
Switzerland	0.68 (0.04) (12)			0.72 (18) (88)	0.82 (0.10) (6)	0.76 (0.16) (41)	0.73 (0.16)	0.01 (0.48)
UK		0.64 (0.09) (271)			0.60 (0.12) (68)	0.72 (0.11) (46)	0.64 (0.10) (385)	–0.09 (–12.50)
All	0.74 (0.11) (567)	0.68 (0.12) (475)	0.70 (0.11) (659)	0.77 (0.15) (224)	0.74 (0.15) (984)	0.73 (0.18) (312)	0.72 (0.14) (3,221)	
Difference (*t*-stat)	0.02 (3.85**)	–0.05 (–7.92**)	–0.02 (–4.18**)	0.05 (5.02**)	0.02 (3.09**)	0.01 (1.04)		

Notes
1 For ownership categories, see Table 2.1.
2 T-tests refer to the differences between the particular category and all the remaining categories.
3 Significance levels: ** 1%; * 5%.

German savings banks (e.g. Brunner *et al.* 2004). Privately owned savings banks often then transformed into joint stock companies. Moreover, cooperative ownership was blamed for inefficiencies because the non-transferability of shares was seen as an obstacle to pursuing efficiency and profit maximization.

The Great Crisis has provided reasons to modify these views. The banks that most distanced themselves from their traditional business—collecting deposits and making loans—and became enmeshed in financial-market-related activities were the most severely hit, at least in the early stage of the crisis. Governments had to step in to provide extensive support to these troubled banks, sometimes even nationalizing them. Overall, it became clear that the high profitability of banking has been achieved through excessive leveraging and taking on undue risks. To be sure, with some notable exceptions, cooperative and savings banks fared much better than their joint stock counterparts through the crisis. Thus, the conventional wisdom of today is questioning the old tenets. But, we ask, were those tenets right even before the recent crisis?

In this chapter, we have utilized a large database of more than 300 banks in 19 European countries from 1994 to 2007 to make a long-term comparison of the performance of banks across different organizational structures. As performance measures, we used profitability, cost efficiency, and loan losses. To fully capture the possible impact of ownership diversity, we made some refinements by re-coding several banks and providing a finer classification of the banks' organizational structures.

The key results of the chapter are at odds with the negative views about stakeholder-owned financial institutions. Even though there is some evidence that stakeholder-owned banks have somewhat lower profitability than shareholder-owned banks, these differences do not generally hold when differences within countries are examined. The results are thus an artefact of the fact that not all types of stakeholder-owned banks exist in all countries. Consequently, it is difficult to argue that stakeholder-owned banks underperform profit-maximizing banks; instead, they often appear to be doing better, especially in terms of cost efficiency and loan losses. These results partly contradict the previous literature. For instance, when compared with the cross-country results of Iannotta *et al.* (2007), our results are more cautious about the profitability advantages of shareholder-owned banks and, with regard to state-owned savings banks, are more positive. Our findings about state-owned banks are closer to those of Micco *et al.* (2004), who show that in developed economies state ownership does not lead to worse performance than private ownership in the banking sector.

Thus, even before the reassessment of the merits of different ownership structures provoked by the crisis, there was no compelling evidence to support the claim that joint-stock ownership was superior to stakeholder ownership in European banking. With respect to loan losses and cost efficiency, it appears that stakeholder-owned banks held the advantage. These results may not be that surprising given that shareholder- and stakeholder-owned banks have co-existed in most European countries for several decades, including more than two decades during the era of financial liberalization. Thus, it seems likely that the survival of the stakeholder model is due to the competitive advantages of the model, rather than to alleged regulatory interference. These findings also provide support for those who argue that the diversity of organizational structures in European banking is worth preserving (Ayadi *et al.* 2009; Schmidt 2009; Llewellyn 2010).

Notes

1 We thank the participants in the Euricse conference on financial cooperatives held in Trento, Italy, June 2010, the IAFEP conference in Paris, July 2010, and the economics departmental seminar at the University of Victoria, September 2010, for constructive comments; we also thank Wim Fonteyne for his suggestions. For a longer version of this chapter with additional details and econometrics, see Ferri *et al.* (2010).

2 Bankscope is a leading global database on banking that includes financial statements and related information for banks and other financial institutions; see Bureau van Dijk (2011).

3 The division of surplus is not necessarily tied to profits only, as many cooperative banks divide the surplus at least partly based on member involvement in operations (such as loans, deposits, and mutual fund stakes). In some countries, members cannot freely decide on the division of surplus since the law requires mandatory outlays to reserves. Italian cooperative banks are probably an extreme case, since the law governing them requires that at least 70 per cent of profits be allocated to non-divisible reserves (Lolli 2010).

4 However, based on a large cross-country survey, Micco *et al.* (2004) find that there are no significant efficiency differences between privately and publicly owned banks in developed countries, whereas in developing countries privately owned banks have an efficiency advantage.

5 A similar conclusion can also be made about studies that have used data from outside Europe; see Hermalin and Wallace (1994), Bongini *et al.* (2000), and Fuentes and Vergara (2007).

6 Building societies and mortgage banks from continental Europe differ in several respects. Building societies nowadays offer a broader range of financial services, while continental mortgage banks are very specialized. The latter are also usually owned by other banks or owned by government (Brunner *et al.* 2004), both of which are arguments for excluding them from the analysis.

7 The exception is size (log of total assets), which is very neatly normally distributed. We think that especially removing the largest banks might bias the results because the largest and most important banks would thereby be eliminated.

8 It is difficult to identify a general criterion for savings banks because they take various legal forms. The criterion we use is that if a savings bank is majority controlled by a foundation and there are no other large owners, then it is classified as a savings bank, even it is a joint-stock company.

9 The arguments made in Prowse (1995) and Kose and Kedia (2006) support the idea that the optimal ownership for banks would involve a high degree of concentration.

10 Cooperative and savings banks often own specialized non-retail banks—e.g. Calyon is the investment banking arm of Credit Agricole Group—that are not included in the analysis.

11 Ferri *et al.* (2010) provides further results in a regression framework. The results are qualitatively similar.

References

Allen, F., Carletti, E., and Marquez, R. (2008) 'Stakeholder capitalism, corporate governance and firm value', Working Paper 09–28, Philadelphia: Wharton Financial Institutions Center, University of Pennsylvania. Online. Available at: http://finance.wharton.upenn.edu/~allenf/download/Vita/JF-MS6731-Revision-corporate-governance-with-figures-16sep09-final.pdf (accessed 7 August 2011).

Altunbas, Y., Evans, L., and Molyneux, P. (2001) 'Bank ownership and efficiency', *Journal of Money, Credit and Banking*, 33(4): 926–54.

Amess, K. (2002) 'Financial institutions, the theory of the firm and organisational form', *The Service Industries Journal*, 22(2): 129–48.

Ayadi, R., Schmidt, R.H., and Carbó Valverde, S. (2009) *Investigating Diversity in the Banking Sector in Europe: the performance and role of savings banks*, Brussels: Centre for European Policy Studies.

Ayadi, R., Llewellyn, D.T., Schmidt, R.H., Arbak, E., and De Groen, W.P. (2010) *Investigating diversity in the banking sector in Europe: key developments, performance and role of cooperative banks*, Brussels: Centre for European Policy Studies.

Beck, T., Hesse, H., Kick, T., and von Westernhagan, N. (2009) 'Bank ownership and stability: evidence from Germany', CFR Seminar Series, Washington, DC: Center for Financial Research, Federal Deposit Insurance Corporation. Online. Available at: www.fdic.gov/bank/analytical/cfr/2009/june/CFR_SS_2009_beck.pdf (accessed 18 August 2011).

Bøhren, Ø. and Josefsen, M.G. (2008) 'Are owners redundant?', Nydalsveien: Norwegian School of Management (BI). Online. Available at: http://finance-old.bi.no/~bohren/wip/Banking_Paper.pdf (accessed 7 August 2011).

Bongini, P., Ferri, G., and Kang, T.S. (2000) 'Financial intermediary distress in the Republic of Korea: small is beautiful?', Policy Research Working Paper 2332, Washington, DC: World Bank Development Research Group, Finance.

Brunner, A.D., Decressin, J., Hardy, D.C.L., and Kudela, B. (2004) 'Germany's three-pillar banking system: cross-country perspectives in Europe', IMF Occasional Paper 233, Washington, DC: International Monetary Fund.

Bureau van Dijk (2011) 'Bankscope: a comprehensive, global database on banks' financial statements, ratings and intelligence', Brussels: Bureau van Dijk. Online. Available at: www.bvdinfo.com/Products/Company-Information/International/Bankscope (accessed 24 October 2011).

Coco, G. and Ferri, G. (2010) 'From shareholders to stakeholders finance: a more sustainable lending model', *International Journal of Sustainable Economy*, 2(3): 352–64.

Crespí, R., García-Cestona, M.A., and Salas, V. (2004) 'Governance mechanisms in Spanish banks. Does ownership matter?', *Journal of Banking and Finance*, 28(10): 2311–30.

Cuevas, C.E. and Fischer, K.P. (2006) *Cooperative Financial Institutions: issues in governance, regulation and supervision*. World Bank Working Paper no. 82, Washington, DC: The World Bank.

Desrochers, M. and Fischer, K.P. (2005) 'The power of networks: integration and financial cooperative performance', *Annals of Public and Cooperative Economics*, 76(3): 307–54.

Fama, E.F., and Jensen, M.C. (1983) 'Separation of ownership and control', *Journal of Law and Economics*, 26(2): 301–25.

Ferri, G., Kalmi, P. and Kerola, E. (2010) 'Organizational structure and performance in

European banks: a reassessment', seminar paper, Victoria, Canada: Department of Economics, University of Victoria. Online. Available at: http://web.uvic.ca/econ/research/seminars/Panu.pdf (accessed 18 August 2011).

Fonteyne, W. (2007) 'Cooperative banks in Europe: policy issues' IMF Working Paper WP/07/159, Washington, DC: International Monetary Fund.

Fuentes, R. and Vergara, M. (2007) 'Is ownership structure a determinant of bank efficiency?', Central Bank of Chile Working Papers No. 456, Santiago: Central Bank of Chile.

García-Marco, T. and Robles-Fernández, M.D. (2008) 'Risk-taking behaviour and ownership in the banking industry: the Spanish evidence', *Journal of Economics and Business*, 60(4): 332–54.

Girardone, C., Nankervis, J.C., and Ekaterini-Fotini, V. (2009) 'Efficiency, ownership and financial structure in European banking', *Managerial Finance*, 35(3): 227–45.

Goddard, J., Molyneux, P., and Wilson, J.O.S. (2004) 'The profitability of European banks: a cross-sectional and dynamic panel analysis', *Manchester School* 72(3): 363–81.

Hasan, I. and Lozano-Vivas, A. (2002) 'Organizational form and expense preference: Spanish experience', *Bulletin of Economic Research*, 54(2): 135–50.

Hermalin, B.E. and Wallace, N.E. (1994) 'The determinants of efficiency and solvency in savings and loans', *RAND Journal of Economics*, 25(3): 361–81.

Iannotta, G., Nocera, G., and Sironi, A. (2007) 'Ownership Structure, Risk and Performance in the European Banking Industry', *Journal of Banking and Finance*, 31(7): 2127–49.

Kontolaimou, A. and Tsekouras, K. (2010) 'Are cooperatives the weakest link in European banking? A non-parametric metafrontier approach', *Journal of Banking and Finance*, 34(8): 1946–57.

Kose, J. and Kedia, S. (2006) 'Design of corporate governance: role of ownership structure, takeovers, and bank debt', Pollack Center for Law and Business Working Paper, New York: New York University. Online. Available at: http://archive.nyu.edu/bitstream/2451/25996/2/06–023.pdf (accessed 18 August 2011).

La Porta, R., Lopez-de-Silanes, F., and Shleifer, A (2002) 'Government ownership of banks', *Journal of Finance*, 57(1): 265–301.

Llewellyn, D.T. (2005) 'Competition and profitability in European banking: why are British banks so profitable?', *Economic Notes* 34(3): 279–311.

Llewellyn, D.T. (2010) 'Cooperative banks and the benefits of diversity', speech presented at the European Association of Co-operative Banks (EACB) convention 'Co-operative banks: key driving force to economic recovery', Brussels, 8 April. Online. Available at: www.eurocoopbanks.coop/pdf/Llewellyn.pdf (accessed 18 August 2011).

Lolli, R. (2010) 'Credit cooperatives in the Italian legislation', paper presented at the International Co-operative Association (ICA) European Research Conference 'Cooperatives' contributions to a plural economy', Lyon, 2–4 September.

Micco, A., Panizza, U., and Yañez, M. (2004) 'Bank ownership and performance: does politics matter?', *Journal of Banking and Finance*, 31(1): 219–41.

O'Hara, M. (1981) 'Property rights and the financial firm', *Journal of Law and Economics*, 24(2): 317–32.

Prowse, S.D. (1995) 'Alternative methods of corporate control in commercial banks', *Federal Reserve Bank of Dallas Economic Review*, 3rd quarter: 24–36. Online. Available at: http://dallasfed.org/research/er/1995/er9503c.pdf (accessed 7 August 2011).

Rasmusen, E. (1988) 'Mutual banks and stock banks', *Journal of Law and Economics*, 31(2): 395–421.

Sapienza, P. (2004) 'The effects of government ownership on bank lending', *Journal of Financial Economics*, 72(2): 357–84.

Schmidt, R.H. (2009) 'The political debate about savings banks', *Schmalenbach Business Review* 61(4): 366–92.

Schure, P., Wagenvoort, R., and O'Brien, D. (2004) 'The efficiency and the conduct of European banks: developments after 1992', *Review of Financial Economics*, 13(4): 371–96.

The Economist (2010) 'Mutual respect: taking stock of Europe's islands of socialist banking', 21 January. Online. Available at: www.economist.com/node/15331269?story_id=15331269 (accessed 18 August 2011).

3 Competition and market power within the Italian banking system[1]

Juan S. Lopez and Stefano Di Colli

During the last decade, competition has been a recurrent topic in the banking literature. In fact, a dynamic process of consolidation within the banking industry that started during the 1990s has been accelerated by the deregulation of capital markets, the harmonization of financial legislation, and a reduction of entry barriers. In Europe, the third stage of the Economic and Monetary Union together with the prospect of a common market and the deregulation of financial services have contributed to important changes in European banking markets by forcing domestic banks to search for higher levels of efficiency, offering diversified services to customers, and imposing economies of scale. In other words, banks have been pushed to increase their size in order to cut costs and gain market share. The wave of mergers and acquisitions in recent years can be explained in this way. This process of consolidation has affected competitive forces in the banking industry and enhanced cross-border capital flows.

Concentration and competition are linked to product markets and geographical areas. Banks provide a multitude of products that do not serve a unique market, and defining a relevant market involves making a preliminary decision about potentially relevant structural characteristics, such as concentration and competition. The relevant market includes all suppliers of a good who are actual or potential competitors, and it has both product and geographical dimensions.

The product definition of a market requires the determination of a range of products, which can be assigned to a particular market based on their substitutability in terms of consumer demand. Likewise, the geographical boundaries of a market are drawn according to existing and potential interactions between actual and potential market participants. These interactions are determined from the customer's point of view and take into consideration individual consumer as well as product characteristics. The mobility of banking customers, and therefore the geographic boundaries of the market, depend on the type of customers and their economic size; the local dimension of a market is relevant for retail banking products and the regional or international dimension is relevant for corporate banking. Product characteristics influence the mobility of customers in that commercial borrowers tend to display greater mobility in their search for financing possibilities than depositors.

Italy, among other European countries, has followed this path. During the last 15 years, the number of banks in Italy has declined by a third, and their average size and branch network have more than doubled. Market structure indicators—such as the Herfindahl–Hirschman Index calculated between 1995 and 2004—suggest a degree of concentration that is larger in Italy than in Germany and the UK, but lower than in France, probably due to an increase in concentration at national level (Drummond *et al.* 2007). The resulting increased concentration may have augmented the market power of active banks. For this reason, measures of concentration and competition are essential for investigating the implications of these developments.

This chapter focuses on the relationship between concentration and market power for the Italian banking market using three econometric techniques—the Panzar–Rosse H-statistic, the Lerner Index, and the Boone Indicator—in order to compare the results. Specifically, the Panzar–Rosse H-statistic is estimated with a dynamic panel technique for two different governance models for banks—cooperative credit and popular. The decision to investigate the relationship between ownership models and competition was made to respond to the claim that non-profit maximizing institutions survive in the market because they enjoy some sort of market power provided by complacent regulation. It is therefore relevant to assess the possible degree of market power enjoyed by different ownership structures as a possible input for competition policies.

Theoretical framework

The literature on the measurement of competition can be divided into two major strands—structural models and non-structural models. The structural approach to measurement of competition involves the Structure-Conduct-Performance (SCP) paradigm and the Efficiency Hypothesis. This approach investigates whether there is a causal relationship between a highly concentrated market and banks' behaviour and performance. Non-structural approaches—the Iwata model (Iwata 1974), the Bresnahan model (Bresnahan 1982; Lau 1982), and the Panzar–Rosse model (Panzar and Rosse 1987)—are derived from Industrial Organization Theory, in particular the so-called New Empirical Industrial Organization.

Structural models

Structural measures of competition may be divided into two types of approaches: formal and non-formal. This section proposes a formal way of measuring the competition-concentration relationship—the Herfindahl–Hirschman Index (HHI). The following section discusses two non-formal approaches to the market structure-market performance relationship—SCP and the Efficiency Hypothesis. These models are considered non-formal because they are not derived analytically.

The formal approach to bank competition is rooted in Industrial Organization theory. The derivations are based on the maximization problem for oligopolistic markets (Cowling 1976; Cowling and Waterson 1976). In this framework, there are n unequally sized banks in the industry producing a homogeneous product. The profit function for an individual bank takes the usual form:

$$\Pi_i = px_i - c_i(x_i) - F_i \tag{3.1}$$

where Π_i is profit, x_i is output, p is output price, c_i are the variable costs, F_i are fixed cost of i-th bank. The inverse demand function is defined as $p=f(X)=f(x_1+$ $+x_2+\ldots+x_n)$. The first order condition for profit maximizing

$$\frac{d\Pi_i}{dx_i} = p + f'(X)\left(\frac{dX}{dx_i}\right) - c_i'(x_i) = 0 \tag{3.2}$$

can be rewritten as

$$p + f'(X)(1+\lambda_i)x_i - c_i'(x_i) = 0 \tag{3.3}$$

where $\lambda_i = d\sum_{j\neq i}^{n} x_j / dx_i$ is the conjectural variation of bank i with respect to all other banks in the market. It allows differentiation between various market forms. In fact, depending on the underlying market form, λ_i can take values between -1 and $\sum_{j\neq i}^{n} x_j / x_i$. In the case of perfect competition, an increase in output by one bank has no effect on the market price and quantity.[2] A bank operating in a Cournot oligopoly expects other banks to remain inactive in response to an increase in total industry output by the same amount.[3] In the case of perfect collusion, a bank i expects full reaction from its competitors in order to protect their market share.[4]

Multiplying Equation 3.4 with x_i and summing the result over all banks yields:

$$\sum_{i=1}^{n} px_i + \sum_{i=1}^{n} f'(X)\left(\frac{dX}{dx_i}\right)X^2\left(\frac{x_i^2}{X^2}\right) - \sum_{i=1}^{n} c_i'(x_i)x_i = 0 \tag{3.4}$$

which can be rewritten as

$$\sum_{i=1}^{n} \frac{(px_i - c_i'(x_i)x_i)}{pX} = -(1+\gamma)HHI / \eta_D \tag{3.5}$$

where $\eta_D = dXp/dpX = p/f'(X)X$, $\gamma = \sum_{i=1}^{n} \lambda_i x_i^2 / \sum_{i=1}^{n} x_i^2$, which represents the average price-cost margin in terms of η_D, the price elasticity of demand, the HHI (being $HHI = \sum_{i=1}^{n} s_i^2$ where s is the bank size measured as a market share) and γ, a term capturing the conjectural variation. This theoretical derivation is in line with the SCP assumptions that a higher degree of concentration in an industry results in higher price-cost margins, and it justifies the use of the HHI as a measure of concentration in S-P relationships, when γ is known and equal for all banks. Estimations of HHI for the Italian banking system are presented below.

The non-formal approaches of SCP and the Efficiency Hypothesis have both been frequently applied in empirical estimations, even though they lack formal theoretical derivation. In its original form, the SCP approach was used to explain market performance by assuming a link between market structure, the behaviour of banks, and profitability (Mason 1939; Bain 1951). Structure and performance are positively related because firms in higher concentrated markets are supposed to have collusive behaviour and greater market power, resulting in better market performance and increasing profits (Goldberg and Rai 1996). In fact, a higher level of concentration is supposed to foster collusion among the active banks and to reduce the degree of concentration.

The SCP approach has been criticized by various authors, including Gilbert (1984), Reid (1987), Vesala (1995), and Bos (2002). They pointed out that a positive relationship between higher levels of efficiency for banks and increasing profits is not necessarily related to growth in market concentration. The one-way causality—from market structure to market performance—implies a positive link between market structure and profitability (Smirlock 1985; Berger 1995; Goldberg and Rai 1996; Molyneux 2003). Empirical studies of SCP for the banking industry do not provide unambiguous evidence supporting the theory: the results of Berger and Hannan (1989), Hannan and Berger (1991), and Pilloff and Rhoades (2002) are in line with SCP predictions, while those of Jackson (1992), Rhoades (1995), and Hannan (1997) are not.[5]

The Efficiency Hypothesis was developed by Demsetz (1973) and Peltzman (1977). It postulates that efficient banks are able to maximize profits and gain market share by reducing prices. Consequently, market concentration increases automatically as the result of the superior efficiency of the leading banks. In fact, a bank with a higher degree of efficiency than its competitors can adopt two different strategies for maximizing profits: maintaining the present levels of prices and company size or reducing prices and expanding the size of the company. In the latter case, the most efficient banks will gain market share and bank efficiency will be the driving force behind the process of market concentration without necessarily reducing competitiveness.

Non-structural models

Non-structural models do not infer the competitive conduct of banks through the analysis of market structure, but rather recognize that banks behave differently depending upon the market structure in which they operate. In this framework, Contestable Markets Theory (Baumol 1982) stresses that a concentrated industry can behave competitively if the barriers for new entrants to the market are non-existent or low. In a perfectly contestable market, entry is absolutely free, exit is completely without cost, and the demands for industry outputs are highly price-elastic. In practice, entering banking markets requires considerable investments in terms of sunk costs. Moreover, regulation poses a justifiable entry barrier from a financial stability perspective. However, in contrast to Canoy *et al.* (2001), we expect that the potential negative consequences of a concentrated banking sector will be largely offset by free entry. Incumbents offer a wide range of products and services via various channels at the same time, whereas new financial players can easily focus on a particular customer or product market with limited distribution channels. Incumbents are always vulnerable to hit-and-run entry when they try to exercise their potential market power. In this framework, a concentrated banking market can be effectively competitive even if it is dominated by large banks. Therefore, policymakers should be relatively less concerned about the market dominance of some types of financial intermediaries in a country's financial system, if the financial markets are contestable.

The New Empirical Industrial Organisation approach tries to test conduct of banks directly by addressing firms' behaviour in three ways: the Iwata model, the Bresnahan model, and the Panzar–Rosse model. The Iwata model estimates conjectural variations for individual banks supplying homogeneous product in an oligopolistic market (Iwata 1974). This measure has been applied to the banking industry (in a two-bank market framework) by Shaffer and DiSalvo (1994).

Bresnahan (1982) and Lau (1982) provide a short-run model for the empirical determination of the market power of an average bank. Utilizing industry time-series data, this model is based on the estimation of a parameter that can be interpreted as a conjectural variation coefficient or the perceived marginal revenue. This parameter represents the behaviour of firms and the degree of their market power (Bresnahan 1982, 1989; Lau 1982; Alexander 1988), as determined by simultaneous estimations of market demand and supply curves.[6] Empirical applications of the Bresnahan model have been conducted by several authors. Shaffer (1989, 1993) applied it to the US and Canadian banking sectors, and Suominen (1994) to the Finnish loan market. Swank (1995) found that both loan and deposit markets for the Netherland were significantly oligopolistic between 1957 and 1990. In their study of nine different deposit and loan banking markets, Bikker and Haaf (2002) were not able to reject perfect competition.

The Panzar–Rosse model is based on the evaluation of the impact of input price variations on firm revenue through an index—the so-called Panzar–Rosse H-statistic. The H-statistic is calculated as the sum of elasticities of the reduced-form revenue with respect to all the factor prices (Rosse and Panzar 1977; Panzar and Rosse 1987). Its value depends on the price elasticity of the demand faced by bank *i*.

The application of the Panzar–Rosse model to banking assumes that banks are single-product companies, using deposits and other funding costs as inputs to produce simply loans and other interest-earning assets. This is consistent with the intermediation approach where banks are considered mainly as financial intermediaries. In theory, a natural monopoly will eventually emerge if only one producer is able to produce all products at minimum cost. If, however, there is space for more than one producer, an oligopoly will obviously develop. Moreover, if the banking market is characterized by increasing returns to scale, the optimum size of an individual bank will constantly increase with expanding demand. In this situation, the consolidation process is the result of a dynamic market process. This natural tendency to concentrate activities would ultimately lead to the survival of only one viable bank and a concentration ratio of one. On the other hand, in the absence of economies of scale and scope for all products and services, it would be possible for several banks to operate in a highly competitive market under certain circumstances.

In particular, the Panzar and Rosse H-statistic is consistent under the assumption that banks operate in a long-term equilibrium. However, bank performance is continuously influenced by the actions of other market participants. Following Bikker and Haaf (2002), the model assumes price elasticity of demand greater than one and a homogeneous cost structure. Bank i maximizes profits where marginal revenue equals marginal cost:

$$R_i(\bar{x}_i, z_i^R) - C_i(\bar{x}_i, w_i, z_i^C) = 0 \tag{3.6}$$

where $R(\bullet)$ and $C(\bullet)$ are the revenue and cost function for bank i, x_i is the output of the i-th bank, w_i is a n-dimensional vector of factor input prices of i-th bank, z_i^R is a m-dimensional vector of exogenous variables shifting the revenue function, while z_i^C is a k-dimensional vector of exogenous variables affecting the cost function. In equilibrium, at the individual level, marginal revenues are equal to marginal costs:

$$R_i'(\bar{x}_i, z_i^R) = C_i'(\bar{x}_i, w_i, z_i^C). \tag{3.7}$$

Under these assumptions, a change in factor input may be reflected in the equilibrium revenues earned by bank i. The H-statistic is a measure of competition given by the sum of the elasticities of the reduced form revenues with respect to factor prices:

$$H = \sum_{k=1}^{m} \left(\frac{\partial \bar{R}_i}{\partial w_{k_i}} \right) \left(\frac{w_{k_i}}{\bar{R}_i} \right). \tag{3.8}$$

The estimated value of the H-statistic is between $-\infty < H \leq 1$. $H < 0$ means that underlying market is a monopoly, $0 < H < 1$ for monopolistic competition and $H = 1$ in case of perfect competition.

This technique analyses directly firms' conduct avoiding indirect inferences about market power based on indicators of concentration, but it needs detailed information about costs and demand. The H-statistic consists of a comparative static analysis and its main advantage is that it requires only firm-specific data on revenues and factor prices.

Empirical framework

A great deal of empirical work has estimated different measures for the level of competition and market power within the European banking market (see Table

Table 3.1 Panzar–Rosse studies for the Italian banking system

	Authors	*Countries*	*Period*
Cross-country studies including Italy	Molyneux *et al.* (1994)	DE, ES, FR, IT, UK	1986–9
	Bikker and Groenveld (2000)	15 EU	1989–96
	De Bandt and Davis (2000)	DE, FR, IT, US	1992–6
	Bikker and Haaf (2002)	23 OECD	1990–8
	Weill (2004)	12 EU	1994–9
	Claessens and Laeven (2004)	50 worldwide	1994–2001
	Casu and Girardone (2006)	15 EU	1997–2003
	Staikouras and Koutsomanoli-Fillipaki (2006)	DE, ES, FR, IT, UK	1998–2002
	Bikker *et al.* (2007)	101 worldwide	1986–2005
Italy-specific studies	Coccorese (1998)	IT	1995–8
	Coccorese (2009)	IT (local markets)	1988–2005
	Drummond *et al.* (2007)	IT	1995–2004
	Gutiérrez (2008)	IT	1995–2004

3.1). This section describes how we compiled our data and estimated the Panzar–Rosse H-statistic and other structural indexes. Our estimation results are then compared to the findings of other studies.

Data description

The detailed dataset used in this study was compiled directly from information in the balance sheets of Italian banks, as reported to the Italian supervisory authority from 1995 to 2004. Taking into account problems due to changes in accounting standards, 1995 was chosen as the earliest observation. Another issue was to make our results comparable with the estimation results of Gutiérrez (2008). The balance sheets and income statements are reported on monthly, quarterly, and half-yearly bases. End-of-year (December) aggregates have been used in order to transform accounting information into yearly data. Table 3.2 provides descriptive statistic for the sample.

The study utilized the consolidated data from commercial, cooperative credit, and saving banks. Observations pertaining to other types of financial institutions were removed. Data from banks in special circumstances—such as holding companies—and banks that were established during the period of the sample were not considered. Following Gutiérrez de Rozas (2007) and in contrast to several previous studies, mergers and acquisitions were taken into account. Each transaction was considered to generate an entirely new institution. In this way, structural breaks in the data were avoided.

Other general consistency checks were undertaken, excluding all observations where banks report missing values and adjusting for outliers. The resulting dataset is a balanced panel composed of 6,015 observations.

Table 3.2 Descriptive statistics

Variables	*Minimum*	*Maximum*	*Mean*	*Standard deviation*
Total interest revenue	70.24	1.0e+07	115,349.9	541,015.5
Interest expenses to total funds	0.0013	0.9863	0.0438	0.0395
Personal expenses to total assets	0.0002	0.2564	0.0177	0.0091
Capital expenses to fixed assets	6.3e–06	4.0224	0.1723	0.1458
Total assets	1.94e+08	0.1013	1,573,420	8,242,706
Capital to total assets	0.0122	1.3898	0.1139	0.0694
Total loans on total assets	0.0001	5.3064	0.5264	0.2297
Deposits on total assets	0.0000	10.0491	0.7864	0.3434

The dependent variable is explained by factor prices and other bank-specific variables that affect long-run equilibrium bank revenues for the years 1995 through 2004. Specifically, the dependent variable (y_{it}) is total interest revenue (or total revenue), ie_{it} is interest expenses to total funds, pe_{it} is personnel expenses to total assets, and ce_{it} is capital expenses and other administrative expenses to fixed assets.

The Herfindahl–Hirschman Index

As defined in the previous section, the HHI has been estimated for the Italian banking system for both loans and deposits. As shown in Figure 3.1, this index

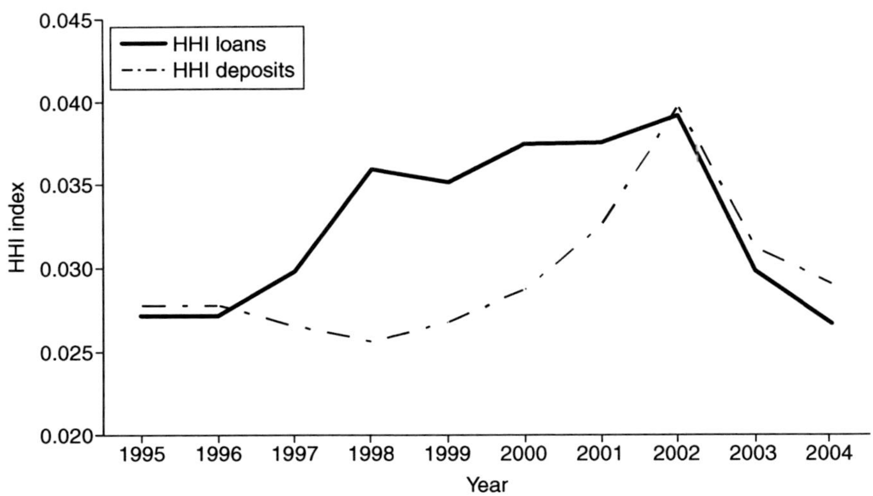

Figure 3.1 Herfindahl–Hirschman Index (HHI) for Italian banking loans and deposits, 1995–2004 (source: authors' calculations based on banks' balance sheet data).

increases during the period from 1995 to 2002 due to mergers and acquisitions that occurred during this period.

One aspect of particular interest for the purposes of this study is the contribution of cooperative credit banks in determining the overall value, calculated as the share of the HHI explained by the market share of cooperative credit banks (see Figure 3.2). Again, the contribution of cooperative credit banks is calculated for each year from 1995 to 2004 for both loans and deposits. The weight of the overall contribution of cooperative credit banks to the degree of concentration of the banking sector is very low (less than 1 per cent of the HHI) but increased during the last part of the sample, after the consolidation process had occurred among the cooperative credit banks. As illustrated above, the HHI has several limitations. The most important is that it can assume the same value in the presence of different market structures. One indicator that is not affected by this limit is the number of banks in the market. Figure 3.3 shows the number of Italian banks and the number of branches from 1995 to 2004. The number of banks gradually decreased between 1995 and 2004, confirming the trend identified by the HHI.

During this period, the number of cooperative credit banks decreased from more than 600 to less than 500 (see Figure 3.4), while the number of branches increased (see Figure 3.5). In particular, the proportion of cooperative credit banks compared to the system decreased (see Figure 3.4), which seems to indicate that the concentration process that involved this type of intermediaries was higher than the rest of the system. At the same time, the share of branches increased compared to the system (see Figure 3.5).

The measures considered so far are concentration indices. Taking into account also the criticisms of the SCP paradigm, an increase or decrease in the

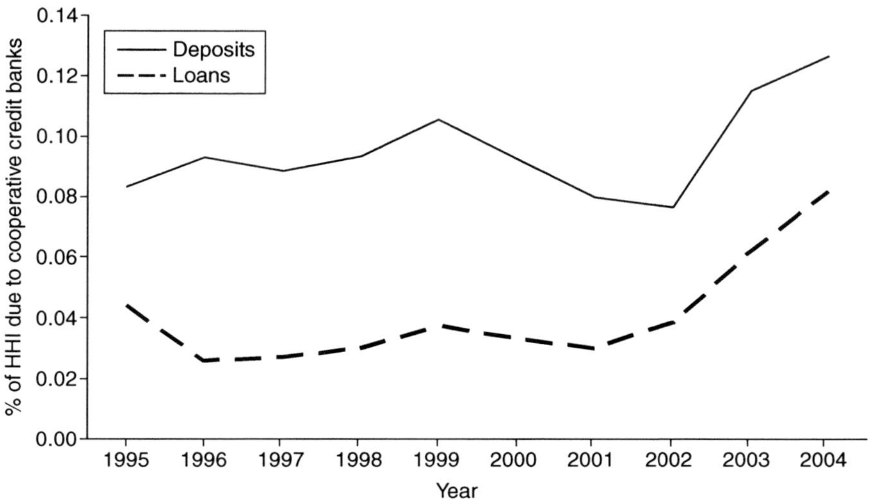

Figure 3.2 Contribution of Italian cooperative credit banks to the HHI, 1995–2004 (source: authors' calculations based on banks' balance sheet data).

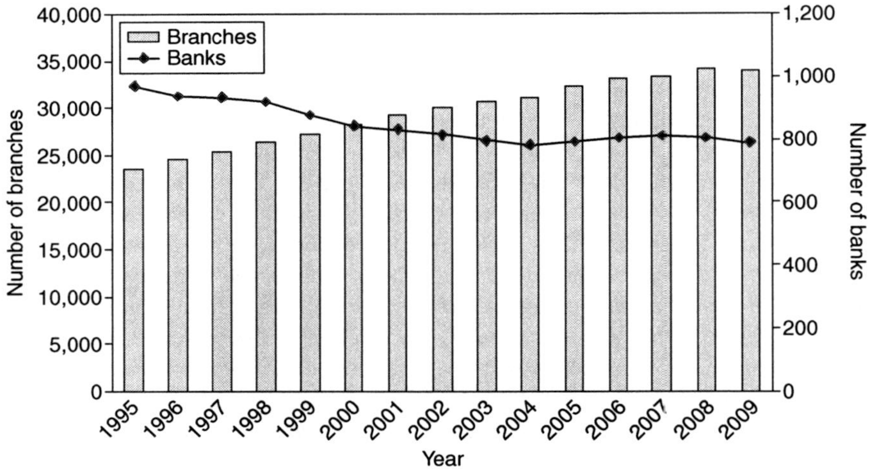

Figure 3.3 Number of Italian banks and number of branches, 1995–2009 (source: authors' calculations based on data from Bank of Italy).

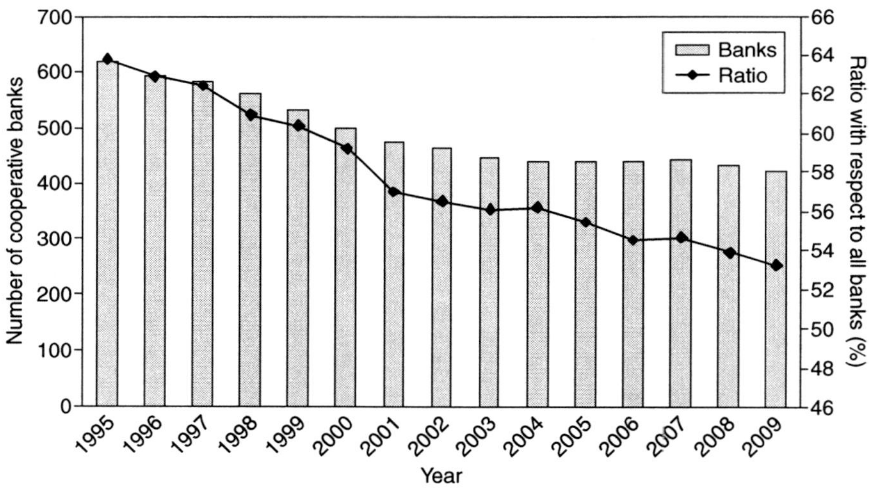

Figure 3.4 Number of Italian cooperative banks in absolute numbers and as a proportion of the system, 1995–2009 (source: authors' calculations based on data from Bank of Italy).

concentration does not imply an increase or decrease in market power of banks.

A simple indicator of market power held by banks is the sum of the absolute values of changes year-over-year in market shares. An increase in the value of the index indicates an improvement in the market competitiveness, and vice versa. In Figure 3.6, this ratio for the Italian banking market is

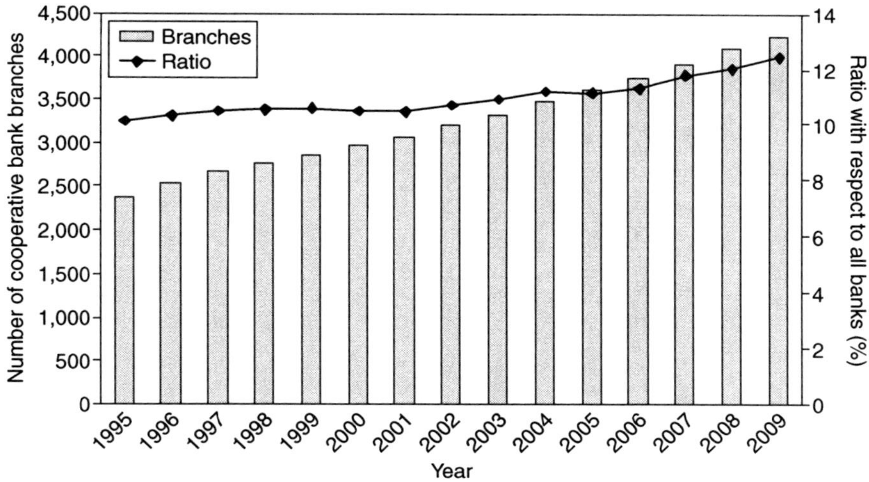

Figure 3.5 Number of branches of Italian cooperative banks in absolute numbers and as a proportion of the system, 1995–2009 (source: authors' calculations based on data from Bank of Italy).

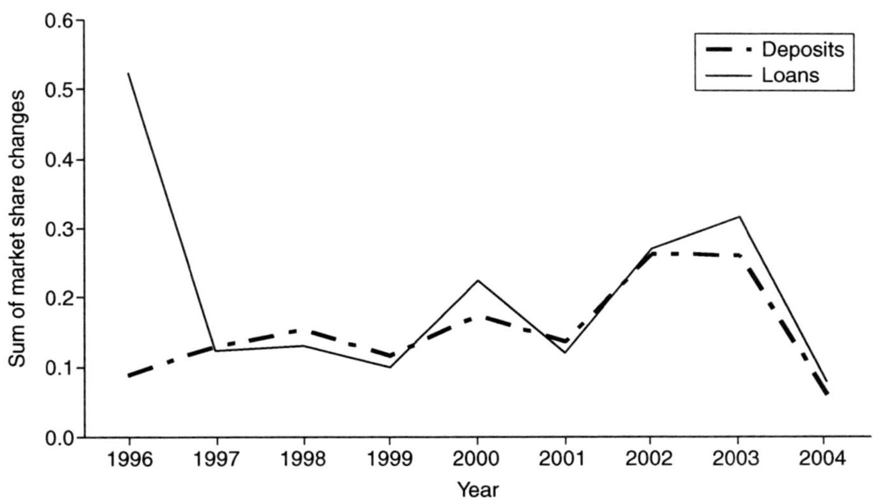

Figure 3.6 Sum of Italian banking deposit and loan market share changes (absolute values), 1995–2004 (source: authors' calculations based on banks' balance sheet data).

reported from 1996 to 2004. It has a constant trend, with the exception of two peaks in 2000 and 2002–3, which were due to large mergers and acquisitions.

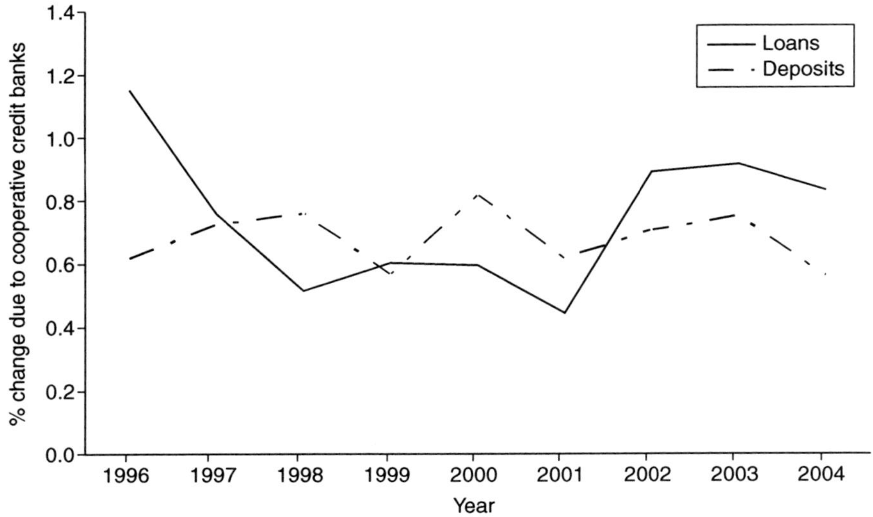

Figure 3.7 Contribution of Italian cooperative credit banks to changes in market shares, 1995–2004 (source: authors' calculations based on banks' balance sheet data).

Figure 3.7 reports the contribution of cooperative credit banks to the total index, calculated as the contribution percentage of changes in market shares of cooperative credit institutions to the total index. The contribution of all cooperative credit banks to the sum of changes in market shares is very low—less than 1 per cent—and stable over time.

One preliminary conclusion that can be drawn from analysing these indicators is that the degree of concentration in the Italian banking market—and cooperative credit banks in particular—increased between 1995 and 2004. At the same time, the market power held by these banks at the aggregate level did not increase and may even have decreased. This provides further confirmation of the weakness of the empirical SCP paradigm. Moreover, cooperative credit banks do not seem to occupy a niche market power over others.

The Panzar–Rosse H-statistic

As shown above, the Panzar–Rosse H-statistic is the sum of elasticities of the reduced-form revenue with respect to all factor prices. In practice, it is usually computed summing elasticity coefficients from fixed effect regressions to panel data for individual firms. Banking input and output are defined following the production approach, which considers banks as firms that use capital and labour to produce loans and deposits. The dependent variable (y_{it}) is total interest revenue (or total revenue). Since deposits are considered as output, the interest expense on deposits is not included in the costs (Berger and Hannan 1989), ie_{it}

represents interest expenses on deposits and other liabilities, pe_{it} is the ratio of personnel expenses to total assets, and ce_{it} is the ratio of non-interest expenses to fixed assets. A number of control variables, are introduced to account for size, risk, and deposit mix differences: total assets (ta_{it}), capital to total assets (ca_{it}), total loans on total assets (tl_{it}), and deposits on total assets (de_{it}).

The empirical application of the Panzar–Rosse approach usually assumes log-linearity in the specifications of the marginal revenue and cost-functions from Equation 3.8. Following the demonstration by Gutiérrez de Rozas (2007), we can rewrite the marginal revenue and cost-function equations as follows:

$$\ln(R_i') = \alpha_0 + \alpha_1 \ln(x_i) + \sum_{m=1}^{M} \gamma_m \ln(z_{mi}^R) \tag{3.9}$$

$$\ln(C')_i = \mu_0 + \mu_1 \ln(x_i) + \sum_{n=1}^{N} \beta_m \ln(w_{ki}) + \sum_{k=1}^{K} \varphi_k \ln(z_{ki}^C). \tag{3.10}$$

For a profit-maximizing bank, the equilibrium output results from Equation 3.8 are

$$\alpha_0 + \alpha_1 \ln(\bar{x}_i) + \sum_{m=1}^{M} \gamma_m \ln(z_{mi}^R) = \mu_0 + \mu_1 \ln(\bar{x}_i) + $$

$$+ \sum_{n=1}^{N} \beta_m \ln(w_{ki}) + \sum_{k=1}^{K} \varphi_k \ln(z_{ki}^C) \tag{3.11}$$

These terms can be re-arranged as

$$\ln(\bar{x}_i) = \frac{1}{\lambda_1}\left(\lambda_0 + \sum_{n=1}^{N} \beta_m \ln(w_{ki}) + \sum_{k=1}^{K} \varphi_k \ln(z_{ki}^C) - \sum_{m=1}^{M} \gamma_m \ln(z_{mi}^R)\right) \tag{3.12}$$

where $\lambda = \mu - \alpha$. From the product of the equilibrium output of bank i and common bank level, given by the inverse demand equation, it is possible to derive the reduced form equation for revenues of the representative bank:

$$\ln(\bar{R}_i) = \omega + \sum_{n=1}^{N} \beta_m \ln(w_{ki}) + \sum_{s=1}^{S} \varphi_k \ln(z_{ki}) \tag{3.13}$$

where z_i is a s-dimensional vector of bank-specific variables. According to Panzar–Rosse,

$$H = \sum_{n=1}^{N} \beta_m \,. \tag{3.14}$$

Empirical applications of the Panzar–Rosse test to the European banking industry have been carried out by several authors. Among others,[7] Vesala (1995) applied the Panzar–Rosse method to Finland, Molyneux *et al.* (1994) to five European countries, Rime (1999) to Switzerland, and Gutiérrez de Rozas (2007) to Spain. They all found evidence of the monopolistic competition hypothesis.

Cross-country studies based on Panzar Rosse that include Italy have been conducted by Molyneux *et al.* (1994), Bikker and Groeneveld (2000), De Bandt and

Davis (2000), Bikker and Haaf (2002), Claessens and Laeven (2004), Staikouras and Koutsomanoli-Fillipaki (2006), and Bikker *et al.* (2007). They all found empirical evidence in favour of monopolistic competition for the Italian banking market, with the exception of Bikker *et al.* (2007), who found evidence of monopoly. Several Italy-specific studies have also found evidence of monopolistic competition (Coccorese 1998, 2009). Gutiérrez (2008) considered different banking governance structures, concluding that cooperative credit banks in Italy hold a higher market power than the rest of banking system because of their local nature.

Consistent with the empirical literature on Panzar–Rosse H-statistic applied to the banking market, we estimated the following bank revenue equation for the Italian banking system:

$$\ln y_{it} = \beta_0 + \beta_1 \ln ie_{it} + \beta_2 \ln pe_{it} + \beta_3 \ln ce_{it} +$$
$$+\gamma_1 \ln ta_{it} + \gamma_2 \ln ca_{it} + \delta_1 \ln tl_{it} + \delta_1 \ln de_{it} + u_{it}. \tag{3.15}$$

The estimation results for Equation 3.15 are reported in Table 3.3, which shows that the monopolistic competition hypothesis is supported by the complete sample and all the subsamples (1996–8, 1999–2001, and 2002–4). Note that the H-statistic increases over time.

Unlike all the studies presented above—except for Drummond *et al.* (2007)—we used the dynamic panel regression technique of Arellano and Bond (1991) with multiple instruments. A crucial point of the Panzar–Rosse approach is, in fact, that the correct identification of the H-statistic be based on the assumption that markets are in long-run equilibrium at each point in time. On the other hand, the micro theory underlying the Panzar–Rosse test relies upon a static equilibrium framework. However, the adjustment towards equilibrium can be less than instantaneous and when this occurs, the market is temporarily out of equilibrium. In a situation of partial but not instantaneous adjustment, a misspecification bias arises, necessitating a dynamic structure with the inclusion of a lagged dependent variable among the covariates. Goddard and Wilson (2009) have investigated the implications for the estimation of H-statistics from this form of misspecification bias in the revenue equation. In a Monte Carlo simulation exercise, they show that the fixed effect estimation for Panzar Rosse of a static revenue equation produces a measured H-statistic that is biased towards zero, reducing the ability of the researcher to distinguish between the three theoretical market structures.

Dynamic panel estimation, on the other hand, permits unbiased estimation of the H-statistic:

$$\Delta \ln y_{it} = \alpha_0 + \alpha_1 \Delta \ln y_{it-1} + \beta_1 \Delta \ln ie_{it} + \beta_2 \Delta \ln pe_{it} + \beta_3 \Delta \ln ce_{it} +$$
$$+\gamma_1 \Delta \ln ta_{it} + \gamma_2 \Delta \ln ca_{it} + \delta_1 \Delta \ln tl_{it} + \delta_1 \Delta \ln de_{it} + \Delta u_{it}. \tag{3.16}$$

Gutiérrez (2008) computed H-statistics to estimate fixed effects regressions for Italian banks, distinguishing between all banks, cooperative credit banks, saving banks, and commercial banks. She found evidence supporting the monopolistic

Table 3.3 Regressions on Italian banking system, 1995–2004

Variable	*Coefficient*	*Within regression fixed effects*				*Pooled least squares*			
		1995–2004	*1996–8*	*1999–2001*	*2002–4*	*1995–2004*	*1996–8*	*1999–2001*	*2002–4*
Constant	α_0	0.2968	–0.2042	0.0740	2.8264	–0.5379	0.0113	–1.0077	–0.3685
		[0.000]	[0.016]	[0.000]	[0.000]	[0.000]	[0.282]	[0.000]	[0.024]
ie_{it}	β_1	0.2859	0.2908	0.2711	0.0858	0.2742	0.2288	0.1246	0.0817
		[0.000]	[0.000]	[0.000]	[0.002]	[0.000]	[0.000]	[0.000]	[0.001]
pe_{it}	β_2	0.3576	0.2936	0.2977	0.0211	0.3081	0.2523	0.2625	0.3046
		[0.000]	[0.000]	[0.000]	[0.726]	[0.000]	[0.000]	[0.000]	[0.000]
ce_{it}	β_3	0.2101	0.0109	0.0258	0.6833	0.0948	–0.0212	0.0048	0.2901
		[0.000]	[0.042]	[0.008]	[0.000]	[0.000]	[0.000]	[0.403]	[0.000]
H-statistic		**0.8536**	**0.5953**	**0.5946**	**0.7902**	**0.6771**	**0.5023**	**0.3919**	**0.6764**
p(F-test)		**[0.000]**	**[0.000]**	**[0.000]**	**[0.000]**	**[0.000]**	**[0.000]**	**[0.000]**	**[0.080]**
ta_{it}	γ_1	0.9759	0.9705	0.8496	0.9749	0.9721	0.9670	0.9756	0.9808
		[0.000]	[0.000]	[0.000]	[0.000]	[0.000]	[0.000]	[0.000]	[0.000]
ca_{it}	γ_2	–0.0938	–0.0785	–0.1485	–0.0695	–0.0811	–0.0940	–0.0917	–0.0112
		[0.000]	[0.004]	[0.000]	[0.015]	[0.000]	[0.038]	[0.000]	[0.548]
tl_{it}	δ_1	–0.0775	0.0384	0.0637	0.0851	–0.0772	–0.0322	–0.0186	–0.0145
		[0.000]	[0.056]	[0.003]	[0.008]	[0.000]	[0.001]	[0.000]	[0.542]
de_{it}	δ_2	–0.1274	0.0153	–0.0655	–0.0678	–0.1080	–0.0867	–0.0683	–0.0260
		[0.000]	[0.742]	[0.007]	[0.013]	[0.000]	[0.166]	[0.000]	[0.024]
# observations		6,002	1,855	1,835	1,726	6,002	1,855	1,835	1,726
R^2		0.92	0.99	0.84	0.74	0.98	0.98	0.99	0.97

Note

The dependent variable (y_{it}) is the ratio of total interest revenue to total assets, ie_{it} represents interest expenses to total funds, pe_{it} is personnel expenses to total assets, ce_{it} is capital expenses to fixed assets, while control variables are total assets (ta_{it}), total capital (ca_{it}), total loans on total assets(tl_{it}), and deposits on total assets (de_{it}).

competition hypothesis and concluded that cooperative credit and saving banks enjoy higher degrees of monopoly power than commercial banks. One criticism of this conclusion is that the H-statistic is not able to capture changes in banking structure and can only be used to test the three theoretical hypotheses discussed above and cannot be used to compare degrees of monopoly (Boone 2000). In addition, the fixed effects regression produces a measured H-statistic that is severely biased towards zero.

Equation 3.16 has been estimated for the Italian banking system as a whole, cooperative credit banks, and for the banking system without the cooperative credit banks by using Arellano and Bond estimators with multiple instruments. First, Arellano and Bond estimation results are in favour of monopolistic competition hypothesis, in line with the main literature on market power within the Italian banking system (see Table 3.4). Furthermore, the results shown in Table 3.5 lead to the conclusion that there is no significant difference between the estimated H-statistic for the banking system and cooperative credit banks. In other words, the hypothesis of the existence of a sort of market power 'niche' for cooperative credit banks in Italy can be rejected.

Conclusions

Many studies have attempted to determine the degree of competition in banking markets. This chapter has applied one of the most popular econometric techniques to a sample of Italian banks—the Panzar–Rosse H-statistic—and estimated it with a dynamic panel methodology in order to avoid the misspecification bias in the revenue equation identified by Goddard and Wilson (2009). Specifically, the

Table 3.4 Estimated Panzar–Rosse H-statistics for the Italian banking system

Studies		*Period*	*H-statistic*
Molyneux *et al.* (1994)		1986–9	−0.61
Bikker and Groeneveld (2000)		1989–96	0.91
De Bandt and Davis (2000)		1992–6	0.51
Bikker and Haaf (2002)		1990–8	0.82
Weill (2004)		1994–9	0.62
Claessens and Laeven (2004)		1994–2001	0.60
Casu and Girardone (2006)		1997–2003	0.41
Staikouras and Koutsomanoli-Fillipaki (2006)		1998–2002	0.67
Drummond *et al.* (2007)		1998–2004	0.71
Gutiérrez (2008)		1995–2004	0.55
This study:	WRFE	1995–2004	**0.85**
	GPLS	1995–2004	**0.68**
	Arellano–Bond	1995–2004	**0.72**

Notes
WRFE, Within Regression Fixed Effects; GPLS, Generalized Pooled Least Squares; Arellano–Bond Dynamic Panel Data Estimation.

Table 3.5 Dynamic panel regressions with Arellano and Bond technique

Variable	*Coefficient*	*All banks*	*Cooperative banks*	*Other banks*
Constant	α_0	–0.0008	0.0006	0.0113
		[0.879]	[0.868]	[0.282]
y_{it-1}	α_1	–0.0055	–0.0156	–0.0028
		[0.232]	[0.000]	[0.664]
ie_{it}	β_1	0.3358	0.3818	0.3501
		[0.000]	[0.000]	[0.000]
pe_{it}	β_2	0.2984	0.2986	0.3011
		[0.000]	[0.000]	[0.000]
ce_{it}	β_3	0.0882	0.0074	0.0950
		[0.042]	[0.100]	[0.040]
H-statistic		**0.7224**	**0.6878**	**0.7462**
p(F-test)		**[0.000]**	**[0.000]**	**[0.000]**
ta_{it}	γ_1	0.9705	0.9749	0.9542
		[0.000]	[0.000]	[0.000]
ca_{it}	γ_2	0.0785	0.0695	0.0807
		[0.004]	[0.015]	[0.038]
tl_{it}	δ_1	0.0384	0.0851	0.0023
		[0.756]	[0.166]	[0.201]
mi_{it}	δ_2	–0.0153	–0.0678	–0.0883
		[0.042]	[0.013]	[0.036]
# observations		3,708	2,929	1,285
AB test AR(2)	0.537	0.243	0.641	

Note
The dependent variable (y_{it}) is the ratio of total interest revenue to total assets, ie_{it} represents interest expenses to total funds, pe_{it} is personnel expenses to total assets, ce_{it} is capital expenses to fixed assets, while control variables are total assets (ta_{it}), total capital (ca_{it}), total loans on total assets(tl_{it}), deposits on total assets (de_{it}).

H-statistic has been estimated for the entire banking system, for cooperative credit banks, for popular banks, and for saving banks. Our results contradict those of Gutiérrez (2008) and show no significant differences between the banking system and cooperative credit banks. The most important finding is that the monopolistic competition hypothesis is confirmed for the Italian banking system for the period from 1995 to 2004. At the same time, the level of competition seems to have increased during this period. Finally, there is no evidence that cooperative credit banks exert a higher level of market power.

Notes

1 The authors are grateful to Anna Di Trapano, Giorgio Gobbi, Claudia Guagliano, Paolo Coccorese, and the participants in the Eighteenth International Conference in Banking and Finance at the University of Rome Tor Vergata (December 2009) and the Euricse Conference on Financial Co-operative Approaches to Local Development through Sustainable Innovation (Trento, June 2010) for their valuable comments and suggestions. The views expressed in this chapter are personal and do not necessarily reflect those of Federcasse.

2 $dX/dx_i = 0 = (1+\lambda_i)$ and hence $\lambda_i = -1$.
3 $dX/dx_i = 1 = (1+\lambda_i)$ so that $\lambda_i = 0$.
4 $dX/dx_i = X/x_i = (1+\lambda_i)$ i.e. an increase in output by bank I by one unit leads to an increase in market output by X/x_i units.
5 For surveys of empirical studies of the SCP model, see Gilbert (1984) and Weiss (1989).
6 $\lambda = (1 + d\Sigma_{i \neq j} x_j / dx_i)/n$ with $0 \leq \lambda_i \leq 1$.
7 See Shaffer (1982, 2002, 2004), Nathan and Neave (1989), Molyneux *et al.* (1994, 1996), Vesala (1995), Coccorese (1998, 2004, 2009), Hondroyiannis *et al.* (1999), Bikker and Groeneveld (2000), De Bandt and Davis (2000), Bikker and Haaf (2002), Gelos and Roldós (2004), Al-Muharrami *et al.* (2006), Casu and Girardone (2006), Matthews *et al.* (2007), and Gutièrrez (2008).

References

Alexander, D.L. (1988) 'The oligopoly solution tested', *Economics Letters* 28(4), 361–4.

Al-Muharrami, S., Matthews, K., and Khabari, Y. (2006) 'Market structure and competitive conditions in the Arab GCC banking system', *Journal of Banking and Finance*, 30(12): 3487–501.

Arellano, M. and Bond, S. (1991) 'Some specification tests for panel data: Monte Carlo evidence and an application to employment equations', *Review of Economic Studies*, 58(2): 277–97.

Bain, J.S. (1951) 'Relation of profit rate to industry concentration: American manufacturing', *Quarterly Journal of Economics*, 65(3): 293–324.

Baumol, W.J. (1982) 'Contestable markets: an unprising in the theory of industry structure', *American Economic Review*, 72(1): 1–15.

Berger, A.N. (1995) 'The profit-structure relationship in banking: tests of market-power and efficient-structure hypotheses', *Journal of Money Credit and Banking*, 27(2): 404–31.

Berger, A.N. and Hannan, T.H. (1989) 'The price-concentration relationship in banking', *Review of Economics and Statistics*, 71(2): 291–9.

Bikker, J.A. and Groeneveld, J.M. (2000) 'Competition and concentration in the EU banking industry', *Kredit und Kapital*, 33(1): 62–98.

Bikker, J.A. and Haaf, K. (2002) 'Measures of competition and concentration: a review of the literature', *Economic and Financial Modelling*, no. 9: 53–98.

Bikker, J.A., Spierdijk, L., and Finnie, P. (2007) 'The impact of market structure, contestability and institutional environment', Discussion Paper Series no. 07–29, Utrecht: Tjalling C. Koopmans Research Institute, Utrecht School of Economics.

Boone, J. (2000) 'Competition', CEPR Discussion Paper no. 2636, London: Centre for Economic Research.

Bos, J. (2002) *European Banking: market power and efficiency*, Maastricht: Maastricht University Press.

Bresnahan, T.F. (1982) 'The oligopoly solution concept is identified', *Economic Letters*, 10(1–2): 87–92.

Bresnahan, T.F. (1989) 'Empirical studies of industries with market power', in R. Schmalensee and R.D. Willig (eds), *Handbook of Industrial Organization*, vol. 2, 5th ed. Amsterdam: North Holland, pp. 1011–57.

Canoy, M., Van Dijk, M., Lemmen, J., De Mooij, R., and Weigand, J. (2001) *Competition and Stability in Banking*, CPB Document no. 15, The Hague: CPB Netherlands Bureau for Economic Policy Analysis. Online. Available at: www.cpb.nl/sites/default/files/publicaties/download/competition-and-stability-banking.pdf (accessed 11 August 2011).

Casu, B. and Girardone, C. (2006) 'Bank competition, concentration and efficiency in the single European market', *Manchester School*, 74(4): 441–68.

Claessens, S. and Laeven, L. (2004) 'What drives bank competition? Some international evidence', *Journal of Money, Credit and Banking*, 36(3): 563–84.

Coccorese, P. (1998) 'The degree of competition in the Italian banking industry', *Economic Notes*, 27(3): 355–70.

Coccorese, P. (2004) 'Banking competition and macroeconomic conditions: a disaggregate analysis', *Journal of International Financial Markets, Institutions and Money*, 14(3): 203–19.

Coccorese, P. (2009) 'Market power in local banking monopolies', *Journal of Banking and Finance*, 33(7): 1196–210.

Cowling, K. (1976) 'On the theoretical specification of industrial structure-performance relationships', *European Economic Review*, 8(1): 1–14.

Cowling, K. and Waterson, M. (1976) 'Price-cost margins and market structure', *Economica*, 43(171): 267–74.

De Bandt, O. and Davis, E.P. (2000) 'Competition, contestability and market structure in European banking sectors on the eve of EMU', *Journal of Banking and Finance*, 24(6): 1045–66.

Demsetz, H. (1973) 'Industry structure, market rivalry, and public policy', *Journal of Law and Economics*, 16(1): 1–9.

Drummond, P., Maechler, A.M., and Marcelino, S. (2007) 'Italy: assessing competition and efficiency in the banking system', IMF Working Paper WP/07/26, Washington, DC: International Monetary Fund.

Gelos, R.G. and Roldós, J. (2004) 'Consolidation and market structure in emerging market banking systems', *Emerging Market Review*, 5(1): 39–59.

Gilbert, R.A. (1984) 'Bank market structure and competition: a survey', *Journal of Money, Credit and Banking*, 16(4): 617–45.

Goddard, J. and Wilson, J.O.S. (2009) 'Competition in banking: a disequilibrium approach', *Journal of Banking and Finance*, 33(12): 2282–92.

Goldberg, L.G. and Rai, A. (1996) 'The structure-performance relationship for European banking', *Journal of Banking and Finance*, 20(4): 745–71.

Gutiérrez, E. (2008) 'The reform of Italian cooperative banks: discussion of proposals', *IMF Working Paper* WP/08/74, Washington, DC: International Monetary Fund.

Gutiérrez de Rozas, L. (2007) 'Testing for competition in the Spanish banking industry: the Panzar–Rosse approach revisited', Banco de España Working Papers 0726, Madrid: Banco de España.

Hannan, T.H. (1997) Market share inequality, the number of competitors, and the HHI: an examination of bank pricing', *Review of Industrial Organization*, 12(1): 23–35.

Hannan, T.H. and Berger, A.N. (1991) 'The rigidity of prices: evidence from the banking industry', *American Economic Review*, 81(4): 938–45.

Hondroyiannis, G., Lolos, S., and Papapetrou, E. (1999) 'Assessing competitive conditions in the Greek banking system', *Journal of International Financial Markets, Institutions and Money*, 9(4): 377–91.

Iwata, G. (1974) 'Measurement of conjectural variations in oligopoly', *Econometrica*, 42(5): 947–66.

Jackson, W.E. (1992) 'The price-concentration relationship in banking: a comment', *Review of Economics and Statistics*, 74(2): 373–6.

Lau, L.J. (1982) 'On identifying the degree of competitiveness from industry price and output data', *Economics Letters*, 10(1–2): 93–9.

Mason, E.S. (1939) 'Price and production policies of large-scale enterprise', *American Economic Review*, 29(1): 61–74.

Matthews, K., Murinde, V., and Zhao, T. (2007) 'Competitive conditions among the major British banks', *Journal of Banking and Finance*, 31(7): 2025–42.

Molyneux, P. (2003) '"Does size matter?" Financial restructuring under EMU', European Integration, Financial Systems and Corporate Performance (EIFC) Working Paper no. 03–30, Maastricht: Institute for New Technologies, United Nations University.

Molyneux, P., Altunbas, Y., and Gardener, E. (1996) *Efficiency in European Banking*, Chichester: John Wiley.

Molyneux, P., Lloyd-Williams, D.M., and Thornton, J. (1994) 'Competitive conditions in European Banking', *Journal of Banking and Finance*, 18(3): 445–59.

Nathan, A. and Neave, E.H. (1989) 'Competition and contestability in Canada's financial system: empirical results', *Canadian Journal of Economics*, 22(3): 576–94.

Panzar, J.C. and Rosse, J.N. (1987) 'Testing for monopoly equilibrium', *Journal of Industrial Economics*, 25(4): 443–56.

Peltzman, S. (1977) 'The gains and losses from industrial concentration', *Journal of Law and Economics*, 20(2): 229–63.

Pillof, S.J. and Rhoades, S.A. (2002) 'Structure and profitability in banking markets', *Review of Industrial Organization*, 20(1): 81–98.

Reid, G.C. (1987) *Theories of Industrial Organization*, Oxford: Blackwell.

Rhoades, S.A. (1995) 'Market share inequality, the HHI, and other measures of the firm composition of a market', *Review of Industrial Organization*, 10(6): 657–74.

Rime, B. (1999) 'Mesure de degré de concurrence dans le système bancaire Suisse à l'aide du modèle de Panzar et Rosse', *Revue Suisse d'Economie Politique et de Statistique*, 135(1): 21–40.

Rosse, J.N. and Panzar, J.C. (1977) 'Chamberlin vs. Robinson: an empirical test for monopoly rents', *Economics Discussion Paper* no. 90, Bell Laboratories.

Shaffer, S. (1982) 'A non-structural test for competition in financial markets', in *Proceedings of a Conference on Bank Structure and Competition, April 12–14, 1982*, Chicago: Federal Reserve Bank of Chicago, pp. 225–43.

Shaffer, S. (1989) 'Competition in the US banking industry', *Economics Letters*, 29(4): 321–3.

Shaffer, S. (1993) 'A test of competition in Canadian banking', *Journal of Money, Credit and Banking*, 25(1), 49–61.

Shaffer, S. (2002) 'Ownership structure and market conduct among Swiss banks', *Applied Economics*, 34(16): 1999–2009.

Shaffer, S. (2004) 'Patterns of competition in banking', *Journal of Economics and Business*, 56(4): 287–313.

Shaffer, S., and DiSalvo, J. (1994) 'Conduct in a banking duopoly', *Journal of Banking and Finance* 18(6): 1063–82.

Smirlock, M. (1985) 'Evidence on the (non) relationship between concentration and profitability in banking', *Journal of Money, Credit and Banking*, 17(1): 69–83.

Staikouras, C.K. and Koutsomanoli-Fillipaki, A. (2006) 'Competition and concentration in the new European banking landscape', *European Financial Management*, 12(3): 443–82.

Suominen, M. (1994) 'Measuring competition in banking: a two-product model', *Scandinavian Journal of Economics*, 96(1): 95–110.

Swank, J. (1995) 'Oligopoly in loan and deposit markets: an econometric application to the Netherlands', *De Economist*, 143(3): 353–66.

Vesala, J. (1995) *Testing for competition in banking: behavioural evidence from Finland*, Bank of Finland Studies E:1, Helsinki: Bank of Finland.

Weill, L. (2004) 'On the relationship between competition and efficiency in the EU banking sectors', *Kredit und Kapital*, 37(3): 329–52.

Weiss, L.W. (1989) 'A review of concentration-price studies in banking', in L.W. Weiss (ed.) *Concentration and Price*, Cambridge, MA: MIT Press, pp. 219–65.

4 Cooperative capital

Why our world needs it

Alan J. Robb, James H. Smith, and J. Tom Webb[1]

A central challenge for anyone seeking to understand the dynamics of cooperative business is to understand both the context in which cooperators and cooperatives exist and the profound differences between cooperatives and other forms of business. Cooperative businesses are islands in a sea of investor-owned firms. As islands, they are impacted by the language and concepts of the world around them even when the language and concepts are inappropriate. Cooperatives are profoundly different from investor-owned firms, and this difference is the key to meaningful understanding of all aspects of cooperative business. Understanding the nature, role, and behaviour of capital in cooperatives can potentially help redress the social damage caused by the global financial crisis that has affected our economic and social lives since 2007.

The evolution and nature of cooperatives

Cooperatives evolved in a number of countries in the mid-nineteenth century in response to the development of the Industrial Revolution and the upheavals this caused in society (Birchall 1997). The rules adopted by the Rochdale Equitable Pioneers Society in 1844 have been influential in the development of cooperative thinking and form the basis of the principles adopted by the International Co-operative Alliance (ICA).

Industrialization and the development of the market economy tore society apart. This occurred in many countries, not just Britain as is sometimes implied.[2] In Britain, landowners used their absolute political power to enclose the common lands, forcing the landless to earn their subsistence through wage labour:

> One by one, all the customary rights that working people had had were stripped away: the right to gather firewood and to hunt game, the right to have their wages set by a magistrate, the right to 'poor relief' if they were unemployed or laid off from agricultural work in the winter, and so on.... Now, for the first time, it was thought acceptable to allow people as individuals to take their chances within a volatile new market economy which could not guarantee survival. As Polanyi (1957) puts it, whereas previously the market had been an adjunct to society, now society became an adjunct to the market.
>
> (Birchall 1997, 2, citing Polanyi 1957)

The response from the affected members of society was the development of trade unions, friendly societies, and cooperatives, and these mutual organizations shared the common aim of ameliorating the injustices of the market economy and its emphasis on the primacy of financial capital.

Mutuality was not a new concept; it lay at the heart of partnerships as a business form. Partnerships have existed as long as businesses have operated (de Roover 1956). Many of the features still found in partnerships were adopted by the founders of cooperatives—e.g. capital was contributed equitably (not necessarily equally), profits were shared in proportion to agreed-upon ratios (not necessarily in proportion to financial capital), and members withdrawing from the partnership would be paid out their contributed capital.

Accountability was also an early value of cooperatives, as it was in sole traders and partnerships. The Rochdale Pioneers' rules of 1844 provided for quarterly general meetings at which members would receive audited financial reports (Birchall 1994, 54).

Parnell (1999) suggests that there are two forms of socio-economic cooperation—mutual and business. Mutual cooperation occurs between individuals who seek to provide a service for themselves; business cooperation takes place between businesses. In a similar manner, Mintzberg *et al.* (2005) identify four types of mutual association: activist, providing advocacy for others; benefit, providing services for others; protection, providing benefits for members; and mutual, providing pleasure or gain for members. Cooperatives are placed in the fourth category. In this chapter, the focus is on cooperative business, although many observations concerning capital may also be relevant to the other forms of mutual endeavour.

The historical development of cooperatives has been shaped by seven key factors:

1. Cooperatives meet needs that are not met by markets or where people face exploitation by those markets.
2. Cooperatives exist to provide benefits to members through their active participation in the cooperative's activities.
3. Members of cooperatives benefit from the strength and solidarity that mutuality confers in markets.
4. Capital is contributed equitably by members, normally in proportion to the use that members make of the services of the cooperative.
5. Interest may be paid on capital contributions—but it should be limited and fixed.
6. Members' capital is repaid by the cooperative when the membership ceases.
7. As democratic organizations, cooperatives operate on the basis of equal voting rights rather than voting in proportion to the amount of share capital held.

The nature of investor-owned businesses

In contrast to cooperatives, the development of the limited liability company in the mid-nineteenth century was designed to facilitate the investment of financial capital. In the UK, the Joint Stock Companies Act 1844 originally contained a number of provisions including the keeping of books of account, the regular preparation and publication of balance sheets, and the appointment of auditors. These 'oppressive provisions' were subsequently removed in 1856 on the grounds that they were 'officious interference of the State' (Johnston and Edgar 1963, 7).

Consequently, company directors were left relatively free from legal obligations of accountability towards shareholders. Historically, directors have resisted any requirement to disclose detailed financial information. The presentation of audited profit and loss reports was not required until after the Royal Mail Steam Packet Company collapsed in 1929. This occurred because the directors had been able to present the appearance that the company was profitable for more than seven years by utilizing undisclosed secret reserves and transfers from off-balance-sheet entities.

Although there has been a move in recent years towards triple bottom-line reporting, the overriding purpose of investor-owned companies remains the maximization of profits, more often than not to the exclusion of any social or other considerations. Not surprisingly, this has resulted in an amoral attitude to business. When asked about the havoc his currency speculation caused to East Asian economies in the crash of 1997, George Soros replied, 'as a market participant, I don't need to be concerned with the consequences of my actions' (Clarke 2003, 32).

For investor-owned businesses, the principal objective is not simply the making of profits, but rather a continual increase in the profits that are made (Friedman 1970). This process may involve replacing employees by automation or by shifting production to lower-cost economies. Profits are often maximized by externalizing the costs of business operations, such as ignoring pollution or worker safety (Goetz and Rupasingha 2006). The shareholder and market pressure on managers to increase profits is usually unrelenting.

When faced with the need or wish to exit a company, an investor must seek an external buyer for the shares held.[3] That sale may be more or less than the equity originally invested and more or less than the net asset backing of the shares.

A key point to note is that exiting shareholders exert little direct influence on the company to perform. Indeed, more influence may be exerted by customers boycotting a company's products. For example, opponents of the so-called New Coke forced the return of the traditional formulation after only a few months in 1985 (Coca Cola n.d.). In 2009, Cadbury's decision to replace cocoa butter with palm oil sparked a similar protest and the decision was reversed within weeks (*Environmental Leader* 2009).

Equally, there is little, if any, direct incentive and no expectation for a shareholder to transact with the company. Because voting is normally proportionate to shareholding, the investor-owned company is essentially undemocratic. The organization responds to the needs of capital rather than the needs of people and communities. An investor-owned company may meet human and community needs, but that is not its primary purpose.

Cooperative differences

Cooperative enterprises differ from investor-owned companies in several important respects:

1 The very idea of cooperation rests on assumptions about the nature of humanity. There is an implicit assumption that people are generally good and wish to do good. This assumption is not based on the naive notion that people are perfect, but rather on the faith that, given an opportunity to make the world a better place, people will generally choose to do so. Without this belief, cooperative activity would be foolish. A second assumption is that people are simultaneously motivated as individuals and as members of a social group or community, and that these two aspects of human nature need to be in some reasonable balance. Successful cooperatives recognize the economic imperative of operating profitably; failure to do so would result in bankrupt ideologists.

In contrast, investor-owned businesses are based on a belief that the overriding motivation of people is economic rationalism. It is assumed that individuals act in their own best interests and seek to maximize the return on their financial resources. The interests of humanity are reduced to financial interests. Consequently, the owners of investor-owned companies treat labour and materials as input costs to be minimized, if return on financial resources is to be maximized.

2 Cooperatives are open to all persons 'able to use their services and willing to accept the responsibilities of membership' (ICA 1995). This does not preclude limiting membership due to constraints on cooperative or financial viability. Members who cease transacting with the cooperative are normally ineligible for continued membership. Mutuality and participation are central to cooperation.

In contrast, investor-owned businesses require no commitment to the activities of the business.

3 Cooperatives require members 'to contribute equitably to, and democratically control, the capital of their cooperative.... Members usually receive limited compensation, if any, on the capital subscribed as a condition of membership' (ICA 1995).

In contrast, investor-owned businesses invite the purchase of share capital as a speculation where the compensation may have no limit. Control of the capital is in proportion to the amount invested.

4 Cooperatives are usually established in response to unfairness in free market economies. Often cooperatives are started as a direct result of exploitation of people by investor-owned businesses. The purpose for which people create cooperatives is to satisfy member and community needs. Businesses should exist for people, not the other way around.

Cooperatives are about justice and fairness for both individuals and the community:

> Co-operatives keep capital in the community where it was generated, while stock companies export capital elsewhere. Since they give surplus

> revenue back to their members, co-operatives keep wealth in their communities. Stock companies do the reverse. By distributing profits to shareholders, they take capital out of the community.
>
> (Gutknecht 2008)

Investor-owned businesses arise in environments of laissez-faire where the concept of *caveat emptor* ('let the buyer beware') is the accepted standard for behaviour. In the eighteenth century, Adam Smith warned of the dangers posed to society of schemes proposed by the promoters of investor-owned companies:

> The interest of [those who live by profit] has not the same connection with the general interest of the society as that of [labourers and landlords].... The proposal of any new law or regulation of commerce which comes from this order [those who live by profit], ought always to be listened to with great precaution, and ought never to be adopted till after having been long and carefully examined, not only with the most scrupulous, but also with the most suspicious, attention. It comes from an order of men whose interest is never exactly the same with that of the public, who have generally an interest to deceive and even oppress the public, and who accordingly have, upon many occasions, both deceived and oppressed it.
>
> (Smith 1776, 155)

Similar criticisms of investor-owned companies and profit maximization are voiced today:

> While this ownership model provides a powerful driver, it also creates a problem. Being effective at delivering private benefit is all very well, but an economy based on the quest for the private benefit of some does not seek the common good of all.... This is even more significant when seen in the context of today's global issues—diminishing natural resources, climate change, and global poverty. It makes little sense to attempt to solve these problems without acknowledging that the pursuit of growth and the maximization of private gain might at best hinder these endeavours, and at worst be a major part of the problem. There is now an urgent imperative to find a different and fairer basis for business—and for business ownership—that does not ignore today's social and environmental concerns...
>
> A system designed to pursue one goal only is likely to achieve that goal; but it may do so at the expense of other potentially legitimate—maybe even more important goals. What economists call the 'negative externalities'—the downstream costs of exploiting natural and human resources in the pursuit of profit—are becoming more recognized and better understood.
>
> (Mills 2009, 1–2)

This implies a need for a better, fairer type of capital.

Cooperative capital

Cooperative capital is equity, in the traditional accounting sense. It is the claim of the members of the entity to the net assets of the entity. The members of a cooperative are entitled to be paid back their equity when they leave the cooperative in exactly the same way that members of a partnership receive their equity (whether designated as 'capital' or 'current' account) upon leaving the partnership.

The obligation to pay a limited amount of interest on capital and the obligation to redeem cooperative capital are two important disciplines on the managers and directors of cooperatives. Capital is not free and must therefore be subject to a capital-rationing discipline to ensure that members' contributions are not wasted. The redemption obligation puts managers under pressure to use capital efficiently and attract new members and to fund the withdrawals of retiring members.

The cooperative companies that belong to the Mondragon Corporation in the Basque region of Spain combine a fair return on capital with a fair wage to the worker members. This has had a major impact on stemming the outflow of people from the area. It has also provided safe and secure work with excellent conditions:

> One hallmark of the Mondragon model is its use of capital. Rather than flowing into the pockets of executives and outside investors, a company's profits are distributed in a precise, democratic way; set aside as seed money for new co-operatives; distributed to regional nonprofits; or pooled into shared institutions like the university and research center. In other words, each individual co-operative gains long-term benefits from the financial assets of the whole.
>
> (Schwartz 2009)

Mondragon's egalitarian pay scale—limiting the top salary in the member companies to no more than nine times the lowest pay of workers—is well documented and consistent with cooperative principles (Kelly and Massena 2009).

The public policy benefits of reduced income inequalities leading to increased social cohesion and improved quality of life are clear (Fahey *et al.* 2005; Wilkinson and Pickett 2009). The GINI Project is a major study of 29 countries by 80 researchers that seeks to 'consider the overall impact of changing inequalities on societies for the longer term and discuss whether agenda setting in politics may undergo structural change' (GINI Project 2010). That such a study should be undertaken shows the extent of concern for an alternative to investor-owned capital in the modern world.

The significance of cooperative financial institutions

Cooperative and mutual financial institutions around the world typically have low profiles, but they can be of significant financial size:

- Credit unions have assets in excess of US$1.4 trillion (World Council of Credit Unions 2011).
- The 400 members of the International Co-operative and Mutual Insurance Federation (2011) have assets approaching US$1.5 trillion.
- There are a considerable number of strong cooperative financial institutions such as the Rabobank Group, an international financial services provider that, in terms of Tier I capital, is among the world's 25 largest financial institutions; CoBank and the National Co-operative Bank in the USA; a network of cooperative banks in Italy; the Caja Laboral Popular in Spain's Basque Country; and the Co-operative Bank in the United Kingdom (part of Co-operative Financial Services). It is safe to estimate that together cooperative financial institutions have assets well in excess of US$2.9 trillion.

Generally, the capital in these financial institutions is fully committed to member services, and it is not available for cooperative development unless the institution makes this choice as a deliberate policy. Where this policy is adopted, society benefits.

From its inception, the Caja Laboral Popular has had a policy of not only providing the workers in Mondragon's cooperatives with a sound financial institution but also financing and making possible the growth and development of worker-owned cooperatives in the Basque Country. The founders of Mondragon wanted to create workplaces that were participatory and to stop the drain of people from the region. From launching its first cooperative in 1956, Mondragon grew to employ a workforce of 92,700 in 2008. The Caja has successfully participated in the growth of the Mondragon cooperatives while achieving solid success as a financial institution. In 1988 it administered €1.3 billion and by 2008 that had grown to €21.5 billion (Caja Laboral Popular 2011). It has also allowed people in the Basque Country to invest in their own future and that of their children.

The pro-active development of cooperatives in southern Spain by the Caja Rural de Almeria similarly illustrates how a cooperative bank can revitalize an economy when it moves beyond a relationship-based model and provides seed finance and know-how in the local community (Giagnocavo *et al.* 2010).

Regulation of capital: implications for cooperatives

Abuse of trust has been a repetitive issue in the raising of capital for investor-owned businesses, and each crisis has led to new regulation of financial industries and stock markets.

Such changes in legislation can have unintended consequences for cooperatives because regulators often know little of the ways in which cooperative business differ from investor-owned companies. When the New Zealand government drafted new companies legislation in 1993, it proposed repealing the existing cooperative companies' law. This would have made it impossible for cooperatives to operate. The New Zealand Co-operatives Association succeeded in persuading the politicians that a separate cooperatives act was required. The

Association drafted the necessary legislation, and it was passed by Parliament in 1996.

A second instance where regulatory change might have had detrimental effects occurred in 2003 when the International Accounting Standards Board proposed changes that would treat all cooperative shares as debt instruments. The ICA mobilized cooperative associations around the world to make submissions, which they did in record numbers. Consequently, changes were made in accounting standards to accommodate and recognize the ways in which cooperative capital differs from investor-owned shares.

The lesson from these two examples is that cooperatives need to be continually vigilant, guarding against adverse effects of regulation from legislators who do not understand the fundamentals of cooperatives and believe they are relics of the past.

The evolving need for capital in cooperatives

The National Co-operative Grocers Association reports that at least 50 per cent of food cooperatives in the U.S. are undergoing some form of expansion. The capital needed for buildings, equipment, and inventory is far beyond these cooperatives' ability to finance growth through retained earnings. To finance this immense natural growth, food cooperatives need to look at acquiring substantially higher levels of capital (Thompson 2009). Similarly, as agriculture becomes more industrialized, the need for capital at the processing and marketing levels increases (Fulton and Hueth 2009).

Traditionally, cooperatives have limited their services and membership to a single group in society, such as farmers, taxi operators, florists, or consumers. This form of organization has meant a dependence on the ability of that group to finance the cooperative. Increasingly, some cooperatives have been widening their membership and so broadening access to a greater range of sources of capital. The new members may be individuals or other cooperatives. Sometimes these are called 'solidarity cooperatives' or 'stakeholder cooperatives' (Co-operative Action 2004).

- The Caja Laboral Popular, Mondragon's powerful and enormously successful financial institution, has cooperatives that are members as well as worker members, and Eroski, Mondragon's retail system, has a board elected by both consumer and worker members.
- The Weaver Street Market in North Carolina has both employees and consumers as members. Indeed, cooperatives owned by both producers and consumers are not unusual in the US.
- Italian social cooperatives often have workers and consumers of their services as members—for example, social workers and former prison inmates.
- Canada has numerous solidarity cooperatives, especially in Quebec, and the Cooperative Act (RSQ cC-67.2) allows for multiple classes of members including investor members.

Impact of investor capital on cooperative businesses

The introduction of investor members creates the potential for disharmony and tension in a cooperative for it brings in capital that may be incompatible with cooperative values. The greatest potential source of tension relates to investor expectations of return. A second source of tension is that the investors will not be transacting parties with the cooperative and so will not be contributing to its business prosperity. Taken together, investor capital is likely to be more transient, moving and seeking a higher return as day-to-day expectations about investment returns change.

Once investor capital is introduced, the cooperative is on a slippery slope. When members realize the cooperative must now maximize the return to a group of investors or provide them with a higher return than members are receiving for their cooperative capital, the perceptions of member benefits are more likely to decrease than increase. Members are likely to question whether meeting their needs is coming second to meeting investors' demands for increasing returns.

If the outside capital is tradable on traditional stock exchanges, then the ability of the cooperative to offer competitive returns compared to investor-owned businesses will be reflected in the share prices. It is likely that only in a weak market will cooperative shares have much chance to increase in value, and if the market is very weak, the cooperative's shares are likely to follow the market down.

These considerations suggest that there will be an inevitable pressure on any cooperative that seeks investor-driven capital to maximize the return to capital as the overriding goal of the business. When profit maximization replaces the primacy of cooperative business purpose, values, and principles, the business has ceased to be a cooperative.

Further pressure to abandon cooperative principles would come from asset strippers seeking to 'unlock value' by demutualizing the cooperative as has happened with building societies in the UK and credit unions in Australia and the United States.

Tradable cooperative capital

An alternative to the introduction of investor capital is the suggestion that cooperative shares be traded on a separate exchange—in other words, that shares should be tradable rather than redeemable (Co-operative Action 2004). The ethical exchange concept would offer those wishing to invest in cooperative shares the possibility to increase the liquidity of their investments. Exchanges for trading shares have two functions: to provide liquidity and to make possible speculative gains by the investor. The latter can include short selling, a feature of the recent global financial crisis.

Introducing a speculative component to capital in cooperatives inevitably has the effect of pressuring the cooperative into a business form where maximization of shareholder returns increasingly becomes the prime driver of the business.

This is an assault on the very fundamentals of what it means to be a cooperative. The purpose of the business has begun to change.

On 30 June 2010, the members of Fonterra Co-operative Group in New Zealand voted for constitutional changes that cancelled the right to redeem shares and allowed trading of shares amongst farmers. The changes include setting up an exchange platform on which the shares will be traded. One or two substantial financial institutions will be appointed to provide volume in the market by buying and selling shares 'in a similar way that banks buy and sell foreign exchange' (Fonterra Co-operative Group 2010). The change has been welcomed by many in the finance industry, but has also been criticized as opening the way for outsiders to make money out of members of the cooperative (Robb 2010).

Future directions

The three major issues that will affect cooperatives in the future are the ability of individual cooperatives to retain adequate capital, the ability of the cooperative sector to grow a pool of capital to assist the development of new cooperatives, and the willingness of cooperatives to support one another.

Retention of capital

Because cooperative capital can be withdrawn when members exit, it is important that cooperatives build up permanent capital from retained surpluses. In some countries, this may be a legal requirement. For example, Italian cooperatives are required to retain 70 per cent of an annual surplus as legal reserves and pay 3 per cent into a fund for the development of new cooperatives. Only the remaining 27 per cent can be distributed as rebates to members, for social purposes, or as dividends. Cooperatives in other countries would do well to consider introducing such a requirement into their laws to strengthen their capital structures.

The need for a cooperative capital fund

One possibility for expanding the availability of cooperative capital could be the creation of cooperative capital funds. Cooperative financial institutions on a regional or national basis could create such funds where a percentage of the funds under their direction could be invested. The resulting pool of funds could be made available for investments consistent with cooperative purpose, values, and principles. Possibilities that could be considered could include shares and loans to cooperative business, home mortgages, loans to not-for-profit businesses, and social economy businesses. As noted above, this is the practice in Italy.

It is essential that the risk level of such funds be along the same cautious lines that credit unions and other cooperative financial institutions have traditionally used. These funds are not meant to be charitable foundations but custodians of member savings that ensure those members that the funds are used for 'good' purposes and receive a fair return that quantifies not only the financial return but also the 'social' return. A selection of funds with varying levels of risk and varying (but not excessive) levels of return or varied purpose may be a reasonable option. Participation in such funds should be open as widely as possible to individuals as well as cooperative institutions.

Although it might seem desirable that such funds should receive favourable tax treatment in light of the public policy benefits they provide, some might argue against this because cooperatives have always believed in the values of self-help and self-responsibility (ICA 1995). The fourth principle of the ICA's Statement on the Co-operative Identity states that cooperatives are 'autonomous, self-help organizations controlled by their members'. The phrase 'self-help' could arguably mean that there is no place in government budgets for resources to advance the role of cooperatives in the economy and that coops should only ever 'go it alone' in everything they do, including raising capital.

We do not agree with such a narrow interpretation of the fourth principle. There are many public policy schemes to encourage investor-driven investment. Cooperative capital should not be left at a disadvantage. One might even argue that there are public policy benefits that flow from business conducted in line with cooperative purposes, values, and principles, and that, as a result, public policy that favours the growth of cooperative capital would be reasonable.

In addition to self-help and self-responsibility, cooperative values include 'democracy, equality, equity solidarity, caring for others, and social responsibility' (ICA 2005). All these values require participation in the democratic processes of the country so that the society in which we live and work reflects the values we believe will benefit the whole community.

The global financial crisis we have experienced, and are still experiencing, shows the antisocial effects of financial markets when regulations are weakened or abolished. Cooperatives and cooperative capital did not contribute to the crisis. They acted responsibly.

All political representatives need to be reminded that cooperatives are socially responsible and that the growth of cooperatives benefits society. Some governments are well aware of this and actively support the growth of cooperatives. Others could do much more. It is not enough simply to have legislation facilitating their formation. There needs to be active financial and other promotion of cooperatives by government departments and agencies.

Those who have read New Zealand history know that dairy industry, which now contributes about 25 per cent of the Gross Domestic Product, really only developed in the 1880s and 1900s because of government support for the cooperative system of dairying (Ward 1975, 10–17).

In many countries there has been much lobbying against cooperatives and mutual organizations by investor-owned businesses, both individually and through organizations such as the Business Roundtable. They claim that cooperatives are inefficient, outmoded, and inappropriate in the modern world (Kerr 1999).

Cooperatives need to be equally active in informing politicians and the public of the truth: cooperatives are efficiently run, they are socially responsible, and their financial capital is benign and not aggressive. Governments should be encouraged to support the raising of cooperative capital funds.

At the same time, cooperative boards need to ensure that they do not depart from cooperative values and principles. They must compete in the market place; but they should guard against losing sight of the ethical values of honesty, openness, social responsibility, and caring for others.

Support of cooperatives by cooperatives

A perusal of the annual reports of a number of cooperatives suggests that they frequently use the services of investor-owned banks, despite the availability of cooperative alternatives. The cooperative movement as a whole should adopt a policy of making cooperatives their 'provider of choice' for financial services in all cases, and supporting the development of financial cooperatives in sectors where they do not already exist. The argument for sourcing short-term financial capital from those committed to cooperative values is as strong as for longer-term capital.

In its broadest sense, cooperative 'capital' includes human resources. A key group in any cooperative is the board of directors. The appointment of independent or external directors can strengthen or weaken a cooperative's human capital. Those who have a commitment to cooperative principles and values, and have a successful track record of management or board participation elsewhere in the cooperative sector, are more likely to contribute to a successful board than directors whose background is in investor-owned companies.

Conclusion

The differences between cooperative capital and investor capital are summarized in Table 4.1. These differences arise from cooperative purposes, values, and principles.

Cooperative capital offers a proven alternative in meeting human needs and reducing the growing income disparity between and within countries. The world of the twenty-first century needs capital that is both socially constructive rather than destructive and more stabilizing than destabilizing.

The creation of some form of tradable cooperative capital may be possible, but it creates risks of undermining what makes the cooperative business model a valuable and proven alternative in our global economy.

Finally, as businesses that are based in communities, and where governance is democratic, cooperatives are well suited to provide capital that meets local and community needs. Cooperatives should explore ways of allowing transacting members and others to direct their savings into cooperative capital.

Table 4.1 Differences between cooperative capital and investor capital

Cooperative capital	*Investor capital*
Purpose:	
• improve the quality of life for transacting members	• create wealth for investors
Control:	
• democratically elected member representatives—one member, one vote	• dominant shareholders—one share, one vote
Motivational drivers:	
• self-help and mutual aid	• personal wealth creation
Return on capital:	
• distributions of surplus in proportion to level of transactions with co-op • limited interest, if any, paid on capital	• profit maximization with optional consideration of ethical issues • dividends paid in proportion to paid up capital • no conceptual limit on dividends
Basis of organization:	
• cooperation and mutuality to mitigate antisocial and unjust effects of unrestricted markets and market failure	• ownership and free movement of financial wealth
Social implications:	
• concern for community a basic principle • community development in employment, education, and well-being • stability sought in fluctuating markets • social goals coequal with financial health	• jobs outsourced to lower-cost countries • externalization of many environmental, health, and safety costs • income inequalities increased • ability to accentuate/exploit fluctuations in share markets, currency markets, and commodity markets • market speculation in currencies and commodities encouraged regardless of social impact

Notes

1 The authors appreciate comments on an earlier version of this chapter from Peter Couchman, Erbin Crowell, Cliff Mills, Ian Reid, and the participants of the Euricse Conference 'Financial Co-operative Approaches to Local Development through Sustainable Innovation', University of Trento, 10–11 June 2010.

2 Birchall (1997) provides extensive coverage of the worldwide development of cooperatives.

3 In some investor-owned companies, existing shareholders may be given a pre-emptive right to purchase the shares; in other cases, the directors may have the power to refuse a transfer of shares.

References

Birchall, J. (1994) *Co-op: the people's business*, Manchester: Manchester University Press.

Birchall, J. (1997) *The International Co-operative Movement*, Manchester: Manchester University Press.

Caja Laboral Popular (2011) 'Consolidated annual accounts to 31 December, 2010'. Online. Available at: www.cajalaboral.com/clweb/pdf/sobre_nosotros/informes/2010/en/2010Consolidated_annual_accounts.pdf (accessed 17 September 2011).

Clarke, N. (2003) 'NS Profile: George Soros', *New Statesman*, 3 June 2003. Online. Available at: www.newstatesman.com/200306020019 (accessed 17 September 2011).

Coca Cola (n.d.) 'Coke lore: the real story of New Coke'. Online. Available at: www.thecoca-colacompany.com/heritage/cokelore_newcoke.html (accessed 20 August 2011).

Co-operative Action (2004) *Co-operative Capital: a new approach to investment in co-operatives and other forms of social enterprise*. Manchester: Cooperative Action.

de Roover, F.E. (1956) 'Partnership accounts in twelfth century Genoa', in A.C. Littleton and B.S. Yamey (eds) *Studies in the History of Accounting*, London: Sweet and Maxwell, pp. 86–90.

Environmental Leader (2009) 'Protests push Cadbury to drop palm oil from milk chocolate', *Environmental Leader*, 18 August. Online. Available at: www.environmentalleader.com/2009/08/18/protests-push-cadbury-to-drop-palm-oil-from-milk-chocolate/ (accessed 13 August 2011).

Fahey, T., Whelan, C.T., and Maître, B. (2005) 'First European quality of life survey: income inequalities and deprivation', Dublin: European Foundation for the Improvement of Living and Working Conditions; available from Luxembourg: Office for Official Publications of the European Communities. Online. Available at: www.eurofound.europa.eu/pubdocs/2005/93/en/1/ef0593en.pdf (accessed 21 August 2011).

Fonterra Co-operative Group (2010) 'Fonterra begins consultation on step 3 of capital structure changes'. Online. Available at: www.fonterra.com/wps/wcm/connect/fonterracom/fonterra.com/our+business/news/media+releases/fonterra+begins+consultation+on+step+3+of+capital+structure+changes (accessed 20 August 2011).

Friedman, M. (1970) 'The social responsibility of business is to increase its profits', *New York Times Sunday Magazine*, 13 September 1970: 32–3, 122–6.

Fulton, M.E. and Hueth, B. (2009) 'Cooperative conversions, failures and restructuring: an overview', *Journal of Cooperatives*, vol. 23: 116–29.

Giagnocavo, C., Aguilera, D.U., and Pérez, L.F-R. (2010) 'Modern agriculture, sustainable innovation and co-operative banks: the development of Almeria (1963–2010)', paper presented at Euricse conference 'Financial Co-operative Approaches to Local Development through Sustainable Innovation', Trento, Italy, 10–11 June 2010. Online. Available at: www.euricse.eu/sites/default/files/db_uploads/documents/1284104993_n694.pdf (accessed 21 August 2011).

GINI Project (2010) 'Growing Inequalities' Impacts'. Online. Available at: www.gini-research.org/articles/research (accessed 17 September 2011).

Goetz, S.J. and Rupasingha, A. (2006) 'Wal-Mart and social capital', *American Journal of Agricultural Economics*, 88(5): 1304–10.

Gutknecht, D. (2008) 'Thinking outside the coop', *Cooperative Grocer*, no. 136 (May–June). Online. Available at: www.cooperativegrocer.coop/articles/2010-07-20/thinking-outside-co-op (accessed 13 August 2011).

ICA (1995) 'Statement on the Co-operative Identity', Geneva: International Co-operative Alliance. Online. Available at: www.ica.coop/coop/principles.html (accessed 20 August 2010).

International Co-operative and Mutual Insurance Federation (ICMIF) (2011) 'Who we are'. Online. Available at: www.icmif.org/who-we-are (accessed 17 September 2011).

Johnston, T.R. and Edgar, G.C. (1963) *The Law and Practice of Company Accounting in New Zealand*, 2nd ed. Wellington: Butterworths.

Kelly, G. and Massena, S. (2009) 'Mondragon worker-cooperatives decide how to ride out a downturn', *Yes! Magazine*, 5 June 2009. Online. Available at: www.yesmagazine.org/issues/the-new-economy/mondragon-worker-co-operatives-decide-how-to-ride-out-a-downturn (accessed 20 August 2011).

Kerr, R. (1999) 'Co-operatives versus corporates', text of speech, Christchurch, 9 November 1999. Online. Available at: www.nzbr.org.nz/site/nzbr/files/speeches/speeches-99/coop_v_corps.pdf (accessed 22 August 2011).

Mills, C. (2009) 'Funding the future: an alternative to capitalism', Elstree, Hertfordshire: Mutuo. Online. Available at: www.mutuo.co.uk/latest-releases/funding-the-future-an-alternative-to-capitalism-by-cliff-mills/ (accessed 20 August 2011).

Mintzberg, H., Molz, R., Raufflet, E., Sloan, P., Abdallah, C., Bercuvitz, R., and Tzeng, C.H. (2005) 'The invisible world of association', *Leader to Leader*, no. 36: 37–45, doi: 10.1002/ltl.126.

Parnell, E. (1999) *Re-inventing Co-operation: the challenge of the 21st century*, Woodstock, Oxfordshire: Plunkett Foundation.

Polanyi, K. (1957) *The Great Transformation: the political and economic origins of our time*, Boston: Beacon Press.

Robb, A.J. (2010) 'Step 3—you pay for it', *New Zealand Dairy Exporter*, 1 May 2010. Online. Available at: www.dairymag.co.nz/article/35674.html (accessed 21 August 2011).

Schwartz, J.D. (2009) 'In Cleveland, worker Co-ops look to a Spanish model', *Time Magazine*, 22 December 3009. Online. Available at: www.time.com/time/business/article/0,8599,1947313,00.html#ixzz0il0JZ9vA (accessed 20 August 2011).

Smith, A. (1776) *Wealth of Nations*, edited by C. J. Bullock, vol. 10 of Harvard Classics, New York: P.F. Collier & Son, 1909–14. Online. Available at: www.bartleby.com/10/ (accessed 21 August 2011).

Thompson, D. (2009) 'Remember the member: co-ops are in a capital revolution', *Cooperative Grocer*, no. 140 (January–February): 22–4.

Ward, A.H. (1975) *A Command of Cooperatives: the development of leadership, marketing and price control in the cooperative dairy industry of New Zealand*, Wellington: New Zealand Dairy Board.

Wilkinson, R.G. and Pickett, K. (2009) *The Spirit Level: why more equal societies almost always do better.* London: Allen Lane.

World Council of Credit Unions (2011) 'Financial Statistics'. Online. Available at: www.woccu.org/memberserv/intlcusystem (accessed 17 September 2011).

Part II

From cooperative banks to local societies

The chapters in this part are case studies that examine the proactive role played by cooperative banks in promoting and supporting the interests of local societies, and hence the development of them. Some chapters examine cases where there are pre-existing and strong community bonds, while others focus on weak communities, where the creation of new social capital has been a challenge. The authors provide interesting insights into the functions of cooperative banking that surpass not only the Hicksian channel of supplying savings for investment, but also the more ample Schumpeterian channel of selecting more efficient investments and entrepreneurs.

In Chapter 5, Cynthia Giagnocavo, Luis Fernández-Revuelta Pérez, and David Uclés Aguilera show how the cooperative bank Cajamar in the Spanish province of Almería has been a proactive force of development since its origins during Francoism. This bank has been a pioneer in developing agriculture, introducing technological innovation, establishing cooperative institutions and networks, filling a vacuum in civil society, and providing cohesion for a cooperative community. The authors reconsider the notion of 'territory' in the context of constructed communities and with respect to the need to reconcile the financial necessities of such communities and the growth strategies of cooperative banks. This analysis represents a useful complement to the mainstream approach to industrial districts, since the shortcomings of this approach have been overcome in Almeria due to the development and growth strategies of the cooperative bank.

In Chapter 6, Rosario Laratta and Sachiko Nakagawa explore the relatively uncharted field of cooperative banking in Japan. They address the central question of what and how Japanese cooperative banks can do to encourage cooperative behaviour between local residents and social enterprises to increase investment in the development of their communities. The authors compare two Japanese cooperative banks which operate in deprived areas and argue that if cooperative banks want to become useful tools for community development and distinguish themselves from ordinary banks, they should fill structural holes and spread bridging social capital by utilizing local expertise to overcome cultural and geographic barriers and promote a spirit of cooperation among local actors.

In Chapter 7, Theodoros A. Katerinakis applies social network analysis to a cooperative bank on the Hellenic island of Crete. He shows why real-life economic decisions cannot always be adequately interpreted under the *homo oeconomicus* approach, especially when the pre-existing social bonds of local agents are particularly strong. He connects trust and integrity with the central value of Hellenic culture *philotimo*, which is a unique sense of honour and pride, as expressed through acts of generosity and sacrifice. He applies social network analysis to the context of cooperative banking and argues that the connectedness that resides in the network structure of cooperative functions is the critical success factor that makes people stay involved with, and add to, community development.

In Chapter 8, Amélie Artis and Holger Blisse draw on the rich experience of France and Germany to challenge the historical capacity of cooperative banks to adapt their operations to highly demanding environments. The authors trace the new financial needs that emerge in local societies and describe specific initiatives to meet them through case studies of cooperative banks and solidarity-based finance. They identify innovative cooperative approaches that have been employed to 'create' capital that can be utilized by local societies. Following this 'outside' perspective on new evolving institutional solutions, the authors add an 'inside' perspective by showing how the annual profits and surpluses that result from a successful business model can remain at the disposal of local members to invest in mutually defined and prioritized projects.

5 The case for proactive cooperative banks and local development

Innovation, growth, and community building in Almería, Spain

Cynthia Giagnocavo,
Luis Fernández-Revuelta Pérez, and
David Uclés Aguilera

The evolution of Almería, a province in southern Spain, is of particular interest in demonstrating the role of cooperative finance in social, economic, and institutional development. In this case study, a cooperative bank is shown to have been a proactive force in developing economic activity and technological innovation, establishing cooperative institutions and networks, filling a civil society vacuum, and playing a cohesive function in the creation of a cooperative community in the midst of a dictatorship. In addition, we reconsider the notion of 'territory' in the context of both constructed communities and the need to reconcile the financial necessities of such communities and the growth strategies of cooperative banks.

We set our discussion against the backdrop of industrial districts due to the historical and theoretical association of this concept with cooperative banks and local development; moreover, the cooperative agricultural economy of Almería is often considered within the industrial district paradigm. We argue that in the case of Almería, traditional shortcomings identified in industrial districts have been overcome by the development and growth strategies of a cooperative bank.

Context

The province of Almería is home to Cajamar, the largest Spanish cooperative bank and the sixteenth largest Spanish bank (Grupo Cooperativa Cajamar 2011). The province is known as an example of rapid development based on smallholdings and the expansion of intensive agriculture. The average landholding sufficient to support a family is a mere 1.5 hectares, and most are held by farmers or small enterprises that are members of agricultural cooperatives. The benefits of this type of development are widely distributed (Downward and Taylor 2007). The Almería model has been 'exported' to various countries and has been studied as an example of cluster support for a successful model of sustainable, non-industrial development.

During the 1950s and 1960s, Almería was known for its abject poverty and arid landscapes, and the region was the subject of exposés in books such as Juan Goytisolo's *Campo de Nijar* (1954) and *La Chanca* (1962) and Gerald Brenan's *South from Granada* (1957), all of which chronicled the dire circumstances of the inhabitants and the harshness of the habitat. In terms of GDP per capita in 1955, Almería ranked last—less than 50 per cent of the national average—in an already poor Spain suffering from the autarky imposed by the Franco dictatorship. Today, Almería ranks among the top third of Spanish provinces in GDP per capita thanks in large part to the development of intensive agriculture.

Theoretical approach

Our primary claim is that this pattern of development cannot be explained or understood without investigating the active involvement of both the local cooperative bank and the cooperative movement of farmers. This development was a result, in large measure, of the innovative practices of the cooperative bank and its proactive involvement in the local economy.

The success and role of cooperative finance is too often framed as issues of trust or information asymmetries or incompleteness. Arguments are thus made in favour of cooperative bank finance based on information and transaction costs efficiencies—i.e. that monitoring is easier because knowledge is more implicit or community/trust-based and, thus, that the risk of 'incompleteness' of both information and contract is reduced (e.g. Dei Ottati 1994; Padoa-Schioppa 1996).

This approach, however, is only one element of the analysis if we wish to understand the role of cooperative finance in local development. In our study, we show that this role includes, but goes far beyond, a relationship-based supply of credit. The cooperative bank was a constant source of, and impetus for, sustainable innovation, both social and technical, as well as the force behind the construction of the social and economic community. This community was not an already pre-existing group defined by territory and cultural ties based on proximity—an observation that has important implications if we wish to consider the role that finance can play in social cohesion and social change.

In a 'control' or information-based model (however much it has been modified to 'fit' the cooperative bank situation), the financial entity gathers as much information as possible through screening and monitoring to limit potential investment risk, all the while providing 'banking services' such as affordable credit, a system of payment, and perhaps insurance and pension fund services. In contrast to this model, we demonstrate a more profound and proactive institutional role for cooperative banks.

The economy of Almería has been examined in various studies of 'industrial districts',[1] albeit as an agricultural industrial district (e.g. Ferraro García and Aznar Sánchez 2008). Moreover, within this district a 'territorially embedded' cooperative bank has played an important role in shaping the local economy.

While this case study is not limited to the context of industrial districts, it is useful to take note of this form of development for the issues that have been highlighted in the last few decades. In the 1980s, a rather optimistic exuberance for industrial districts could be found in academic literature, particularly with respect to Italy. Piore and Sabel (1984) lauded a production model where small and medium enterprises embedded in local territories could compete in global markets. Becattini's work on the 'Marshallian Industrial District' (1979, 1987) provided a framework, and the term 'industrial district' was defined as a 'social-territorial entity ... characterised by the active presence of both a community of people and a population of firms in one naturally and historically bounded area' (Becattini 1990, 38).

Porter (1998, 78) made the term more generic by broadly defining 'clusters' as 'geographically proximate groups of interconnected companies and associated institutions in a particular field', linked by common industries and complementary products. This definition is 'agnostic as to territorial scale' (Whitford and Potter 2007, 4) and has been criticized for stretching the concept to any scale and reducing it to a 'world-wide fad, a sort of academic and policy fashion item' (Martin and Sunley 2003, 6). However, the insistence on a more orthodox Marshallian industrial district is somewhat limited by its rootedness in the particular experience of relatively culturally cohesive regions, as in Italy (Whitford and Potter 2007, 5).

In this chapter, we are not so concerned about arguing for one specific definition of *industrial district*. What interests us is leaving the conceptual door open to a model that allows 'considerable room for geographic and historical variations' (Zeitlin 1992, 280). Simply put, we treat Marshall's or Becattini's models as ideal types and look to other elements that contribute to success and innovation, which in our case are the activities of cooperative banks.

Above all, we want to avoid the trap of treating districts, and thus the financing within them, as a static unit of analysis with formal characteristics. Instead, we prefer to view districts as a 'unit of initiative' (Brusco 1992, 195). When they 'are successful, [industrial districts] are creative, display originality, are often able to discover new markets [and] continuously introduce incremental innovations' (Brusco 1992, 196). This non-static approach to clusters/industrial districts or local development ties into other characterizations, such as the cooperative movement or other 'collective entrepreneurship' initiatives of which the industrial district and cooperative business are only two amongst many forms.

In the Italian industrial district literature, cooperative credit banks are seen as 'intermediate institutions' that provide cheaper access to credit, thus lowering default rates through the close ties—extensive knowledge of clients and trust—that banks have with the local community (Brusco and Righi 1989; Ferri 1997). While we do not dispute that cooperative banks play this role, we argue that their more important and creative role occurs in the development of local economies.

We show that cooperative credit not only contributed to the developmental success of the area through both traditional and innovative methods, but also provided part of the solution when problems began to emerge; indeed, these problems arguably had their origins in classic industrial district characteristics. Bellandi and Caloffi (2006, 466) characterize such problems as 'the structural deficits of an economy heavily dependent on small firms and a sectoral specialization weighted towards relatively mature products that are particularly exposed to low-wage competition'. Brusco (1992, 196) points out that industrial districts are 'slow to adopt new technologies, lack expertise in financial management, have little knowledge required for basic research, and are unable to produce epoch-making innovation'. Local banks operating in industrial districts seem to be undermined by consolidation in a financial system afflicted by weak organization and unprepared to compete with rivals (Ferri 1997; Padoa-Schioppa 1996).

These traditional failings were avoided in the development of Almería in large part due to the strategic and active participation by the local cooperative bank, which helped prevent the tendency of mature industries (which intensive agricultural later became) to maintain the status quo rather than 'retooling to capture emergent opportunities elsewhere' (Whitford and Potter 2007, 6). Because Cajamar assumed the role of developing, encouraging, and incorporating innovation, and because it had a direct interest in both the short term success of its individual members and the long term success of the entire sector, it was not content with simply supplying interest-bearing credit. The growth strategy of the cooperative bank, though perhaps controversial for those who advocate 'local' banks based on strictly circumscribed territories, was crucial for avoiding the decline of the largely cooperative community.

In addition, if we accept that the success and resilience of industrial districts was due to both their embeddedness in local areas and simultaneous participation in international (later global) marketplaces, we can observe the role of cooperative credit in these two processes. Furthermore, the task of continuously adapting and adjusting production processes was largely assumed by the cooperative bank, from its initial push for cooperative commercialization channels to the establishment of experimental farms and a research institute.

Central to our analysis is the assertion that the local cooperative bank filled a civil society vacuum and acted as the impetus for community building and social cohesion, thereby contributing to its success. It is noteworthy that the local agricultural sector was never the recipient of large subsidies or state aid compared to the rest of Andalucía, Spain, or the European Union.[2] Moreover, Cajamar has always been steadfastly non-political, often to the chagrin of local politicians.

Cajamar (then Caja Rural de Almería) began during a dictatorship, a regime that had decimated a large proportion of its citizens through inept economic policies and cruel political repression. Specific social, economic, and institutional deficiencies that were caused by the regime illustrate how Cajamar acted as the catalyst in the rebuilding of the province's social economy. As a result of the brutal Spanish Civil War, Almería was a wasteland during the 1950s and early 1960s since many people migrated out of the region, and those who remained had little sense of civic or cultural community and a profound distrust of basic institutions such as the state and the Church, which was aligned with the regime.

In addition to its role in strengthening civil society, the cooperative bank contributed to remedying the social, economic, and institutional deficiencies by encouraging entrepreneurship, creating and sustaining social and cooperative networks, addressing emerging external challenges, and introducing technology, knowledge production, and information dissemination.

Conceiving of the cooperative bank as more than just a local source of capital avoids several problems inherent in both the territorial and the economics of information approaches. In other words, since the limited control-based, territorial model is premised on transaction costs efficiencies due to proximity, any advantage that cooperative banks may have will be seen as disappearing as soon as the cooperative bank experiences significant growth or expands beyond its original territory. However, in some circumstances growth may actually be key to capturing more funds to finance the original territory's financing needs. A non-territorial approach to growth strategies, while firmly based in cooperative values and the rational of sustainable community needs, is an alternative to the view that cooperative banks operate within a defined geographical region with a static notion of what constitutes 'a community'.

By approaching the role of cooperative banks as co-generators of development and as important contributors to civil society and the creation of community, it leads us to re-examine our notion of 'territory' and 'local development'. For example, if we look to how 'territories' or 'communities' may be constructed in the case of 'ethical banks', we can see that they rely on a community that shares values but not necessarily physical proximity. Perhaps we can redefine the societal role of finance by using 'active' cooperative banks as an example. The unique inherent characteristics of cooperative banks allow them to fulfil certain social and developmental goals when 'territory' is conceived as a community of values that these banks help to construct rather than as a pre-existing relationship within a geographic area. Indeed, given the migration patterns of those involved in Almería's development, the sense of 'community' is something that arguably had to be created. At least at the beginning, this sense of community was more about economic activity than it was about any particular 'embeddedness' in the pre-existing social fabric. Consequently, cooperative finance played an important role in defining and building community, and not the other way around.

Economic landscape

While the Franco years may be known for their harsh political repression,[3] what has been less documented is the economic 'terror' and suffering caused by failed policies that resulted in mass starvation and dire poverty. In the post-Spanish Civil War years of 1939 to 1945, 200,000 Spaniards died of starvation, while between 1935 and 1945 real incomes dropped by 66 per cent. In 1950, disposable incomes in Spain were 40 per cent lower than in Italy, which had yet to experience its 'economic miracle'. Economic reforms in 1952 did little to ease the economic disaster (Cazorla Sánchez 2010, 12). Within the already poor context of Spain, the Province of Almería, a former republican stronghold in the southeast corner of Andalucía, was the poorest, with a level of income 50 per cent lower than the national average (Sánchez Picón 2005, 76).

After 20 years of economic failure, Franco implemented the 1959 Stabilization Plan, which opened up the market to capitalistic practices but left the dictatorship untouched (Cazorla Sánchez, 2010, 12). Spain's economy as a whole began to improve as the country eased its economic isolation: foreign investment began to flow in, jumping from $40 million in 1960 to $697 million in 1970. However, income disparity increased and the benefits of economic and social development were unevenly distributed geographically. The poorest areas were the rural parts of Andalucía (which includes Almería), Extremadura, and La Mancha (Cazorla Sánchez 2010, 14). In contrast, the industrial areas of the Basque region, home to the internationally known Mondragon cooperative, along with Catalonia and Asturias, ranked first among the wealthier regions.

As Spain's economy grew and became more industrialized and urban, Franco's policies played an important role. As Cazorla Sánchez (2010, 15) observes:

> Francoism created an affordable, disciplined workforce which was achieved by the killing of union leaders, by the destruction of genuine, representative organizations and by instilling fear and pessimism in the general population. The combination of these factors made possible the optimum exploitation of employees by both the state and capital interests. The state guaranteed employers a 'business friendly' environment with a docile and cheap workforce.

Spanish businesses enjoyed low taxes, inexperienced labour, and a captive and undemanding consumer market (Cebrián Villar 2001, 277–300). In 1965, public expenditure in Spain was 15 per cent of GDP, compared to an average of 31 per cent in the OECD. In 1970, public expenditure in Spain was 20.1 per cent of GDP, compared with France, 51.0 per cent; Italy, 43.3 per cent; the UK, 53.2 per cent; and Germany, 36.8 per cent (Carreras and Tafunell 2005, 877).

This state of affairs—the absence of labour leaders, desperate but docile workers, and a lack of public expenditure and investment—are all important for understanding the influential role that the cooperative bank would later play.

'Co-evolution' of the cooperative bank and the cooperative sector

Almería has experienced a huge transformation during the last 40 to 50 years. Between 1970 and 2000, the rate of population increase of the province was 90 per cent more than that of Spain as a whole, 84 per cent more in production, and 130 per cent more in employment growth. During this period, the GDP of the province grew by 20 per cent.

We describe four stages to illustrate the functions assumed by the cooperative bank and the changing role of finance in the development of Almería: pre-1975, post-Franco 1975 to 1990, 1990 to 2000, and 2000 to present.

Pre-1975

With its arid land, extensive out-migration, lack of infrastructure, geographical isolation, and subsistence level of livelihood, the coastal area of Almería was not the best candidate for agricultural development.

During the 1940s, a large expanse of land within the province was declared a 'zone of national interest' in order to exploit the water reserves beneath the arid surface. The Regime was interested in increasing agricultural production, and a government programme was implemented to provide wells and pumps. A few hundred hectares were eventually supplied with water by small gasoline pumps, since reliable supplies of electricity were not available (Sánchez Picón 2005, 82). In 1956, crops were planted with abysmal results since the saline subterranean water was not well suited for irrigation (Cazorla Sánchez 1999, 229).

Poor farmers who had come from the interior part of the province and resettled in coastal regions introduced a 'technological innovation' that consisted of putting down a layer of fertilizer, and then covering this with a layer of sand in order to keep roots moist and filter the salty water. Coming from inland mountain regions, they were accustomed to grape production using trellises, so they started building structures with wooden posts and galvanized wire and covering them with cane to reduce the vicious effects of the strong winds that sweep through the region. With the arrival of plastic sheeting, a clear plastic sheet was put overhead. These structures served as the first rudimentary greenhouses. Perhaps seemingly insignificant to the outsider, this basic innovation revolutionized the economy of the area.

In 1961, the government introduced an electrification plan, allowing more efficient water pumps, and thus a model of development based on exploiting subterranean water was put into motion. More importantly, increased agricultural activity attracted people from the mountains or the interior, many of whom had few other economic prospects. Pursuant to the 'colonization programme' (the Regime's odd term for agrarian reform), the barren land which was considered otherwise useless was sold to families (a maximum of 3.5 hectares)[4] for cultivation. It should be emphasized that without irrigation and at least rudimentary greenhouse technology—both of which required financing—it was impossible to support a family on such small parcels of land. The 'colonization programme' was not intended to improve the lives of such farmers, but rather to exploit the existing resources of cheap labour and underground water; by design, farmers were expected to work part-time for themselves and provide cheap labour for others.

With increased production, it was obvious that families needed to sell their products. Problems faced by the farmers in commercialization—controlled as it was by large, sometimes foreign multinational, groups—were significant and difficult to overcome without independent financing and organizational strength. Local firms solicited to be officially allowed to export, but were denied by the Regime's administration.[5] Commercialization was thus controlled by large regime-friendly companies that could buy Almería's products and re-export them under false labels (Cazorla Sánchez 1999, 232).

On the initiative of entrepreneurial intermediaries, some auction houses backed by foreign and local capital eventually began to operate, and some of these even implemented a type of 'financing' in which they would front the costs of seeds and supplies and subtract it from revenues upon harvest. However, lack of transparency in prices and price fixing between large auction houses occurred, and farmers were left in dire circumstances if they had a bad harvest, and they risked having their land seized. The auction houses would then resell or rent the land to young farmers with exclusive purchasing contracts, allowing the auction house to fill up their warehouses with products and undermine marketing efforts by farmer cooperatives (Cazorla Sánchez 1999, 234).

Economists describing this period often offer the following observations about Almería: in general, financing needs were low and there was very little linkage between financial and agricultural sectors. Production depended on natural factors (availability of water, cheap land, and a sunny climate), an abundance of cheap young labour, and low capital requirements given basic technology and the absence of a marketing structure. Agricultural activity is described as being squarely within the primary sector and value was added through sheer labour effort. The little financial intermediation that existed was largely available through private auction houses (Cortés García 2003–4; Molina Herrera 2005).

Dependent as it is on the notion that 'financing' is about available quantities of credit, this analysis does not highlight that there was a crucial need (however low) for financing by the farmers.[6] Those who had no capital needed a way to turn the only thing they did have—labour—into capital. Moreover, they also needed capital and an organization to create a system of commercialization that did not exploit them. While technology was basic, it was still significantly more expensive than non-irrigated farming.

The development model set up by the Regime was unsustainable, relying as it did on the overly exploitive use of water; under-investment technology, infrastructure, and commercial avenues; and no investment in the people actually working the land. Farmers endured atrocious living conditions, without proper housing or sanitation. Children had to work alongside parents, often not attending school at all (Cazorla Sánchez 2010, 107).

It was against this backdrop that the cooperative bank changed the economic and social landscape.[7] In 1963, the Caja Rural Provincial de Almería commenced activities on the initiative of a few local people, amongst them a young lawyer named Juan del Águila Molina, who worked with various agricultural 'unions'.[8] Knowledgeable about the needs of small farmers in Almería and aware of cooperative credit organizations in other countries, Águila Molina sought a development path between the models advocated by the Fascist Falange and the outlawed Communist Party. He began to visit farmers in the small, scattered towns, informing them of the possibility of setting up agricultural cooperatives. It soon became apparent that adequate financing was not available. Other sources of finance in the province would lend only to businesses and land owners who could provide security or guarantees. Even if the farmers did have land, such land was often not worth enough to secure loans.

As the cooperative 'bank' was not officially set up to perform financial transactions, the founder withdrew the funds from a commercial bank account every morning, circulating amongst the farmers to do their banking.[9] Deposits from farmers in the interior towns were used to finance the emerging needs of the 'new' irrigated farms on the coast.[10] At the close of business, he would return to the commercial bank and deposit the money. In this way, a network of customers was created and knowledge about the farmers and their farms was acquired. This informal process continued until the cooperative bank was officially constituted in 1966. When it gained official status, it could only give credits or make loans to agricultural cooperatives. Consequently, it followed a strategy of creating cooperatives in many small towns and villages, dedicating resources and personnel to the task. There was a dual objective: to find new clients and to create an agricultural cooperative network throughout the province.[11]

Cajamar broke the rules of traditional finance and gave unsecured loans, based solely on the promise of labour. By operating in this way, labour could be turned into capital and the cooperative bank assumed a different position than that of a traditional provider of credit or capital, since it had a far higher stake in making certain that whatever activity the farmers undertook was worth financing.[12] This simple, though radical, approach has informed the strategy of the cooperative bank ever since.

In the absence of union leaders and political organizers coupled with a distrust of institutions and authority, the cooperative bank served as the impetus for farmers to organize. Even though 'cooperatives' were still cooperatives under a dictatorship, the fact that their members were small enterprises with the support of independent financing was the start of a new paradigm in the region. For many of these people, the cooperative bank was the first institution to earn their trust outside of the family.

The first formal loan on its own account was made by Caja Rural de Almería in 1967. In 1970, the cooperative expanded its operations to many of the small towns of the province; the new 'branches' were usually housed in modest buildings amongst the greenhouses. In 1972, the cooperative bank opened its own office in the city of Almería, and in 1974, it began the process of information development and signed an agreement for the acquisition of its first computer.

In a little over a decade, the cooperative bank had started up, began to make 'official' loans, helped to develop an agricultural cooperative movement with production still in the hands of family farms, and established innovations in both information and agricultural technologies. Its 'financial' activity was quite straightforward—the simple credits and loans of traditional banking. The growth of the bank was extraordinarily rapid: in1970, agricultural loans amounted to 200 million pesetas; three years later, this activity had grown to 1,268 million pesetas; by 1975, it was worth 2,490 million pesetas (Caja Rural de Almería 1974, 1976). In contrast, in 1975 the well-established savings bank of Almería had a volume of only 862 million pesetas in agricultural loans.

While these results would be impressive under any circumstances, what is remarkable is that this cooperative movement and cooperative bank managed to achieve these results during a dictatorship in which capital and social structures were tightly controlled by the Regime and there had not been a pre-existing cohesive community embedded in a particular territory. It operated 'under the radar' and by the time the Regime noticed, it was already well entrenched as an institution in the province.

In 1975, Franco died and Spain began the transition to democracy.

Post-Franco: 1975 to 1990

It is tempting to think that with the end of the dictatorship the economy and society would immediately improve. While there was a clear improvement in terms of political freedoms, the economic path upwards proved more complicated. Unemployment was high, the culture of investing was weak, Spain was isolated, and only a muddled vision of the way forward existed with the loss of the paternalistic state and little sense of external international competitiveness. Not to mention fear of further violence and instability if the delicate process of transition failed.

The Almería agricultural model began to show signs of stress, particularly in the most concentrated areas. Demand for land grew and prices rose. At the same time, underground water supplies were overexploited and the saline content was increasing due to seawater seepage. Mineralization of the soil increased, pesticides accumulated, crops quality declined, erosion spread, and waste disposal became an increasing problem. Agricultural production started to decrease and energy prices began to climb (Cazorla Sánchez 1999, 264). Supply started to overtake demand as other areas of Spain also had increased production. Countries that had favoured status within the European Common Market and those that had agreements that gave them preference were serious competitors. Spain's weakening position gave more market power to large agro-food companies (Cazorla Sánchez 1999, 264–5). The challenges for cooperative farmers at this stage of development included not only the adjustments to be made in the transition to a market economy and to a democracy, but also the need for innovation on social, economic, and strategic levels. The cooperative bank was a partner for farmers in this process, and instigated them to take action.

A key strategic decision was taken in 1975: three experimental farms were initiated and fully financed by Cajamar with the goal of increasing the technical level of local agricultural cooperatives by testing, developing, and sharing results with cooperative member farmers. The purpose of the project was to transfer part of the experimental and crop risks—thus, financial risks—from the farmer to the credit cooperative. Sustainable technologies were an important area of research and at this time, there was no university or research centre that could have fulfilled this research function. In addition, the research dealt with pressing environmental issues such as the increasing overuse and salinization of underground water supplies and general environmental degradation; this research was necessary from a sustainability point of view, but was an activity that family farmers were not able to undertake themselves, financially or technically.

The viability of the new technologies was tested beginning in 1975–6 by a service financed by the cooperative bank. The aim was to provide information on establishing adequate finance mechanisms for each new technology that was adopted; essentially, it was a system of risk assessment (Galdeano Gómez 1994–5, 278). While certain technologies were indeed innovative, it was uncertain whether they were—or potentially could be—profitable. The role of finance at this stage in both production and marketing had a dynamic character, providing for the incorporation of new technologies and above all the incorporation of market information in the production process.

The technological projects undertaken by the experimental farms not only significantly increased production but also allowed products to enter the market two months earlier, a factor that was key when faced with increased competition by other countries. The assumption of research expenses and experimental risk by the cooperative bank not only spared farmers from such uncertainties but also created a sense of community through a shared knowledge base. Moreover, it was an example of a financial institution working directly for the benefit of their community and class, something that had been unheard of until then.

The cooperative movement contributed to changing the mentality of the farmers in that they were now participants in the commercialization process, with a deeper understanding of the workings of the market and consumer demand. The pressures that they could now begin to exert as producer-exporters at the level of the national administration, which was dominated by other producer areas of Spain, became stronger as the sector grew and they found themselves with a political voice and power not previously experienced.

1990 to 2000

This decade was important not only in terms of economic growth, but also for an important cultural shift that occurred: the disappearing agricultural identity was replaced by an agro-industrial model. Entrance into the European Union coupled with the increasing globalization after the Marrakech Agreement of 1995, which replaced the GATT agreement and liberalized world trade, created new challenges for the sector. Adapting to these conditions required larger infusions of capital than had previously been the case in order to meet increased demand and enable farmers and cooperatives to compete internationally.

These challenges were met in several ways, including an expansion strategy to a neighbouring province that was prompted by the failure of the province's credit cooperative. Investment in research and technology increased, as technological advances occurred ever more rapidly. Many of the technologies focused on sustainability—for example, increased efficiency in water use, biological rather than chemical pest control, and eco-friendly fertilizers—or technological advances—such as computerized greenhouse controls, structural improvements in greenhouses, and long-life hybrids.[13] Environmental solutions were sought for waste collection and recycling. The function of the cooperative bank in calculating the economic implications of the adoption of such technologies became an even greater contribution.

During this period, there was a widespread adoption of production technology and business management applied to farms, and with these changes there was the gradual conversion of 'peasants' into 'agricultural entrepreneurs'. The cooperative bank contributed to the creation of new lines of business in the cooperatives, supporting business associations linked to agriculture not only by providing financial support and advice but also by utilizing its network of institutional contacts for the development of projects. Services and infrastructure became similar to that of industrial districts. Support for other institutional entities—such as universities, associations of exporters, chambers of commerce—was also part of the strategy, whether through direct funding or indirect support and coordination. The infrastructure for direct commercialization was also put in place. An institute of social and economic studies was created in 1998 in an attempt to achieve a more profound understanding of both local and international economic and social perspectives. These efforts complemented the technical research and innovation carried out on the experimental farms.

Notably, and contrary to the experiences of other industrial districts, the role of the cooperative bank did not decrease when firm size (in this case, sector size) grew and the cooperative bank's reputation became more established. Its proactive role continued as the productive sector began to develop and mature.

2000 to present

Since 2000, the development and maturity of the agricultural support and services industry can be seen to have given rise to sectoral diversification and the creation of a local production system. Looking forward, it is expected that following the financial crisis and the implosion of the construction sector, there will be a new focus on the agro-food industry. In addition, most likely this industry will have to deal with an ever-increasing opening of markets and competition from countries where labour is cheaper. Current areas of emphasis concern food safety, creating value-added products designed to meet consumer demand, research and development and innovation, energy production (from agricultural waste), and renewable energy. Above all, there is a recognized need for strategic expertise and a growing concern with distribution and logistics. The response of the cooperative bank has been to invest more in research and education and to diversify its areas of activity, without leaving behind the agricultural sector.

Growth and expansion strategy

In order to understand the chronological story set out above, it is important to examine the growth strategy of the cooperative bank. As illustrated in Figure 5.1, cooperative bank growth and agricultural growth (represented almost entirely by fruit and vegetable production) went hand in hand. While until the early 1990s the amounts of deposits, credits and production were almost equal—which, in other words, is indicative of a rather self-sustaining financial system—from 1996, and particularly from 2004, the credit demand was more pronounced.

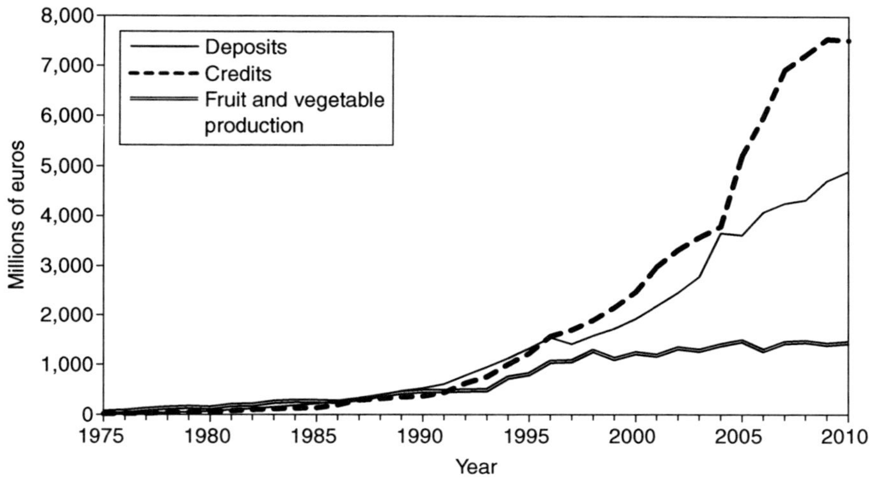

Figure 5.1 Cajamar deposits and credits and agricultural production in Almeria, 1975–2010 (source: Junta de Andalucía (2010) and Cabrera *et al.* (2010)).

Subsequently, the Almería economy required credit beyond the amount that agricultural production alone could generate in order to finance research and development, other auxiliary and cluster activities, and construction and infrastructure investment.

In 1989, a strategy to seek growth outside the province of Almería was taken by the cooperative bank. To access more sophisticated services and financial products, the rural credit cooperatives in Spain decided to work together as an association in 1989–90; however, as Cajamar grew, conflict arose between it and this association, a key issue being an agreement to prohibit entry into the territory of other rural credit cooperatives.

The success of intensive agriculture in the 1990s necessitated a search for additional markets. Cajamar grew rapidly through mergers and synergies as complementary territories were sought out. However, its merger in 2007 with a rural cooperative bank in a distant province altered this tendency, since this cooperative bank was situated in a distinct territory with a type of agriculture unlike that of Almería: the region's population was older and less risk averse; they also had higher levels of savings and, thus, different financial needs. This strategic merger provided an injection of much needed capital into Cajamar and helped to feed the expanding economy of Almería.

The growth phase in which Cajamar now finds itself is a result of the policies of the Bank of Spain and the real estate crises. The Bank of Spain, desiring more manageable and less risky credit cooperatives, instituted the System of Institutional Protection (SIP), which provides for the grouping of small credit cooperatives and the unification of their balance sheets and their systems of risk management. Cajamar decided to head its own SIP, converting itself into a Cooperative Group.

In light of the above, the strategic mergers of Cajamar imply a different concept of the role of credit cooperatives in local development. If we restrict the notion of 'local' to a necessary link between a given community and territory, an expansion of cooperative bank activity beyond the community and territory 'breaks' such bonds. However, if we view the activity of financing as being capable of creating communities and being an impetus for sustainable innovation—and indeed, survival—the emphasis on territorial restriction is reduced. In order to support the cooperative community with which Cajamar had 'grown up', expansion was a necessary development. From a strategic point of view, it has avoided a common pitfall of territorial and sectoral concentration, which renders local finance vulnerable to volatility.

Whether politically mandated mergers and growth are in keeping with this philosophy or a threat to sustainable cooperative finance and the corresponding cooperative community is an open question.

Conclusion

This case study has illustrated the evolution of the role and activities of a cooperative bank in the development of a community as it moved from a primarily agricultural system to a sophisticated local production system. The arguments developed in this chapter support the following observations:

- Sustainable development was the result, in large part, of innovative practices and proactive involvement by the cooperative bank in the local economy. Providing more than a relationship-based supply of credit, the cooperative bank was a constant source of, and impetus for sustainable technological, social, and economic innovation.
- Cooperative finance can act as a catalyst in the creation of community, particularly when the cooperative bank fills a vacuum created by an absence of civil society institutions.
- Our case study can be seen as an example of an industrial district portrayed as a 'unit of initiative'.
- Cooperative banks have a potential role to play in the incorporation of new technologies, management training, and the creation of an innovative knowledge/technology-based society. We have shown the need for flexibility, assumption of risk, and commitment to supporting local economies and production activities.
- The cooperative bank was part of the solution when problems, having their origins in classical industrial district characteristics, began to arise. A growth strategy was included in these solutions as the cooperative bank actively sought to capture funds outside its original territory to finance the growing cooperative and auxiliary business sector.

As a result, when exploring the role of cooperative banks in local development, we suggest shifting the focus not only from 'whether a supply of credit exists' to 'what kind of credit institution exists', but also to an investigation of the extent to which the credit cooperative is implicated in both the local and broader economies.[14]

As a proactive agent of technological, economic, and social innovation, Cajamar has fulfilled a central institutional role in civil society for a population left vulnerable by an economically and politically repressive regime. It has done so by pursuing the following strategies:

- committing itself financially and socially to a vulnerable community such that initially the only 'security' it had was to make sure that the activities of its members were worthwhile funding, thus implicating itself in profound ways into the economic and social life of the community;
- encouraging the establishment of a cooperative economic 'fabric' through the establishment of cooperatives and the coordination of family and other small and medium enterprises;
- building upon, but moving far beyond relationship-based finance, through proactive production and dissemination of technical, economic, and social knowledge;
- shifting and transforming individual economic risk (including technological and experimental risk) to community risk, thus involving not only the cooperative bank, but also the community in shared success;
- recognizing the transformation from 'peasant' to 'agricultural entrepreneur' and providing management and financial training as well as support for other institutional players;
- assuming the role of mediator among international, EU, and domestic politics and policies for community members;
- pursuing organic growth strategies in order to sustain innovation and sector growth amongst its members and to diversify its activities beyond local specialization (both sectoral and territorial), and thus to protect against potentially volatile concentration; and
- pursuing strategic growth strategies in response to government imposed integration in order to maintain its strength both inside and outside its original territory.

In observing these strategies, we note that many of the shortcomings of industrial districts that have been cited in the literature have been addressed and overcome in large part due to the proactive role of cooperative finance. In addition, we have shown how a cooperative bank, in concert with a cooperative movement, has been able to co-construct an economically stable community through sustainable innovation.

Notes

1 As noted by Goglio (2009), what little attention has been paid to the function of local finance has often concentrated on industrial districts. Even so, it should be stressed

that the supply of credit and the financial system providing support is only one factor in local development.

2 As a percentage of agricultural subsidies over agricultural income in 2004: Almería, 1.2 per cent; Andalucía, 17.5 per cent; Spain, 22.2 per cent; and the EU, 18.7 per cent (Torrente 2005).

3 Fifty thousand people were executed for political reasons in Spain following the civil war in 1939.

4 Some people were ineligible, even if they possessed the resources. A selection process declaring prospective purchasers 'fit to work' was required, and these selection processes served as political screening since people convicted of previous political activity or considered subversive were excluded. As Cazorla Sánchez (2010, 107) observes, 'the ideal new farmers were deemed to be apolitical and supportive of the regime'.

5 The Regime reasoned that they did not meet minimum conditions (citing lack of an official quota and poor railway service, two things within the Regime's control) and that they were not in operation long enough (Archivo Histórico Provincial de Sevilla, Memorias del Sindicatos de Frutos, 1951–76 G198–201).

6 It should be noted that before the beginning of the cooperative bank, there were other sources of finance operating in the region: regular commercial banks, savings banks linked to the Church, as well as some public finance in the form of development programmes. None of these lent to poor farmers. While the savings bank was involved in social programmes—such as schools, residences, social housing, and seniors clubs—it also did not lend to poor farmers, although in 1956 it began to offer some lines of credit to the established and profitable inland grape and citrus producers in cooperation with the Servicio Nacional del Crédito Agrícola (Cazorla Sánchez 1999, 262; Titos Martínez 2005, 578).

7 It is useful to provide some background on cooperative bank legislation under the Regime: in 1942 through its Law of Cooperatives, the Regime recognized the importance of having 'a' cooperative movement that was structured to be consistent with the Regime. This initiative should not be confused with recognizing the importance of 'the' cooperative movement. The cooperative movement under Franco hoped to structure society so that both labour and management held their proper 'place' in society—cooperatives were to serve as a method to control and contain labour, giving them small titbits of choice, such as voting within the cooperative. In 1957, a National Caja Rural (rural cooperative credit bank) was created and took under its wing the already existing cooperative rural banks operating in Spain. In 1962, a new law for the regulation of the finance sector generally in Spain was passed, and in 1964 the National Caja Rural was reorganized, strengthened, and placed under the supervision of the Minister of Finance. Important benefits were available to those credit cooperatives that fulfilled certain requirements (5 years of operation, prohibition on being a second level cooperative, and maintenance of assets superior to 100 million pesetas.) This created a big impetus for rural cajas as they had the opportunity to access official agricultural credits and to restructure with a more solid base (Titos Martínez 2005).

8 These *sindicatos* were not really labour unions, but rather regime-sponsored associations used to control and politically categorize workers.

9 Interview with D. Juan del Águila by C. Giagnocavo, 19 March 2010, Almería.

10 Interview with D. Juan del Águila by Cazorla Sánchez, cited in Cazorla Sánchez (1999, 261).

11 As the regulatory legislation was progressively relaxed, the commercial strategy became more varied. For example, in the 1980s members did not have to be farmers and the amount of non-agricultural credit could be up to 50 per cent. Efforts were made to make the majority of its clients cooperative members, regardless of what sector they worked in.

12 Interview with D. Juan del Águila by C. Giagnocavo, 19 March 2010, Almería.

13 One important advance, although seemingly 'low-tech', was the introduction of

colonies of bees that could survive in greenhouses. The task of pollination until 1991 was done by hand, flower by flower, row by row, hectare by hectare—an amount of manual labour now almost unimaginable.

14 However one wishes to define 'local', we suggest that it is not necessarily a pre-existing community tied to a particular territory.

References

Becattini, G. (1979) 'Dal "settore" industriale al "distretto" industriale: alcune considerazione sull´unitá d'indagine dell´economia industrial', *Rivista di Economia e Politica Industriale*, 5(1): 7–21.

Becattini, G. (1987) (ed.) *Mercato e forze locali: il distretto industriale*, Bologna: Il Mulino.

Becattini, G. (1990) 'The Marshallian industrial district as a socio-economic notion', in F. Pyke, G. Becattini, and W. Sengenberger (eds) *Industrial Districts and Inter-firm Co-operation in Italy*, Geneva: International Institute for Labour Studies, pp. 37–51.

Bellandi, M. and Caloffi, A. (2006) 'Distretti industriali italiani e internazionalizzazione fra gli anni novanta e la prima metà del nuovo decennio', in *L'italia nell'economia internazionale: rapporto ICE 2005–2006*, Rome, Istituto Nazionale per il Commercio Estero, pp. 466–82.

Brenan, G. (1957) *South from Granada.* London: H. Hamilton.

Brusco, S. (1992) 'Small firms and the provision of real services', in F. Pyke and W. Sengenberger (eds) *Industrial Districts and Local Economic Regeneration*, Geneva: International Institute for Labour Studies, pp. 177–96.

Brusco, S. and Righi, E. (1989) 'Local government, industrial policy and social consensus: the case of Modena (Italy)', *Economy and Society*, 18(4): 405–24.

Cabrera, A.M., Marzo, B., Uclés, D., Molina, J., Gázquez, J.C., and García, R. (2010) 'Análisis de la campaña hortofrutícola de Almería: campaña 2009/2010', Almería, Spain: Fundación Cajamar.

Caja Rural de Almería (1974) *Informe Anual* [Annual Report], *1973*, Almería, Spain: Caja Rural de Almería.

Caja Rural de Almería (1976) *Informe Anual* [Annual Report], *1975*, Almería, Spain: Caja Rural de Almería.

Carreras, A. and Tafunell, X. (eds) (2005) *Estadísticas Históricas de España: siglos XIX y XX*, Bilbao: Fundación BBVA.

Cazorla Sánchez, A. (1999) *Desarrollo sin Reformistas: dictadura y campesinado en el nacimiento de una nueva sociedad en Almería, 1939–1975*, Almería: Instituto de Estudios Almerienses.

Cazorla Sánchez, A. (2010) *Fear and Progress: ordinary lives in Franco's Spain, 1939–1975*, Chichester, West Sussex: Wiley-Blackwell.

Cebrián Villar, M. (2001) 'Las fuentes del crecimiento económico español, 1964–1973', *Revista de Historia Económica* 19(extraordinario): 277–300.

Cortés García, F.J. (2003–4) 'El papel de las entidades de crédito en el desarrollo económico almeriense', *Revista De Humanidades y Ciencias Sociales*, no. 19: 59–94.

Dei Ottati, G. (1994) 'Trust, interlinking transaction and credit in the industrial district', *Cambridge Journal of Economics*, 18(6): 529–46.

Downward, S.R. and Taylor, R. (2007) 'An assessment of Spain's Programa AGUA and its implications for sustainable water management in the province of Almería, southeast Spain', *Journal of Environmental Management* 82(2): 277–89.

Ferraro García, J. and Aznar Sánchez, J.A. (2008) 'El distrito agroindustrial de Almería: un caso atípico', in *Los Distritos Industriales*, Almería, Spain: Fundación Cajamar, pp. 353–82.

Ferri, G. (1997) 'Introduzione' in F. Cesarini, G. Ferri, and M. Giardino (eds) *Credito e sviluppo: banche locali cooperative e imprese minori*, Bologna: Il Mulino, pp. 17–55.

Galdeano Gómez, E. (1994–5) 'Caja Rural de Almería: evolución, análisis comparado dentro del sector andaluz y política de futuro', *Boletín del Instituto de Estudios Almerienses*: *Ciencias*, no. 13: 277–300.

Goglio, S. (2009) 'Local credit and territorial development: general aspects and the Italian experience', in A. Bonoldi and A. Leonardi (eds) *Recovery and Development in the European Periphery (1945–1960)*, Bologna: Il Mulino, pp. 241–80.

Goytisolo, J. (1954) *Campo de Nijar*, Barcelona: Seix Barral.

Goytisolo, J. (1962) *La Chanca*, Paris: Librería Española.

Grupo Cooperativa Cajamar (2011) *Informe Anual* [Annual Report] *2010*, Almería, Spain: Grupo Cooperativa Cajamar. Online. Available at: www.grupocooperativocajamar.es/es/informacion-corporativa/informacion-financiera/informe-anual/informe-anual.pdf (accessed 21 October 2011).

Junta de Andalucía (2010) *Indicadores económicos de Andalucía* [Economic Indicators of Andalusia]. Seville, Spain: Instituto de estadística y cartografía de Andalucía, Consejería de Economía, Innovación y Ciencia, Junta de Andalucía. Online. Available at: www.juntadeandalucia.es/institutodeestadisticaycartografia/bd/indea/index.jsp?tema=8 (accessed 23 October 2011).

Martin, R. and Sunley, P. (2003) 'Deconstructing clusters: chaotic concept or policy panacea?', *Journal of Economic Geography*, 3(1): 5–35.

Molina Herrera, J. (2005) 'Claves para la interpretación económica de la provincia de Almería', in *La Economía de la Provincia de Almería*, Almería, Spain: Caja Rural Intermediterránea, Instituto de Estudios de Cajamar, pp. 13–41.

Padoa-Schioppa, T. (1996) 'Il credito cooperativo in Italia: realtá e problemi', *Cooperazione di Credito*, 152(3): 223–53.

Piore, M.J. and Sabel, C.F. (1984) *The Second Industrial Divide: possibilities for prosperity*, New York, NY: Basic Books.

Porter, M.E. (1998) 'Clusters and the new economics of competition', *Harvard Business Review*, 76(6): 77–90.

Sánchez Picón, A. (2005) 'De frontera a milagro. La conformación histórica de la economía almeriense', in *La Economía de la Provincia de Almería*. Almería, Spain: Caja Rural Intermediterránea, Instituto de Estudios de Cajamar, pp. 43–84.

Titos Martínez, M. (2005) 'El sector financiero en Almería', in *La Economía de la Provincia de Almería*, Almería, Spain: Caja Rural Intermediterránea, Instituto de Estudios de Cajamar, pp. 563–623.

Torrente, R.G. (2005) 'El sector agrario', in *La Economía de la Provincia de Almería*, Almería, Spain: Caja Rural Intermediterránea, Instituto de Estudios de Cajamar, pp. 153–208.

Whitford, J. and Potter, C. (2007) 'Regional economies, open networks and the spatial fragmentation of production', *Socio-Economic Review*, 5(3): 497–526.

Zeitlin, J. (1992) 'Industrial districts and local economic regeneration: overview and comment', in F. Pyke and W. Senenberger (eds) *Industrial Districts and Local Economic Regeneration*, Geneva, International Institute for Labour Studies, pp. 279–94.

6 Cooperative banks and community development in Japan

Rosario Laratta and Sachiko Nakagawa

Community development occurs when social relationships change such that fewer people are systematically excluded from the benefits that their societies deliver to others, and these reductions in exclusion—and enhancements in self-fulfilment—become more durable (Bebbington 2002). Only with this strategic goal in mind do efforts to foster participation, establish social enterprises, and promote community-driven development make sense. An effective community development agenda aims to change aggregate structures of social capital such that the distribution of power in society begins to favour the excluded. The term *social exclusion* is defined in the literature as the process that deprives people of the resources necessary to participate in society and limits their life choices systematically (e.g. Hills *et al.* 2002; Pierson 2002; Silver 2007). Social exclusion is a serious global issue at both the individual and societal levels.

In order to address the issue of social exclusion, two main approaches are taken to community development—needs based and asset based (Kretzmann and McKnight 1995; McKnight 2003). The former, and more traditional approach, aims to identify, mainly through needs surveys, the deficiencies or social problems within a particular community. Only after these needs are clearly mapped can a strategic plan or programme be established to address the community's problems. Supporters of this approach argue that identifying problems is an effective beginning point for a community development process since recognition is half of the solution. This approach has been criticized by opponents who argue that it only passively involves residents in the community development process (Chirisa 2009). If community residents and external actors focus only on trying to identify and fix problems, they may miss or ignore the real causes of those problems. In addition, a problem-focused approach may lead residents to believe that their community is incapable of addressing the big issues, promoting a culture of 'assistentialism'.

The alternative approach, asset-based community development (ABCD), reverses the needs-based approach by starting from the identification of the existing assets and capacities of a community. ABCD is based on the assumption that by adopting a positive approach and assuming everyone is treated equally, communities can find their own solutions to many of their problems. This approach recognizes three central building blocks for community development: the capacities of all individuals within the community; the power and the work of associations of citizens operating in that community; and the assistance and support of local institutions. ABCD helps communities to adequately map and utilize their resources, including existing assets unlikely to be recognized by other approaches. The ABCD concept can be likened to the familiar drinking glass analogy: if the community recognizes its assets, it will perceive the glass as half-full; hence, its members will adopt a positive approach to further development. However, if they concentrate only on their deficiencies, they will perceive the glass as half-empty, which may not be a problem in itself but often leads to the expectation that someone else will fill it.

Two key theories underpin the ABCD approach: social capital and structural holes. Based on his studies of Italy and the US, Putnam (1993, 1995, 2000) defines social capital as features of social life—such as networks, norms, and trust—that enable participants to act together to pursue shared objectives more effectively. According to Putnam (2000), there are two types of social capital: the first is *bonding social capital*, which brings closer together people who already know each other; the second is *bridging social capital*, which unites people or groups who did not previously know each other. The latter type has similarities with the concept of 'weak ties' suggested by Granovetter (1973), especially in relation to his research on labor markets and opportunities for mobility. Many studies suggest that social capital, especially bridging social capital, is an essential element for successful community development. By gathering multiple resources and capacities from various people, problems within a community can be easily solved because there is a shared feeling of responsibility due to the shared roles by the members of that community (e.g. Keyes *et al.* 1996; Wilson 1996; Johnson and Farrell 1997; Temkin and Rohe 1998). Briggs (1998) argues there is a positive correlation between the number of ties present in a given territory and the level of development of that community.

Structural holes theory refers to individuals who do not connect with others and to the unused financial resources in a community (Burt 1992; Walker *et al.* 1997). Discovering ways in which these structural holes can be filled provides benefits for both individuals and their communities (Gittell and Vidal 1998). Indeed, according to Burt, what is required to enhance the development of a deprived community is the establishment of organizations by individuals who have broader social interests and are seriously committed to filling the existing structural holes. Lupton and Power (2002) point to the negative consequences of not having in place organizations and individuals willing to fill structural holes. Scholars who adopt this approach argue that discovering ways in which bridging social capital can be implemented is a crucial objective if deprived communities are to be transformed into sustainable communities.

Based on the assumption that every community has an untapped pool of skills, knowledge, and work experiences that can be used in local development efforts, the ABCD approach views community development as a cooperative process: it is not somebody's task, but rather a task for the entire community. In order to activate the cooperative process, these assets first need to be discovered, then mobilized, and finally connected. According to the supporters of this approach, rich and poor communities do not exist since each community has its own set of assets upon which to draw (McKnight 2003). The key issue is whether these assets are recognized by the community's residents and used effectively.

Some scholars disagree with this approach. They argue that in many developed areas, and not just in the developing world, the gap between rich and poor communities is still very large because in some areas there is a concentration of assets while in others they are quite scarce (Deininger and Olinto 2000). In Japan, for instance, the average wage in the richest areas is about two-and-a-half times higher than that of the poorest areas (Cabinet Office 2009). In terms of financial assets, there is an enormous gap in Japanese prefectures between metropolitan and provincial areas. The former have sufficient resources from independent revenue to implement effective policies and provide a variety of welfare services for their residents. Conversely, the latter depend on subsidies from the central government for approximately 80 per cent of their revenue (Ministry of Internal Affairs and Communications 2007). Indeed, the number of prefectures where the bank loan–deposit ratio exceeds the mean is only four out of 47, and of these four only one is not located in a metropolitan area (Ministry of Land, Infrastructure and Transport 2005). This means that the savings of many provincial residents, which should be an asset for their communities, flow from their local banks into metropolitan areas without contributing at all to the development of the areas where the banks are located.

One explanation for this transferring of financial assets from provincial to metropolitan areas is that following the Second World War the central government in Japan concentrated all of its operations—from politics to the economy and from culture to information—to the capital city. This policy had an enormously positive impact on the growth of the national economy, allowing Japan to become one of the greatest economic powers in the world. At the same time, however, it diverted the attention of peripheral prefectural administrations away from local issues and needs resulting in an under-utilization of local resources.

Recently, cooperative banks in Japan have introduced initiatives that aim to prioritize the revitalization of local communities, and by so doing they have been able to use investments from residents to improve their local communities and stem the flow of funds to central metropolitan areas. Although Japanese cooperative banks are small in scale and ill-equipped to offer the kind of innovative financial services available in some other countries, they are attracting interest domestically as institutions that have the potential to fight social exclusion in deprived areas (Defourny and Monzón Campos 1992; Carr and Tong 2002). From the perspectives of the ABCD approach, we argue in this chapter that cooperative banks have the potential to connect people who have not previously known each other and, consequently, to spread bridging social capital through their activities.

Nevertheless, we need to be conscious of the fact that having many cooperative banks in a defined locality does not necessary mean that the community is developed. In addition to organization, local people must be involved (Amin *et al.* 2002; Bridge *et al.* 2009). Bhatt *et al.* (2002) found that more than 30 per cent of cooperative banks in California in 1996 were no longer in existence in 1998 due to a lack of cooperation among people in the community. Thus, we should not limit our investigation to mapping cooperative banks as the sole means for understanding their level of diffusion, but rather we should go further to discover the ways in which these banks can successfully connect people within their communities.

There has been a lot of research that investigates how cooperative banks contribute to the improvement of individual's quality of life (Thomas 1990; Rossiter 1997; Morduch 1999; Gross and Silva 2002). However, there have been relatively few studies that focus specifically on how cooperative banks contribute to bringing people together with a view to promoting community development. This chapter seeks to contribute to this literature by comparing two Japanese cooperative banks that operate in deprived areas.

An overview of cooperative banks in Japan

As institutions that are rooted in, and circulate money at, the local level, cooperative banks can contribute to creating sustainable communities. But what does *sustainability* mean? In this chapter, *sustainability* is defined as that level of economic development within a defined community that would allow it to meet the needs of the local population now and in the future (United Nations General Assembly 1987).

We know that cooperative banks differ greatly both between and within countries. For example, the Desjardins Group was established in 1900 as the first and largest cooperative bank in Quebec and North America, and it provides a wide range of services to its six million members, including loans, accounts, savings, investments, and life and health insurance services (Desjardins Credit Union 2011). In contrast, the SEWA Bank was established in 1974 to help women in India become financially independent and start their own economic activities. As of 2008, this bank provided savings, credit, and insurance services for about 60,000 poor, often illiterate, mainly self-employed women (SEWA Bank 2009). Despite these differences in mission, cooperative banks do share some common elements: they are customer-owned entities; their aim is to provide the best products to their members, not maximizing their own profits; they are internally characterized by a participatory governance structure; they can and actually do distribute profits among members; and their mission includes the development of the community where they operate.

Japanese cooperative banks are no exception to this operational framework. However, due to strict governmental regulations of the commercial banking sector, cooperative banks in Japan are not regarded as proper banks and play only a marginal role in providing financial services. Indeed, the Japanese Financial Services Agency permits only stock companies that have a capital of more than $22 million to engage in banking activities aimed at stabilizing the market economy. Japanese cooperative banks are not subject to any of these strong restrictions by the government. However, in the last five years, some governmental agencies have started to show interest in cooperative banks by including them in policies aimed at building more sustainable and healthy communities. For example, the Ministry of Environment implemented a pilot project to promote environmentally friendly business by utilizing investments from a cooperative bank in 2007–8. In the National Spatial Strategies Programme (2008, 23–4), the Ministry of Land, Infrastructure and Transport described cooperative banks as promoters of community development initiatives run by and for local citizens.

As of August 2011, there were 13 cooperative banks in Japan and most of them had track records on investment (see Figure 6.1).

As shown in Table 6.1, cooperative banks differ greatly in terms of their legal forms[1]: non-profits (voluntary associations and so-called specified non-profit corporations), intermediate corporations, cooperatives, incorporated associations, and public interest incorporated associations. Cooperative banks choose among these legal forms depending upon the benefits and constraints offered. For example, if a cooperative bank chooses the business cooperative form then it has to follow the *Cyushokigyo tou kyoudou kumiai hou* (Medium/Small-size Enterprises and Co-operatives Law of 1949), which requires an organization to obtain authorization from the Ministry of Finance and other government agencies in its service area. In addition, within two weeks following the general meeting on settlement, cooperatives are required to submit to the authorities several documents including a report on their activities, an inventory, a balance sheet, and a profit-loss statement. If these requirements are not met, the cooperative will be dissolved.

Cooperative banks that choose the specified nonprofit corporation form under the *Tokutei hi-eiri katsudou sokusin hou* (Specified Nonprofit Activities Promotion Law) are also subject to numerous requirements. When a bank applies for

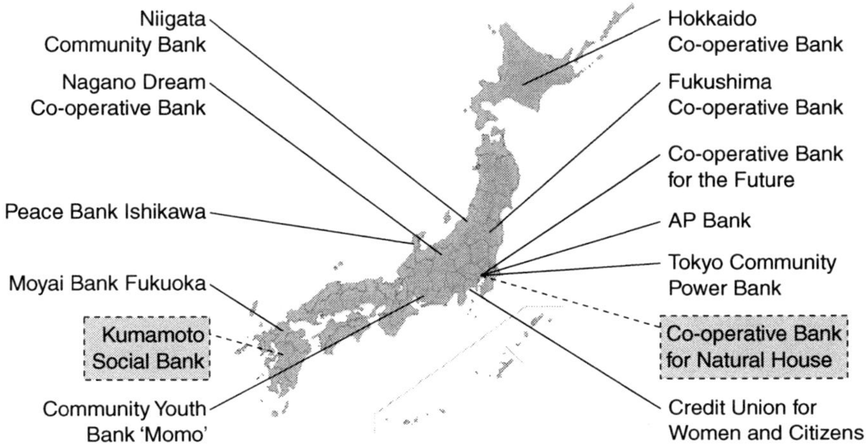

Figure 6.1 Location of Japanese cooperative banks, 2011.

Note
The cooperative banks highlighted in grey do not have track records on investment.

Table 6.1 Profiles of 13 Japanese cooperative banks, 2011

Name	*Location*	*Date established*	*Legal form*	*Terms for loans*	*Credit limit (US$)*	*Interest rate (%)*
Co-operative Bank for the Future	Tokyo (Metropolitan Area)	July 1994	Voluntary association	(1) being a member (2) social enterprises which engage in environmental preservation or welfare service or community development in the country	100,000	3
Credit Union for Women and Citizens	Kanagawa (Metropolitan Area)	August 1998	Voluntary association	(1) being a member (2) not being a social enterprise with the legal form of a for-profit organization (3) social enterprises especially managed by women or individual people in Kanagawa	111,000	2

Hokkaido Co-operative Bank	Hokkaido (Provincial Area)	October 2002	Specified non-profit corporation	(1) being a member (2) not being a social enterprise with the legal form of a for-profit organization (3) social enterprises implementing social purpose activities and aiming to bring benefits to the community in Hokkaido	22,000	2
Ap Bank	Tokyo (Metropolitan Area)	June 2003	Intermediate corporation (past), incorporated association (now)	(1) social enterprises and individual people especially acting for environmental preservation in the country	55,000	1

continued

Name	*Location*	*Date established*	*Legal form*	*Terms for loans*	*Credit limit (US$)*	*Interest rate (%)*
Nagano Dream Co-operative Bank	Nagano (Provincial Area)	August 2003	Specified non-profit corporation	(1) being a member (2) not being a social enterprise with the legal form of a for-profit organization (3) social enterprises implementing social purpose activities and aiming to bring benefits to the community in Nagano	33,000	2–3
Tokyo Community Power Bank	Tokyo (Metropolitan Area)	September 2003	Voluntary association	(1) being a member (2) not being a social enterprise with the legal form of a for-profit organization (3) social enterprises and individual people in Tokyo	111,000	1–2.5

Niigata Community Bank	Niigata (Provincial Area)	July 2005	Voluntary association	(1) being a member (2) social enterprises and individual people implementing social purpose activities, disaster recovery, and aiming to bring benefits to the community in Niigata	22,000	3
Community Youth Bank 'Momo'	Aichi (Metropolitan Area)	October 2005	Voluntary association	(1) being a member (2) social enterprises and individual people engaging in community development and sustainable community in Aichi, Gifu, and Mie prefectures	55,000	2–2.5
Kumamoto Social Bank	Kumamoto (Provincial Area)	February 2008	Voluntary association	(1) social enterprises implementing social purpose activities and aiming to bring benefits to the community in Kumamoto	33,000	3

continued

Name	*Location*	*Date established*	*Legal form*	*Terms for loans*	*Credit limit (US$)*	*Interest rate (%)*
Co-operative Bank for Natural House	Tokyo (Metropolitan Area)	June 2008	Voluntary Association	(1) being a member (2) individual people who are going to purchase a natural house with energy-saving and eco-friendly furniture and home electrical appliances	33,000 (for natural houses) 11,000 (for energy-saving and eco-friendly furniture and home electrical appliances)	2
Moyai Bank Fukuoka	Fukuoka (Provincial Area)	April 2009	Voluntary Association	(1) being a member (2) social enterprises and individual people engaging in social purpose activities and specified non-profit activities defined by the NPO law and aiming to bring benefits to the community in Fukuoka	33,000	2–3

Fukushima Co-operative Bank	Fukushima (Provincial Area)	January 2010	Incorporated Association	(1) social enterprises and individual people engaging in social purpose activities and aiming to bring benefits to the community in Fukushima	33,000	5
Peace Bank Ishikawa	Ishikawa (Provincial Area)	April 2010	Voluntary Association	(1) being a member (2) social enterprises and individual people engaging in social purpose activities and specified non-profit activities defined by the NPO law and aiming to bring benefits to the community in Ishikawa	33,000	1–3

Source: Based on authors' research results in 2011.

incorporation, for example, it must provide many documents to the authorities including its articles of incorporation, a list of funders and ten or more members, certification of the purposes of the organization and non-affiliation with criminal organizations, a prospectus, and operating plans and budget estimates for the year of incorporation and the following year. The Specified Nonprofit Activities Promotion Law not only identifies the activities in which the specified non-profit corporation can engage, but also specifies that the main purpose of the non-profit's activities cannot be religious or political and that the organization cannot make a profit for an individual, corporation, or other organization, though it can engage in profit-making projects as long as the profit is reinvested in its non-profit activities (Specified Nonprofit Activities Promotion Law, Articles 2, 10, and 28). Every year, a specified nonprofit corporation is required to prepare, keep, and submit to the competent agency the following documents: an activities report, an inventory of assets, a balance sheet, a statement of revenue and expenditure, lists of officers and of those who receive remuneration, and the names and addresses of at least ten members.

The cooperative banks that choose the intermediate corporation form have to follow an even more complicated regulatory framework. Under the *Chuukanhojin hou* (Intermediate Corporation Act) enacted in 2001, these organizations could not distribute profits among their members, but they could engage in various activities as hybrid organizations having the characteristics of both for-profits and non-profits.

These two legal forms were abolished in 2008 and organizations that had retained this legal status were forced to take the form of *Ippan shadan hojins* (incorporated associations) or *Koeki shadan hojins* (public interest incorporated associations). These two new legal forms were introduced with three new acts adopted in December 2008: the Act on General Incorporated Associations and General Incorporated Foundations; the Act on Authorization of Public Interest Incorporated Associations and Public Interest Incorporated Foundations; the Act concerning Special Measures for enforcement of General Incorporated Associations/Foundations Act and Public Interest Incorporated Associations/Foundations. Under these acts, the status of all *Koeki hojins* (Public Interest Corporations)—i.e. the traditional Japanese nonprofit sector which had been regulated by the Civil Code of 1898 and controlled by the national government—was revoked, and these organizations had to re-register under the new legislation. The new laws allow these organizations to be re-registered in the form of *Ippan shadan hojins* (incorporated associations) or *Ippan zaidan hojins* (incorporated foundations). The former type can be established if there are at least two members and have no minimum financial requirements. In addition to existing public interest corporations re-registered as incorporated associations or incorporated foundations, any organization—including a cooperative bank—that claims not to operate in the pursuit of profit, regardless of whether it has a charitable purpose, is allowed to file for this legal designation. These organizations are recognized as *Koeki shadan hojins* (public interest incorporated associations) or *Koeki zaidan hojins* (public interest incorporated foundations).

The government also set out a scheme in which Public Interest Corporation Commissions evaluate general incorporated associations or incorporated foundations. Organizations that satisfy the requirements are declared eligible to receive tax-deductible contributions from corporations and individuals, as some of the current public interest corporations already do. Before the enactment of the 2008 laws, acquiring public benefit status was not a separate procedure under Japanese law. This is no longer the case for associations and foundations. Under the Association and Foundation Law of 2008, citizens can form an association or foundation even if the organization's activities are not in the public interest. The Law on Recognizing Organizations as Public Interest delineates a range of requirements for associations and foundations to be recognized as serving the public interest. Moreover, the Public Interest Corporation Commission screens applications from organizations and authorizes or rejects the public interest status of each. Cooperative banks that receive the incorporated association status can engage in a wide range of activities, but they cannot distribute profit among their members. The Fukushima Co-operative Bank is currently operating as an incorporated association, and despite the many requirements it is planning to get the public interest incorporated association status.[2]

Choosing one legal status rather than another can obviously influence the ownership structure of the cooperative bank. For example, those banks such as Hokkaido Co-operatve Bank and Nagano Dream Co-operative Bank that operate under the specified non-profit corporation legal status will attract greater investment from the government.

Table 6.1 shows that cooperative banks differ greatly in terms of their loan policies, credit limits, and interest rates. A further difference among cooperative banks is their target borrowers. For example, the Credit Union for Women and Citizens, provides loans to social enterprises managed by women who encounter obstacles in borrowing money from commercial banks; the Ap Bank to non-profit organizations, limited companies, and stock companies who work for environmental preservation of the country; and the Cooperative Bank for Natural House to individuals who purchase houses that have energy-saving systems and eco-friendly furniture and appliances.

These findings show that there are some differences among cooperative banks in terms of target clientele, organizational structure, and management. There are, however, also important similarities. The first is that when cooperative banks make decisions to lend money, they attach great importance to community needs, such as the creation of new employment opportunities for local residents. The second is that they focus on small loan services and their interest rates are lower than those of commercial banks. The third is that they are forced to depend on voluntary labour because they cannot make enough income to hire staff. For example, in the Co-operative Bank for the Future, eight volunteers discussed online and identified the social enterprises that would constitute their cooperative's main target for investing its money. The extensive utilization of voluntary labour allows cooperative banks to operate at a very low cost; for instance, our previous research found that Hokkaido Co-operative Bank was able to run its management activities at a cost of only US$300 a month (Nakagawa and Laratta 2010).

Research design

This study compared two of the 13 Japanese cooperative banks whose profiles are presented in Table 6.1—Hokkaido Co-operative Bank and Nagano Dream Co-operative Bank. There were two reasons for selecting these banks: first, both of them have the same legal form of specified non-profit corporation and similar regimes for lending money. Moreover, Nagano Dream Co-operative Bank was inspired by Hokkaido Co-operative Bank and its vision of social enterprises networking with each other to develop local communities. Second, unlike other cooperative banks, these two banks are located in provincial areas where revitalization is a more crucial issue than in metropolitan areas. For example, both areas have suffered from a

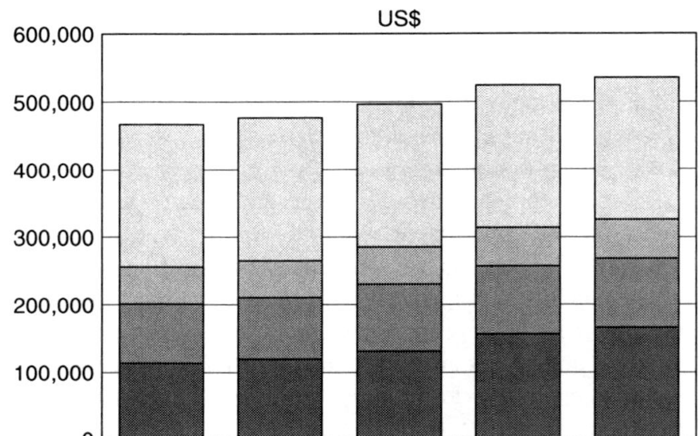

	2005	2006	2007	2008	2009
Prefectural and municipal governments	210,530	210,530	210,530	210,530	210,530
For profit organizations and other local organizations	56,000	55,680	55,470	55,470	55,470
Social enterprises	87,110	90,890	99,000	101,530	103,470
Local residents	113,940	120,050	131,730	156,570	165,840

Figure 6.2 Breakdown of investments in Hokkaido Co-operative Bank, 2005–9 (source: figure created based on interviews with bank officials and data drawn from the bank's newsletter).

decline in population and a lack of infrastructure, and they both have local economies that are highly dependent upon central government subsides (Association for Raising the Youth in Hokkaido 2009; Nagano Prefectural Government 2009).

Despite the similarities between Hokkaido Co-operative Bank and Nagano Dream Co-operative Bank, they differ in their relationship with their local communities. From 2005 to 2009, Hokkaido Co-operative Bank had a progressive increase in the number of local investors and the amount of investments coming from local residents and social enterprises (see Figures 6.2 and 6.3). During the same period, Nagano Dream Co-operative Bank had a gradual increase in the number of local residents and social enterprises as investors, but the amount of investments from these two groups actually decreased (See Figures 6.4 and 6.5).

These initial findings led to the main research question investigated in this study: why has Hokkaido Co-operative Bank been more successful in attracting investments from local residents and social enterprises than Nagano Dream Co-operative Bank?

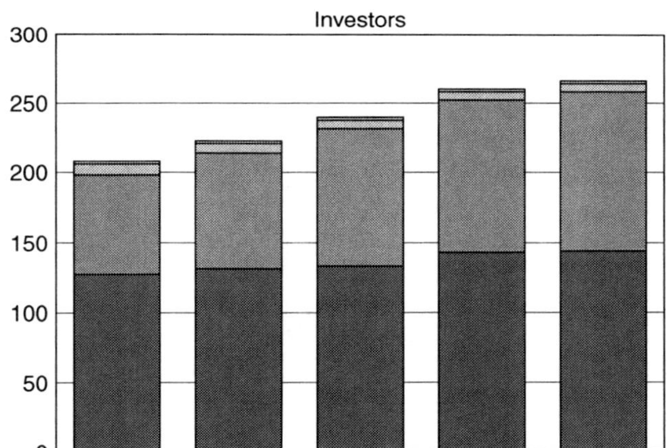

	2005	2006	2007	2008	2009
Prefectural and municipal governments	2	2	2	2	2
For profit organizations and other local organizations	8	7	6	6	6
Social enterprises	71	83	99	109	114
Local residents	127	131	133	143	144

Figure 6.3 Breakdown of investors in Hokkaido Co-operative Bank, 2005–9 (source: figure created based on interviews with bank officials and data drawn from the bank's newsletter).

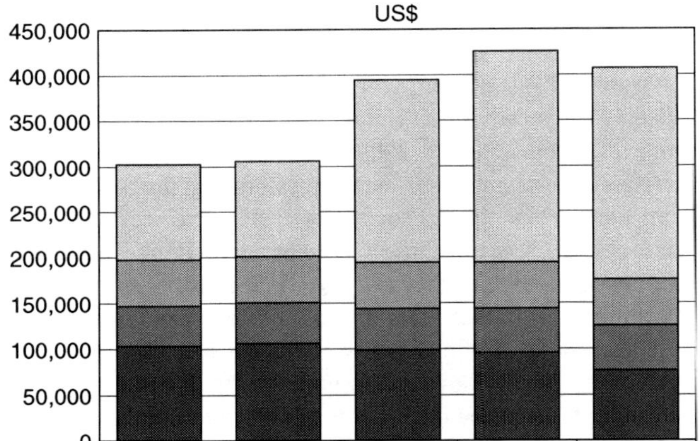

	2005	2006	2007	2008	2009
Prefectural and municipal governments	105,260	105,260	200,000	231,580	231,580
For profit organizations and other local organizations	50,320	50,320	50,320	50,320	50,320
Social enterprises	44,110	44,740	45,260	48,210	48,740
Local residents	103,160	106,110	98,740	95,580	76,420

Figure 6.4 Breakdown of investments in Nagano Dream Co-operative Bank, 2005–9 (source: figure created based on interviews with bank officials and data drawn from the bank's newsletter).

Data collection

Data was collected using both quantitative and qualitative methods. First, we conducted a survey among the two target groups of investors—local residents and social enterprises—for both Hokkaido Co-operative Bank and Nagano Dream Co-operative Bank. In total, we sent out 229 questionnaires between September 2007 and April 2008 and we obtained 108 responses—a response rate of 47 per cent.

Using the sets of questions reported in Tables 6.2 and 6.3, the survey investigated two main factors: *the general level of participation*—i.e. direct/indirect or passive/active—by local residents and social enterprises in the activities of cooperative banks and *the general level of satisfaction*—i.e. positive or negative feelings—of local residents and social enterprises as investors in these cooperative banks. We then compared the data by using the chi-square and Wilcoxon rank-sum tests, respectively, in order to identify and understand the factors that have

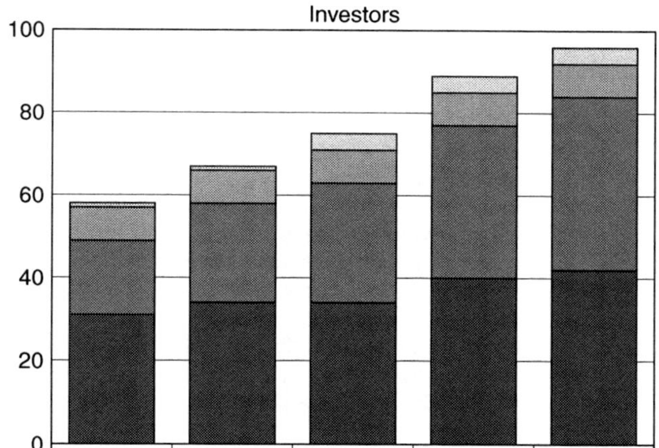

	2005	2006	2007	2008	2009
Prefectural and municipal governments	1	1	4	4	4
For profit organizations and other local organizations	8	8	8	8	8
Social enterprises	18	24	29	37	42
Local residents	31	34	34	40	42

Figure 6.5 Breakdown of investors in Nagano Dream Co-operative Bank, 2005–9 (source: figure created based on interviews with bank officials and data drawn from the bank's newsletter).

Table 6.2 Level of participation by local residents and social enterprises in their cooperative banks

Factors investigated:	
1	I read the newsletters and website of the cooperative bank
2	I read books and magazines about the cooperative bank
3	I participate in the general meetings of the cooperative bank
4	I participate in other events of the cooperative bank
5	I engage as staff or as a volunteer of the cooperative bank
6	I give advice on management and activities to the cooperative bank
7	I do not take any action, except that of investing in this bank
8	Other

Source: Developed by the authors for this study.

Table 6.3 Level of satisfaction of local residents and social enterprises as investors in their cooperative banks

Factors investigated	
1	Did you feel your investment was a positive contribution to your community?
2	Did you think that your investment was a more effective way to use your money for community development?
3	Has your level of interest in investing and donating for your community increased after your investment in this bank?
4	Did you feel that your investment has contributed to increase collaboration between investors, social enterprises, and the cooperative bank for the development of your own community?
5	As an investor of this bank, do you understand the mission and organizational structure of cooperative banks?
6	Has your expectation for cooperative banks as means for community development increased as a consequence of your investment in this bank?
7	Has your willingness to support social enterprises increased as a consequence of your investment in this bank?

Source: Developed by the authors for this study.

influenced the level of investment by local residents and social enterprises in the two banks.

The second stage of this research consisted of semi-structured interviews conducted by the authors between December 2007 and July 2009 with board members of both Hokkaido Co-operative Bank and Nagano Dream Co-operative Bank and with 30 investors, including local residents, social enterprises, and governments. During the interviews with the board members, we gathered further information from documents that the respondents provided.

Findings

The findings are based on analyses of documentary materials and survey findings.

Documentary materials

As Figure 6.6 illustrates, Hokkaido Co-operative Bank and Nagano Dream Co-operative Bank both have the legal form of specified non-profit corporation, which means that their mission is divided into two distinct activities: collecting investments and lending money. The reason for this division is that the Japanese government prohibits specified non-profit corporations from collecting investments.

Table 6.4 compares the loan programme requirements for the social enterprises of Hokkaido Co-operative Bank with those enforced by the Hokkaido Labour Bank and the Sapporo Municipal Office.

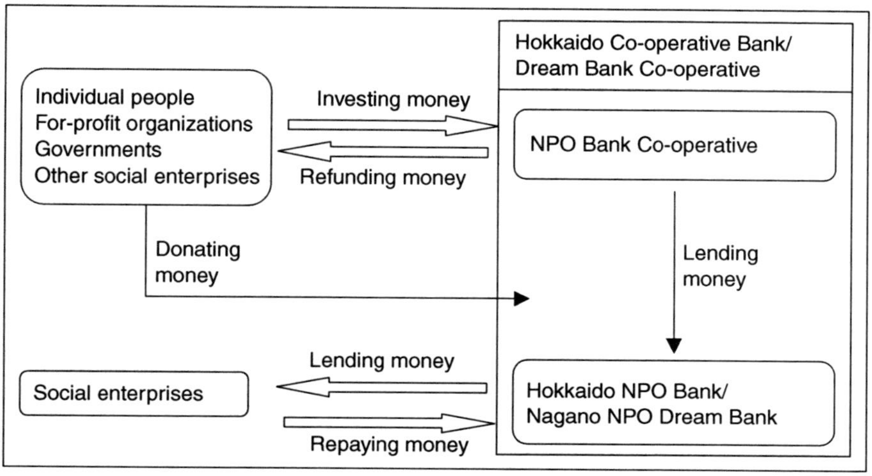

Figure 6.6 Lending Scheme of Hokkaido Co-operative Bank (source: developed by the authors based on information in Hokkaido Co-operative Bank (2007: 5–12)).

Note
The same scheme applies to Nagano Dream Co-operative Bank

Survey data

In this section, we summarize the results of the survey of the two target groups of investors. The findings in Table 6.5 demonstrate that investors participate differently in the two banks. In Nagano Dream Co-operative Bank, 38 per cent of the respondents said that they were not involved in any aspect of their cooperative banks, other than as investors. The opposite was true in Hokkaido Co-operative Bank, where many of the respondents seemed to be more directly and actively participating in the activities of their bank.

Overall, the responses of the target investors to our questions were quite positive (see Tables 6.6 to 6.12). Respondents in both banks saw their investments as a contribution for the development of their community (see Table 6.6). However, for the remaining six questions, the respondents differ to a certain degree with a more positive level of satisfaction among the investors of Hokkaido Co-operative Bank compared to those of Nagano Dream Co-operative Bank. These findings indicate that there are differences in terms of the investors' feelings toward the impact of their investments.

Discussion

Our first aim was to identify differences between the two groups of respondents, especially with regard to whether the level of investor satisfaction was the result of a particular attitude of the two banks towards their local communities. In order to determine this, we ascertained whether each of the banks assumed the

Table 6.4 Comparison among loan programmes for social enterprises

Name of providers	*Terms of a loan*	*Target usage*	*Credit limit (US$)*	*Rate of interest (%)*
Hokkaido Co-operative Bank	1 being a member 2 not being a social enterprise having the legal form of a for-profit organization 3 social enterprises implementing social purpose activity and aiming to bring benefits to the community in Hokkaido	1 working funds 2 equipment funds 3 opening funds	$22,000	2.0
Sapporo Municipal Office	1 having the office in Sapporo city 2 having the legal form of the specified non-profit corporation 3 having more than 3 years of track records	1 working funds 2 equipment funds	without collateral: 1 working funds $56,000 2 equipment funds $56,000 with collateral: 1 working funds $56,000 2 equipment funds $556,000	2.0–3.075
Hokkaido Labour Bank	1 having an office in Hokkaido 2 having the legal form of the specified non-profit corporation 3 having more than 3 years of track record 4 having more than one fiscal year report before the SE can terminate its activities	1 working funds 2 equipment funds	without collateral: 1 working funds $56,000 2 equipment funds $56,000 with collateral: 1 working funds $56,000 2 equipment funds $556,000	2.375–3.875

Source: Developed by the authors based on information contained in Hokkaido Co-operative Bank (2007, 17).

Table 6.5 How do you usually participate in the activities of your cooperative bank? (%)

	No action	*Reading newsletters/ websites on CB*	*Reading books/ magazines on CB*	*Participating in the general meetings of the CB*	*Participating in other events of the CB*	*Engaging as staff or volunteer for the CB*	*Giving advice on management and activities to the CB*	*Others*
Investors of Hokkaido Co-operative Bank	0.0	39.1	13.0	4.3	8.8	4.3	8.8	21.7
Investors of Nagano Dream Co-operative Bank	38.0	20.7	10.3	20.7	0.0	6.9	0.0	3.4

Notes
Sample size of investors of Hokkaido Co-operative Bank=11; sample size of investors of Nagano Dream Co-operative Bank=23; Chi-square=21.76894, level of significance=0.05, P-value=0.002784.

Table 6.6 Do you feel your investment is a positive contribution to your community? (%)

	Strongly agree	*Agree*	*Neither agree nor disagree*	*Disagree*	*Strongly disagree*
Investors of Hokkaido Co-operative Bank	27.3	27.3	18.1	27.3	0.0
Investors of Nagano Dream Co-operative Bank	8.7	21.7	39.2	21.7	8.7

Notes
Sample size of investors of Hokkaido Co-operative Bank = 11; sample size of investors of Nagano Dream Co-operative Bank=23; W=161, P-value=0.238553.

Table 6.7 Do you think that your investment is the most effective way to use your money for community development? (%)

	Strongly agree	*Agree*	*Neither agree nor disagree*	*Disagree*	*Strongly disagree*
Investors of Hokkaido Co-operative Bank	63.6	9.1	27.3	0.0	0.0
Investors of Nagano Dream Co-operative Bank	4.3	26.1	21.7	34.8	13.1

Notes
Sample size of investors of Hokkaido Co-operative Bank=11; sample size of investors of Nagano Dream Co-operative Bank=23; W=102, P-value=0.000686.

Table 6.8 Has your level of interest in investing and donating to your community increased after your investment?(%)

	Strongly agree	*Agree*	*Neither agree nor disagree*	*Disagree*	*Strongly disagree*
Investors of Hokkaido Co-operative Bank	45.5	36.3	9.1	9.1	0.0
Investors of Nagano Dream Co-operative Bank	9.1	22.7	27.3	27.3	13.6

Notes
Sample size of investors of Hokkaido Co-operative Bank=11; sample size of investors of Nagano Dream Co-operative Bank=22; W=115, P-value=0.005115.

Table 6.9 Do you feel that your investment has contributed to increased collaboration between investors, social enterprises, and the cooperative bank for the development of your community? (%)

	Strongly agree	*Agree*	*Neither agree nor disagree*	*Disagree*	*Strongly disagree*
Investors of Hokkaido Co-operative Bank	54.5	45.5	0.0	0.0	0.0
Investors of Nagano Dream Co-operative Bank	0.0	40.0	40.0	15.0	5.0

Notes
Sample size of investors of Hokkaido Co-operative Bank=11; sample size of investors of Nagano Dream Co-operative Bank=20; W=86, P-value=$9.98 \times 10^{-0.5}$.

Table 6.10 As an investor of this bank, do you understand the mission and organizational structure of cooperative banks? (%)

	Strongly agree	*Agree*	*Neither agree nor disagree*	*Disagree*	*Strongly disagree*
Investors of Hokkaido Co-operative Bank	72.7	27.3	0.0	0.0	0.0
Investors of Nagano Dream Co-operative Bank	8.7	56.5	17.4	8.7	8.7

Notes
Sample size of investors of Hokkaido Co-operative Bank=11; sample size of investors of Nagano Dream Co-operative Bank=23; W=99.5, P-value=0.000259505.

Table 6.11 Has your expectation of cooperative banks as means for community development increased as a consequence of your investment in this bank? (%)

	Strongly agree	*Agree*	*Neither agree nor disagree*	*Disagree*	*Strongly disagree*
Investors of Hokkaido Co-operative Bank	81.8	18.2	0.0	0.0	0.0
Investors of Nagano Dream Co-operative Bank	31.8	40.9	18.3	4.5	4.5

Notes
Sample size of investors of Hokkaido Co-operative Bank=11; sample size of investors of Nagano Dream Co-operative Bank=22; W=120.5, P-value=0.006196.

Table 6.12 Has your willingness to support social enterprises increased as a consequence of your investment in this bank? (%)

	Strongly agree	*Agree*	*Neither agree nor disagree*	*Disagree*	*Strongly disagree*
Investors of Hokkaido Co-operative Bank	63.6	27.3	9.1	0.0	0.0
Investors of Nagano Dream Co-operative Bank	9.5	47.6	19.0	23.9	0.0

Notes
Sample size of investors of Hokkaido Co-operative Bank=11; sample size of investors of Nagano Dream Co-operative Bank=21; W=108, P-value=0.002317.

role of 'community organizer' or simply acted as a traditional bank providing financial services. Our interviews show that Hokkaido Co-operative Bank was regularly involved in two areas of activity that identify it as a 'community organizer'. In the following sections, each of these areas are discussed and contrasted with Nagano Dream Co-operative Bank.

Promoting community development

The first activity undertaken by Hokkaido Co-operative Bank consisted of implementing programmes to promote community development through local initiatives. Prior to the launch of a loan programme, the bank established other organizations within their community designed to increase citizens' level of independence in taking decisions and actions to develop a sustainable community system in the region—for example, the Assembly to Promote a Citizenship Movement and Social Enterprises in Hokkaido. These initiatives followed several visits between 1995 and 1997 by bank board members to social enterprises and voluntary organizations in the US working on community development and, with the support of local residents, resulted in a number of advocacy campaigns for community development aimed at local governments.

In addition, bank board members held online and street campaigns to encourage a commitment by local residents to community development through individual action and participation in local non-profit organizations, social enterprises, and seminars. In March 1998, they established the Center for Supporting Social Enterprises in Hokkaido, an organization that specifically focused on administrative work such as compiling legal documents, accounting and management, and providing opportunities for cooperation among social enterprises. This continuous engagement by the board of Hokkaido Co-operative Bank with issues of community development increased the level of trust among local residents and social enterprises. As one of the investors stated:

> Looking at a series of attempts by Hokkaido Co-operative Bank aimed at developing our community, I was moved by their incredible effort. I strongly thought that I wanted to participate in community development as one of the residents of Hokkaido. This was the main reason why I invested my money in this bank.[3]

In contrast, Nagano Dream Co-operative Bank never engaged in advocacy works for either prefectural or municipal governments nor carried out programmes to raise awareness among local residents regarding the importance of their commitment and initiatives with respect to building a sustainable community. The board of this bank is composed of the usual financial experts and administrators, but lacks any practitioners directly involved in community development. The board was also found to have a very hierarchical structure, their decisions were made top-down, and their primary concern was how to improve the loan programme. As the chief director stated, 'As leader, I believe that we must implement the loan programme strictly'.[4]

Peer consultations

The second area of activity consisted in implementing peer consultations within communities. These consultations provided opportunities for local residents and social enterprises to share experiences with, and knowledge about community development. Hokkaido Co-operative Bank has actively held such peer consultations since 2001. For example, in the period from October to November 2008 they invited seven social enterprises from six different communities in Hokkaido to review what local residents and social enterprises could do to promote community development. Moreover, in March 2009, under the bank's coordination, several social enterprises began a programme to fight social exclusion of vulnerable people. This was organized through community restaurants where speakers gave presentations and shared ideas about their activities for community development with local residents and social enterprises in other communities of Hokkaido.[5]

Similar activities were not organized by Nagano Dream Co-operative Bank for the development of its local community. According to the bank's chief director, local residents and social enterprises were reluctant to invest their money because they regarded it as against their own interests. He reasoned that investors tended to ask acquaintances before deciding to make an investment. It emerged during the interview that since the investors did not invest their money voluntarily, they failed to experience the sense of fulfilment that might come from cooperation among investors and social enterprises. The director explained that his bank had to depend on subsidies from prefectural and municipal governments in order to sustain its loan programme.

In our case study, it clearly emerged that more than half of the board members of Hokkaido Co-operative Bank were responsible for social enterprises involved with community development at different levels, including work integration, environmentally friendly tourism, and managing local radio stations. This was not the situation with the Nagano Dream Co-operative Bank. These results suggest that if a cooperative bank takes the role of community organizer, and in so doing changes the state of a community from deprived to sustainable, its board must include members who are actively involved in—or have previous experience with—social enterprises operating in the area. By directly involving themselves with local people in deprived communities, social entrepreneurs have the knowledge and experience to specify which issues need to be urgently addressed within their communities. In addition to this, social entrepreneurs understand the monetary and non-monetary resources and networks that are available in each community, and how these may be utilized for the development of the area. This knowledge is indispensable for cooperative banks if they are to master the *how* of solving community problems and attract investments from local people and social enterprises.

Conclusion

This chapter has shown that having local residents and social enterprises actively participate in the mission of cooperative banks requires that investors be more than passive observers of the community development process. The cooperative banks' willingness to work in partnership with investors, their commitment to the local community, the extent that have earned their clients' personal trust, and their reputations all have a bearing on whether local residents and social enterprises will decide to invest and actively participate. The behaviour or attitude of these cooperative banks clearly reflects the level and type of participation and satisfaction of its investors. If a cooperative bank focuses only on its financial activities, as commercial banks normally do, it is highly likely that the banks' reputation among investors and the community at large will decrease.

On the other hand, if a cooperative bank *facilitates community-led development*, as does Hokkaido Co-operative Bank, it will be able to attract new investors and, at the same time, increase the amount of investment by its existing investors. Moreover, the bank's investors will be encouraged to engage in a mobilization process that helps develop their community. As the case of Hokkaido Co-operative Bank illustrates, including members on a bank's board from, or having a background in local social enterprises should be a priority since this factor helps the cooperative bank achieve its mission. Through their direct involvement with local people in deprived communities, social entrepreneurs have the knowledge and experience to specify which issues need to be addressed most urgently within their communities.

If cooperative banks understand the value of social entrepreneurs in achieving their mission, they can prioritize those activities that support local social enterprises by engaging in consultancy activities, such as providing the legal expertise necessary at the time of their establishment, assisting with the management of administrative work during their operating life, and helping to create a network for the expansion of their activities through an exchange of ideas with similar organizations.

Since social enterprises and cooperative banks share the overall goal of helping their local communities to develop, it would be a failure for them to exclude local residents from their decision-making processes. Keyes *et al.* (1996) emphasize that community development cannot be fully achieved without the engagement and commitment of citizens. Flora *et al.* (1992) make a similar point by arguing that community development can only occur when residents believe that working together can make a difference and organize collectively to address their shared needs. A first step to ensure that the community is engaged in this process is to help local residents understand how they can contribute to community development and the important role that social enterprises and cooperative banks can play in mobilizing resources. Where it is possible, cooperative banks should also provide the opportunity for local residents and social enterprises to coordinate with social enterprises operating in other communities so that an exchange of ideas, knowledge, and experience can help tackle community development issues and implement positive actions.

Notes

1 We should clarify that in Japan there are no legal forms for social cooperatives, although the legal form of 'business cooperatives' exists as a sort of hybrid: non-profits that are allowed to become stock companies and distribute up to 10 per cent of their profit among their members, while being managed according to the democratic rule of 'one member, one vote'. At present, however, no cooperative banks are registered as 'business cooperatives' in Japan. Consequently, cooperative banks are forced either to operate without a legal status, for example as voluntary associations, or to choose organizational forms that are not well adapted to their activities.

2 These requirements include incorporated associations and foundations being recognized as necessities to increase public interest by the Public Interest Corporation Commissions, which consist of well-informed persons and exist in the Cabinet Office and in each prefecture. If an incorporated association or foundation has one office in a prefecture, it is evaluated by a Public Interest Corporation Commission in that prefecture. If it has more than one office, it is evaluated by a Public Interest Corporation Commission in the Cabinet Office. If organizations become public interest incorporated associations, they have to be evaluated by Public Interest Corporation Commissions every year.

3 Interview by R. Laratta and S. Nakagawa with an investor of Hokkaido Co-operative Bank, Hokkaido, 5 December 2007.

4 Interview by R. Laratta and S. Nakagawa of the Chief Director of Nagano Dream Co-operative Bank, Nagano, 11 December 2007.

5 This followed a proposal in 1998 by the Nonprofit Organization Training and Resource Center, a non-profit think tank, as one of the methods for tackling social exclusion. This programme provided opportunities for marginalized people such as the physically and mentally challenged, the elderly, the young, women, and the unemployed. It helps these people strengthen their social relationships and achieve economic and social independence.

References

Amin, A., Cameron, A., and Hudson, R. (2002) *Placing the Social Economy*, London: Routledge.

Association for Raising the Youth in Hokkaido (2009) 'Hokkaido no toshika to kasokano shinkou [Progress of Urbanization and Depopulation in Hokkaido]', Hokkaido, Japan: Hokkaido Seishounen Ikusei Kyokai.

Bebbington, A. (2002) 'Social Capital/Social Development/SDV', note prepared for the workshop 'Social capital: the value of the concept and strategic directions for World Bank lending', 1 March 2002, Washington DC, International Finance Corporation.

Bhatt, N., Painter, G., and Tang, S.-Y. (2002) 'The challenges of outreach and sustainability for U.S. microcredit programs', in J.H. Carr and Z.Y. Tong (eds) *Replicating Microfinance in the United States*, Washington, DC: Woodrow Wilson Center Press, pp. 191–222.

Bridge, S., Murtagh, B., and O'Neil, K. (2009) *Undestanding the Social Economy and the Third Sector*, Basingstoke: Palgrave Macmillan.

Briggs, X.d.S. (1998) 'Brown kids in white suburbs: housing mobility and the multiple faces of social capital', *Housing Policy Debate*, 9(1): 177–221.

Burt, R.S. (1992) *Structural Holes: the social structure of competition*, Cambridge, MA: Harvard University Press.

Cabinet Office (Japan) (2009) *2006nendo kenmin keizai keisan* [Prefectural Economy in the fiscal year of 2006]', Tokyo: Cabinet Office.

Carr, J.H. and Tong, Z.Y. (eds) (2002) *Replicating Microfinance in the United States*, Washington, DC: Woodrow Wilson Center Press.

Chirisa, I. (2009) 'Prospects for the asset-based community development approach in Epworth and Ruwa, Zimbabwe: a housing and environmental perspective', *African Journal of History and Culture*, 1(2): 28–35.

Defourny, J. and Monzón Campos, J.L. (eds) (1992) *Économie sociale: entre économie capitaliste et économie publique/The Third Sector: cooperative, mutual and nonprofit organizations*, Brussels: De Boeck.

Deininger, K. and Olinto, P. (2000) 'Asset distribution, inequality, and growth', Policy Research Working Paper no. 2375, Washington, DC: World Bank.

Desjardins Credit Union (2011) '2010 Annual Report', Toronto: Desjardins Credit Union. Online. Available at: www.desjardins.com/en/dcu/a_propos/rapan2010.pdf (accessed 1 September 2011).

Flora, C.B., Flora, J.L., and Houdek, E. (1992) *Rural Communities: legacy and change*, Boulder, CO: Westview.

Gittell, R. and Vidal, A. (1998) *Community Organizing: building social capital as a development strategy*, Thousand Oaks, CA: Sage.

Granovetter, M.S. (1973) 'The strength of weak ties', *American Journal of Sociology*, 78(6), 1360–80.

Gross, A. and de Silva, S. (2002) 'Social fund support of microfinance: a review of implementation experience', *World Bank Social Protection Discussion Paper* no. 215, Washington, DC: World Bank.

Hills, J., Le Grand, J., and Piachaud, D. (eds) (2002) *Understanding Social Exclusion*, Oxford: Oxford University Press.

Hokkaido Co-operative Bank (ed.) (2007) *Co-operative bank wo riyoushite social enterprise wo tsukurou* [Let's Create Social Enterprises by Using Co-operative Banks], Kyoto, Japan: Showa-do.

Johnson, J.H. and Farrell, W.C. (1997) 'Snapshots of income inequality in metropolitan Los Angeles', *Looking Ahead*, 19(2–3): 34–40.

Keyes, L., Schwartz, A., Vidal, A.C., and Bratt, R.G. (1996) 'Network and nonprofits:

opportunities and challenges in an era of federal devolution', *Housing Policy Debate*, 7(2): 201–29.

Kretzmann, J.P. and McKnight, J.L. (1995) *Building Communities from the Inside Out: a path toward finding and mobilizing a community's assets*, Evanston, IL: Institute for Policy Research, Northwestern University.

Lupton, R. and Power, A. (2002) 'Social exclusion and neighbourhoods', in J. Hills, J. Le Grand, and D. Piachaud (eds) *Understanding Social Exclusion*, New York: Oxford University Press, pp. 118–40.

McKnight, J. (2003) 'Regenerating Community: the recovery of a space for citizens', IPR Distinguished Public Policy Lecture Series, Evanston, IL: Institute for Policy Research, Northwestern University.

Ministry of Internal Affairs and Communications (Japan) (2007) 'Zentodoufuken no shuyou zaisei shihyo [Financial indicators of prefectural governments]', Tokyo: Ministry of Internal Affairs and Communications. Online. Available at: www.soumu.go.jp/iken/zaisei/xls/H19_chiho_3.xls (accessed 1 September 2011).

Ministry of Land, Infrastructure and Transport (Japan) (2005) 'Ginko no kenchoshozaichi ni okeru yokaritsu [Bank Loan Deposit Ratio of Prefectures]', Tokyo: Ministry of Land, Infrastructure and Transport. Online. Available at: www.mlit.go.jp/singikai/kokudosin/keikaku/10/04.pdf (accessed 1 September 2011).

Ministry of Land, Infrastructure and Transport (Japan) (2008) 'Kokuyuchi no senryaku keikaku [National Spatial Strategies Programme]', Tokyo: Ministry of Land, Infrastructure and Transport.

Morduch, J. (1999) 'The microfinance promise', *Journal of Economic Literature*, 37(4): 1569–614.

Nagano Prefectural Government (Japan) (2009) 'Naganoken no kasochiku no gaiyou [Overview of Depopulated Areas in Nagano]', Nagano, Japan: Nagano Prefectural Government.

Nakagawa, S. and Laratta, R. (2010) 'How can cooperative banks spread the spirit of cooperation in deprived communities?', *Social Enterprise Journal*, 6(2): 162–80.

Pierson, J. (2002) *Tackling Social Exclusion*, London: Routledge.

Putnam, R.D. (1993) *Making Democracy Work: civic traditions in modern Italy*, Princeton, NJ: Princeton University Press.

Putnam, R.D. (1995) 'Tuning in, tuning out: the strange disappearance of social capital in America', *Political Science and Politics*, 28(4): 664–83.

Putnam, R.D. (2000) *Bowling Alone: the collapse and revival of American community*, New York: Simon & Schuster.

Rossiter, J. (ed.) (1997) *Financial Exclusion: can mutuality fill the gap?* London: New Policy Institute.

SEWA Bank (2009) *A Bank for Self Employed Women Workers—SEWA Bank*. Online. Available at: www.sewabank.com/images/financial%20counseling.pdf (accessed 1 September 2011).

Silver, H. (2007) 'Social Exclusion: comparative analysis of Europe and Middle East Youth', Middle East Youth Working Paper no. 1, Washington, DC: Wolfensohn Center for Development, Brookings Institution and Dubai: Dubai School of Government.

Temkin, K. and Rohe, W.M. (1998) 'Social capital and neighborhood stability: an empirical investigation', *Housing Policy Debate*, 9(1), 61–88.

Thomas, D. (1990) 'Intra-household allocation: an inferential approach', *Journal of Human Resources*, 25(4), 635–64.

United Nations General Assembly (1987) 'Report of the World Commission on Environment and Development: our common future', UNGA Resolution no. A/RES/42/187. Online. Available at: www.un.org/documents/ga/res/42/ares42–187.htm (accessed 24 August 2011).

Walker, G., Kogut, B., and Shan, W. (1997) 'Social capital, structural holes and the formation of an industry network', *Organization Science*, 8(2): 109–125.

Wilson, W.J. (1996) *When Work Disappears: the world of the new urban poor*, New York: Knopf.

7 *Homo dictyous* transforms *homo oeconomicus*

The social network culture of Hellenic cooperative banking in Crete[1]

Theodoros A. Katerinakis

The modern *homo communicans* seems to prefer to be connected to, and stay in contact with, his surrounding world. Mutuality and social cohesion through sustainable finance, especially at a decentralized local level, function as security mechanisms in the current era of turbulence. Following Illouz (2009), several theorists identify *emotional capitalism* as the cultural process by which new interactional-emotional scripts of economic relationships are illustrated 'by the cultural frames of cooperation or team work'. In cooperation, most major 'purchases' take place among kin, friends, or acquaintances who substitute impersonal markets, especially when decisions involve high levels of uncertainty. Chang (2005) analyses how social networks are the most frequent sources of saving and investment information and are most utilized by those who have the least wealth. As this research suggests, connectedness rather than expertise prevails in important matters; in other cases, risk favours reliance on friends and relatives in order to make and sustain decisions.

This chapter argues that connectedness resides in the network structure of establishing and functioning as a cooperative. Every national culture possesses and reflects a core value that is at the centre of its collective self and shared mindset. The USA is devoted to 'freedom' (e.g. Kengor 2004) and Canada to the concept of 'social justice' (Kernaghan 1995). In Hellenic culture, this central value is *philotimo*, which is an untranslatable and unique cultural virtue of honour and pride idiosyncratic to Hellenes (Kourvetaris 1971; Vassiliou and Vassiliou 1973; Mavreas *et al.* 1989; Triandis 2000; Hoban and Hoban 2004; Koutsantoni 2004; Obama 2010).

Culture consists of relatively specialized lifestyles, values, beliefs, artefacts, forms of behaviour, and patterns of communication. Culture includes anything that a group has produced and developed—i.e. language, religion, laws, ways of thinking, art, communication patterns, rituals, styles, and attitudes (DeVito 2006, 31). Hofstede (1997, 288) provides an operational definition of culture: 'A collective programming of the mind which distinguishes one group from another … [a type of] mental programming … [with] patterns of thinking and feeling and potential acting'. Culture defines a moral frame with standards about how to belong to and be an upstanding member of a group. Culture is transmitted through intra- and inter-generational communication, and the way people define and understand issues, perform transactions, and cooperate is realized in their interactions (Fisher 1997, 22). Culture is not easily acquired; it is a process of growing into a society and evolves with the economy, learning values, following rituals, modelling oneself in comparison with role models or community protagonists, and understanding symbols (Jones 2007, 3). These ingredients of culture are acquired from childhood.

Cross-cultural differences in business environments are determined by the following five dimensions (Hofstede and Hofstede 2005; Hall 1997):

- *power distance* is the extent of tolerance to an unequal distribution of power and wealth;
- *individual and collective orientation* is the aptitude to work alone or in groups;
- *masculinity* is the degree to which traits such as authority, assertiveness, performance, and success are preferred to attributes such as personal relationships, quality of life, service, and welfare;
- *uncertainty* avoidance is the tendency to bypass lack of structure and insufficient information towards future orientation and destiny;
- *long-term orientation* is the valuation of thrift and perseverance over tradition and social obligations.

When people interact and exchange transactions they may disclose different aspects of their private, public, collective, and inner 'self'; cultural, societal, institutional, and deeper value factors interfere with and organize their perception of their actions. If virtues are ethical messages, then culture is the propagation channel of these virtues. In the case of the social networks that people identify with,[2] the constituent elements of individuals and their relationships promote reciprocity in ethical behaviour and facilitate the supplier–customer interaction. Such an interaction communicates 'ethos' as dependability, in the traditional sender–receiver model of communication (Shannon 1948).

The Hellenic mindset of *philotimo*

Since antiquity, Hellenes have considered economics (governing the *oikos*) as part of their inquiry into ethics, politics, and social organization (Petrochilos 1999). Traditionally Hellenic economic thought is placed within the Mediterranean tradition that perceives the economy as embedded in a web of social and political institutions that are regulated by religious and ethical norms (Baeck 1994, Constantelos 2005). Therefore, the economy contributes to developing interpersonal relationships based on the mutual respect of oral commitments, pride, and honouring the virtue of *philotimo* that generates bonds of trust (Ioannou 2009).

Emphasis on integrity (*akeraiotita*), the primary layer of current *philotimo*, has been a constant value for centuries (Psaropoulos 2009). Integrity originally reflected public pressure to behave uprightly, a norm of the responsible citizen (*politis*). In this sense, while profit making can be considered legitimate and part of the atomistic system, profiteering is punished (Doukas 2007, 222–3). It would be unthinkable that someone without integrity—in terms of honesty, justice, and truthfulness—is admired. *Philotimo* seems to have earned the status of a collective conscience in modern Hellas, where people no longer philosophize about it or try to impose it on others, but rather take it for granted and assume its widespread existence.

Philotimo is defined as an innate faculty that may motivate people to do more than what is expected, without expecting anything in return. Hence, *philotimo* is a life principle for Hellenes; it is interpreted as love for honour—honour 'to show' for others and honour 'to receive' from others—and is a characteristic that is intense in small communities on the Hellenic periphery. It is a case of an ideal occurrence where participants generally accept a norm based on the foundation of that normative society, as defined by Habermas (1996). This type of normative ethics transcends the deontology of duties and rules, as well as consequentialism. In this sense, *philotimo* closely corresponds to the virtues and moral character that define virtue ethics. Furthermore, in its various manifestations, the three central concepts of virtue ethics—virtue, practical wisdom, and eudaimonia—are comprehensible, objective, and empirically truthful (Held 1980). *Philotimo* is a virtue that corresponds with credibility, with the tendency to cooperate, and with the ritual of keeping your word (face and commitments) without writing a contract;[3] it is a way of life with *ethos*, consistent with the teleological approach of Aristotle.

This attribute of personal integrity, maintaining face, and trust is essential for all banking practices and acquires institutional support through community networks that form cooperative banks with elements of collective rationality. It is a script of a collective programming of mind (Hofstede and Hofstede 2005, 25) for Hellenes, a determinant of the foundation of cooperative and credit-related institutions in European Mediterranean culture and the Hellenic tradition. In monetary transactions and intimate relationships, trust is mutually cogenerated and goes beyond the *homo oeconomicus* of 'rationality', 'calculation', and 'efficiency' as impersonal economic imperatives.

Moral aspects of *philotimo* in routine language

The community of members of the Co-operative Bank of Chania (CBC) lives by the notion of *philanthropia* as the gist of *philotimo* in several respects. In social enterprises and community-based markets, corporate governance issues are manifested as compatible with the concepts of accountability, reliability, and transparency. This widespread reference to *philanthropia* reflects the primary issue of *philotimo*: the collective self is explicitly related to approaches of trust. Trust can be described as reflex (Salem 2009, 73), as a fixed expectation of culture, sometimes as being learned and situational. Trust is also considered as a resource of social capital, power, and social support. Salem (2009, 163) suggests that trust emerges from communicative interaction; trust and communication are interdependent and lead to 'a probability of structural coupling' between humans. This type of engagement is the essence of business relationships, especially in the banking sector. Moreover, in cooperative banking, trust is the intangible connection that guarantees concrete relationships of membership.

Therefore, individual partners of a cooperative bank achieve a sense of 'betweenness' that has its roots in ethical ties of well-informed client-members. Throughout Hellenic society, the premise of moral equality interacts with strategies to gain advantage among widely separated class or professional interests (Herzfeld 1991, 77). As Campbell (1964) describes it, there is a nuance in *philotimo*, a dependability of moral respect and social asymmetry. Moral respect is simultaneously a mask and a condition of mutual dependence (and exchange) of shepherds, merchants, and politicians. Lyberaki and Paraskevopoulos (2002, 5) are critical of the 'elusive boundaries between social trust and its [Hellenic] substitutive notion of *philotimo*', especially when small communities are examined. It is a type of critique that supports the fusion of trust with *philotimo* at a group level beyond the criteria of the individual; this argument could be interpreted as a notion of institutional *philotimo*.

In rural areas, honour and the lack of it takes dimensions that embrace the whole family, whereas in the cities it becomes more confounding and individualized. The only social class that does not consider honour of such primary importance is the urban middle class. This is consistent with Herzfeld's idea that names are semiotic markers for moral boundaries (in non-urban settings), since those boundaries are themselves highly flexible: what is considered evidence of socially acceptable morality (*philotimo*) in one individual may be treated as its very opposite in another. This morality contagion is a projection of an implicit culture to an explicit identity (Hofstede 2009).

Tracing the roots of community-based moral contagion in contemporary Hellas, there are several junctures that created an amalgam of Hellas with its 'oriental' self in the post-antiquity period. The pre-Islamic Arabs were proud of their pastoral way of life that gave birth to *murū'a* (Shahîd 2009, 31), the Arab concept of *virtus*, which embodies courage in war, hospitality in peace, independence of spirit, and love of liberty. A similar connotation is found in Turkish for 'honour': *seref*, *izzet*, *haysiyet*, and *onur*. The most common word denoting pride is *gurur* whereas *onur* is connected with *philotimo*, respectively (Van Eck 2003, 21).

In decentralized Hellenic society, such effects in moral values are reinforced in local communities, and the value of *philotimo* is relayed through the social networks that shape people's lives (Fowler and Christakis 2009):

- Hellenes prefer self-organization in commons where they recognize common attributes forming networks of affiliation.
- Love thy neighbour: the Hellenic state is organized in geographically dispersed local communities, starting from the 'neighbourhood'. Thus, a solid fabric of connected members is typical in the Hellenic periphery.

- Communal protection cultivates bonding in Hellas.
- Hellenes are social—so inevitably connected—animals following Aristotle's principles.

Again, it is important to distinguish an honour of position, which is an ascribed category related to possessions, and a discrete moral category that devolves from achieving reputation among social peers. In egalitarian contexts, male competitions subsumed by honour may be expressed in terms of 'seniority', or 'respect' and 'honour' (Gilmore 1982). In recent years, *philotimo* has become an ideal; it is the consciousness of superiority of mental achievements against material interests in life, a subconscious voice of authentic humanism with its own rationale. Personal dignity is the consciousness of ultimate sacredness of the corporeal human, but for the Hellenes it is the axiom that directs life (Vakalopoulos and Vakalopoulos 2003, 13). *Philotimo* is one of the ideals that traditional nuclear Hellenic families aim to implant in the generations that follow, and it is frequently invoked when asking someone to 'come to one's senses' or to correct an undesirable attitude. Similarly, the urge—conscious or not—to prove worthy of the nationally praised characterization of *philotimos* might function as a self-fulfilling prophecy. It involves a collective sense of belonging (Social Issues Research Centre 2007, 3), and the positive experience of this identity was the efficiency by, and dithyrambic recognition of Hellenic volunteers during the Athens Olympic Games of 2004.[4]

Along these lines, it is characteristic to read a press release that CBC sent out in the summer of 2009, a period of reasonable seasonal income for its members: 'We have to be realistic.... In all cases where the global crisis is the problem we are going to refinance. We are stepping down to our customers to discuss, consult, advice and refinance. Synergy and symmetry are the corner stones and their sustainability is our strategy' (Marakakis 2009; author's translation). CBC promotes relationship-based transactions; CBC's 'know your customer' (KYC) policy involves constant communication with depositors and borrowers to increase awareness. This process is not routinely implemented by mainstream banks. As Alexopoulos and Goglio (2009) explain, this kind of lending complements standardized credit policies based on verifiable and transmittable data. The lack of a credit record, fully documented revenues, and sufficient collateral is compensated by operational sources of repayment that connects the individual borrower-member of the bank with their collective relations.

Cooperatives as social economy

The above examples indicate that the traditional Hellenic value of *philotimo* is the origin of security, faith, and status that are very important for Hellenes in business, in addition to their need for self-esteem (Bourantas and Papadakis 1996). These cultural traits explain to some extent the phenomenon of small, family-owned firms. In such settings of collective dispersion of ownership, community-based companies or common business ventures entail increased solidarity, accountability, and professionalism. Furthermore, symmetry in action, impact, and rule enforcement are pre-conditions for efficiency. Local societies activate the spirit of survival as collectives with a common teleology to rediscover community. A reflection and extension of the socially organized business finds an exemplary application in cooperative economy and banking.

The same notion seems to be the cultural foundation recognized by the Nobel Prize for the institution of Grameen Bank. The bank is self-financing and makes a profit with a high repayment rates as borrowers maintain face in their communities, guaranteeing normality and solvency in the bank's operations. This process is a typical example of an amalgam of social and value capital supported by a banking network that redefines entrepreneurship and the social fabric in small communities: 'social business will be a new kind of business ... a non-loss, non-dividend company' (Yunus 2006).

The nature of social business is closely associated with the return of material capital not in monetary units, but in units of social capital—such as resources, solidarity, mutual recognition, respect, and the sense of belonging and contributing—that are embedded in the structure of social entrepreneurship. Cooperative banks are the major types of enterprises in which money transactions are complemented with service agreements as active reciprocal relations among their members. These banks are important in order to stimulate sustainable characteristics in the society in which they operate, providing the material base to ensure the reproduction of monetary and social capital (Lin 1999).

Such grass roots ventures function as a social network in which individual actors gain from the support and protection of the group, and the group gains from the contribution of individuals to the pool of its shared resources. The fabric woven leads beyond instrumental self-interest and enriches the socially motivated ends of self-help and shared interests that form the essence of cooperation. The cooperative movement represented a complementary, ethically motivated incentive for this response to early capitalism and, with its ideals of local support, mutuality, and democratic participation, became a driving force in the twentieth century and beyond. Robert Owen, the father of cooperation, defined social structures and not individuals as responsible for 'the moral degradation of capitalism' (Donnachie 2000, 32). These social structures are still present mostly in non-urban communities in the periphery of Mediterranean Europe, Africa, and regions of Asia. Cooperation is still a challenge for several societies, but in cases like Hellas it became a necessity as resource sharing, information, and knowledge exchange was the only feasible response to productivity gaps. Moreover, cooperatives covered the lack of awareness about standard banking transactional frameworks in local communities. In 2007, after a successful increase in capital, the CBC board addressed the members visiting the new headquarters: 'your trust as our members and stakeholders, who shared our vision, is a lasting relation. Cultivating our roots in Chania, we embrace Crete, and we extend our message of cooperation prioritizing you, the people.' (Co-operative Bank of Chania 2007; translated by author).

Cooperative doctrine as identified by the seven International Co-operative Alliance (ICA) principles of open voluntary membership, democratic member control and economic participation, independence, education-training-information, inter-cooperatives cooperation, and community concern are embodied in CBC's constitutional agreement (Bantourakis *et al.* 2007, 5–19). Following Owen's organizational settings experiments, Thomas (1997) applied the ICA's principles to define the members of a cooperative in the banking context. This cooperative globe represents his notion of the Inclusive Partnership Approach (IPA) to business illustrated in Figure 7.1.

The IPA identifies seven partners to whom companies, including banks, have a responsibility: shareholders/members, customers, employees and their families, suppliers and partners, the community at large, wider/global society, and the past and future generations of cooperating entities. This approach was officially accepted by the Hellenic cooperative network as an institutional declaration of commitment in 1999 by the Association of Co-operative Banks of Greece (2011b). In the tradition of their founders, cooperative members believe in the ethical values of honesty, openness, social responsibility, and caring for others. These cooperative values clearly define the network components using the traditional factory and community studies of Radcliffe-Brown, as described by Scott (2000). Using this definition of a cooperative organization, Wellman's network analytic principles can be applied to cooperative banking. Wellman's (1983, 172–8) principles can be adjusted to fit a cooperative network as follows:

- 'Ties are often asymmetrically reciprocal, differing in content and intensity': values connecting cooperative members and entities are founding ties that fulfil these attributes.

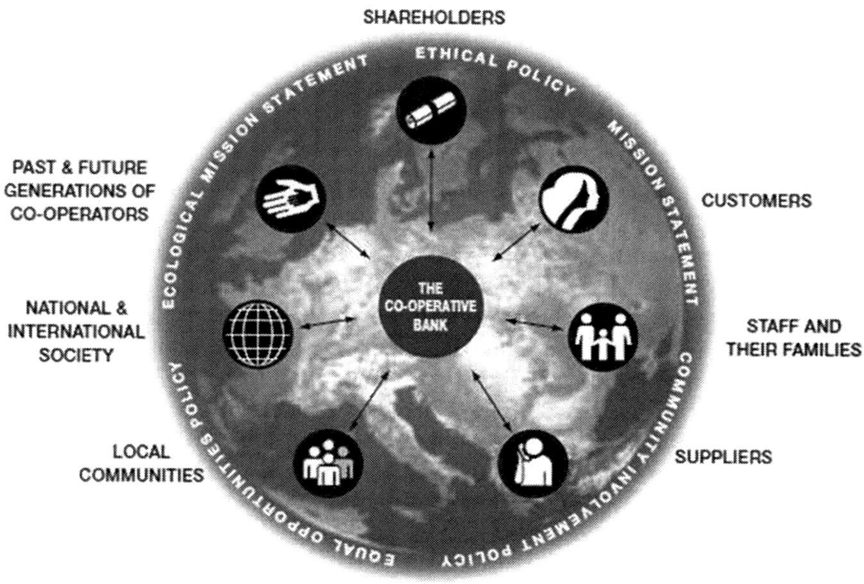

Figure 7.1 Cooperative bank partners according to Owen (source: adapted from Thomas (1997, 18)).

- 'Ties link network members indirectly as well as directly; hence ties must be analysed within the context of larger network structures': cooperative members are linked together directly when transacting and indirectly when engaging in exchange of resources and services.
- 'The structuring of social ties creates non-random networks: so boundaries, network clusters and cross linkages arise': all cooperative entities participate in different subgroups that are inter-related and offer ascribed and acquired characteristics for individual and collective members that are united in the cooperative organization.
- 'Cross linkages connect clusters as well as individuals' (the nodes can be clusters of ties, countries, or shareholders): the IPA introduces explicitly the various layers of cross-linkages in a cooperative network, consisting of individual and collective entities as well.
- 'Asymmetric ties and complex networks distribute scarce resources separately' (resources do not flow evenly or randomly in a social system, and non-symmetric connections and fragmented subgroups of nodes direct the flow of resources): resource sharing is asymmetrical because it starts from the principle of the need value, and subjective individual needs assess the value of resources for each member that may be disproportional, as mutuality and satisfaction are cumulative and not instantaneous elements in cooperatives.
- 'Networks formulate collaborative and competitive activities to secure scarce resources' (antagonism for allocation of resources is inherent in the social system and a source of social change): collaboration is equivalent to cooperation in terms of the IPA, in each cooperative. However, different cooperatives compete for the allocation of the shared or non-sharable resources.

Cooperative banking in Hellas

The cooperative banking sector was a late but well-adopted institutional harmonization that triggered the second stream of deregulation of the market in the banking sector (Gortsos 1998). Cooperative credit began to develop in the 1990s.[5] After raising the required minimum capital and fulfilling certain institutional conditions, credit cooperatives can apply and obtain a bank permit from the Bank of Greece to operate as 'credit institutions'; as such, cooperative banks can operate as local scope commercial banks restricted in their legal status. They are restricted to the use of the term 'Cooperative Bank' in their incorporation. The minimum amount of capital required was raised four times between 1993 and 2007, while the demographics of most Hellenic counties did not follow the same patterns. The regulations governing the evolution of credit cooperatives, mainly shaped by the commercial banking sector, did not always acknowledge their distinct role. Cooperative banks, initially established as member-only institutions,[6] provide all banking services with the exception of immediate underwriting in initial public offerings. Hence, the principal aspect of their communal entity is the full implementation of KYC principles developed by the Bank for

International Settlements (Basel Committee on Banking Supervision 2004). Cooperatives consist of a network of members registered after a screening procedure that affirms their origin and familiarity with the local community.

The importance of cooperative banks for financial stability in the regions they serve is widely accepted, under the provision that cooperative banks are not motivated to take on risk strategies despite their relatively lower profitability. On the other hand, their stability reflects the mutual support mechanisms that many cooperative banks have created (Alexopoulos and Goglio 2009).

Empirical observation of the cooperative reality in Hellas extends DiMaggio's conclusions on consumer transactions (DiMaggio and Louch 1998): the Hellenic paradigm shows that people make significant 'purchases' (like money banking transactions on deposits and investment) from people (bank employees) with whom they have prior non-commercial relationships, as members in a society (banking cooperative) they trust. Banking transactions with 'social contacts' are effective because they embed exchanges in a web of obligations and reciprocity based on a mutually accepted constitution. In addition, such transactions hold the cooperative bank (seller) network responsible and dependent on effective performance and returns to its customers. In the economic transaction, return and benefit on capital are crucial because the bank is financed by mutual-collective (share and deposited) capital owned by its own members. Thus, capital inefficiency is equivalent to a cannibalistic self-shrinking operation. Furthermore, while banking transactions and products are perceived as 'risky' in small communities with low financial transaction awareness, within-cooperative network exchanges are more likely to occur as cooperative membership is the social guarantee for what is perceived as of 'high uncertainty' (Yunus 2006). Consequently, banking preferences are in line with performance quality for banking products, and 'sellers' and 'buyers' share social and commercial ties. Both sellers and buyers are participants in the same cooperative that contributes to augmenting their social capital by broadening membership and their material capital for the bank.

Alexopoulos (2004) examined the performance of Hellenic cooperative banks and their importance for the development of the local areas they serve. The 1990s is the first decade in which Hellenic cooperative banks emerged and had their initial success. At the beginning of the decade, three credit cooperatives evolved into cooperative banks when the legal framework changed in 1992 and made this feasible. By 2001, there were 17 cooperative banks, all located in provincial towns. Within the first decade, these banks had managed to build their apex institutions, a national association, and their 'central' bank. From an economic point of view, cooperatives effectively reduce market barriers that would typically impede some groups—such as professional societies or special groups of civil society—in developing and transformational countries from fully participating in the economic arena (US Overseas Cooperative Development Council 2007). Moreover, cooperatives help combat usury, a common practice in informal 'shadow' markets in Hellas following the Second World War.

Cooperative banks offer these efficiencies as part of a privileged membership package that is shared as a 'homopolar' (give-take-contribute) bond among members: the more they use the bank, the more they benefit from the bank and develop ties further. Membership and active transaction-participation become members' common ties; these ties are cemented from close contact and services during the extended banking hours, emotional intensity in terms of dependability (bank to customer), and reciprocal service (members complete their transactions and reciprocate benefits with deposits and bank services that illustrate their preferences). This strengthening procedure is consistent with the notion of 'tie strength' described by Granovetter (1973) and complements findings of consumer preferences (e.g. DiMaggio and Louch 1998). The set of principles and values in the IPA combined with the sense of belonging and contributing (for members) are constructive elements of affiliation that expand the social lifeworld of cooperative banks in the case of Hellas.

The sense of belonging builds networks with actor-members who are connected with their bank in a sustainable way. In other words, cooperatives are user-owned (users finance the cooperative), user-controlled (an elected board of directors serves as the liaison between the membership and management), and user-centred (members benefit when patronage funds are returned to members based on the amount of business conducted with the cooperative). Trust is likely to be built and strengthened when the 'business is owned by those who use its services, is governed by elected leaders who are users, is locally owned and controlled and whose customers democratically elect their policy body' (US Overseas Cooperative Development Council 2007, 4). Membership and trust are fundamental components of identity between owners and users and between banks and customers, and they are the core elements in sustaining loyalty to the cooperative. Furthermore, these elements structure concrete network ties that homogenize people with various socio-demographic, behavioural, and personal characteristics and define a homophily attribution (McPherson *et al.* 2001). Homophily is cultivated in two dimensions creating social capital—similarity of interest, transaction demands, and ethics among members of society—and institutional familiarity with the notion of 'being in cooperation' and synergy that dictates acceptance and use of other non-financial cooperative organizations in the same community. It is an indication of preference, customer solidarity, and loyalty.

In many respects, cooperatives are just like other banks. The important difference is that cooperatives are the only banks that give customers transparency in how their money is managed. Consequently, cooperative banks have achieved their differentiation by drawing a generic identity from the philosophy of the cooperative movement, and thereby given themselves a unique identity within the banking industry (Wilkinson and Balmer 1996); cooperative identity becomes a social brand.

Co-operative Bank of Chania

In an era of turbulence, domino effects in the globalized economic environment, and interconnected institutions, established economic entities and local communities are flailing. Banking is dominated by resolutions and a 'back to basics' approach in business is widespread. Unlike investment banking and rating agencies, an alternative and less visible approach that supports local communities is cooperative banking. The CBC is one such bank headquartered in the Hellenic island of Crete, which is a region where strong communities ameliorate weak institutions, the transactional ethos is grounded in keeping one's word and face, and being accountable is a poetics of living (Lascelles 2011, 12–14). In the historic capital of Crete, the CBC is a protagonist of economic activity, builds on pre-existing strong community bonds, and defends its founding principles through its actions, values, policies, measures, expectations, and outcomes, indicating that healthy networks of families and friends play an essential role in local communities. In other words, the CBC is built upon integrity concerns woven into in a cohesive web of members that make it resilient and less vulnerable than most of the banking industry.

The CBC operates under the supervision of the Central Bank of Greece[7] and is a relatively small bank with exemplary conditions and a leading position in the western region of Crete, as it has managed to engage more than 50 per cent of the professionally active population of the island. In 2008–9, it had a solvency ratio of 28 per cent, well beyond the Hellenic national operational requirement of 10 per cent for commercial banks and 12 per cent for cooperative banks. The CBC retains all the guarantees for individual members and all investors in the bank's share capital; its institutional protection is based on the Hellenic Deposit and Investments Fund, as do all non-cooperative commercial banks (Hellenic Deposits and Investment Guarantee Fund n.d., 13). As of 2008, the CBC had 24 branches, 200 highly qualified personnel, 40,000 deposit accounts, 8,000 credit accounts, and 21,000 members (Co-operative Bank of Chania 2009, 3). This small scale along with its innovative technology, electronic document management processes, and e-payment systems give this bank a comparative advantage. The CBC has implemented a one-stop-shop policy, applies direct follow-up to customers in a two-day period, and is almost paperless in workflow, with state-of-the-art communication technology. Each employee is responsible for several tens or hundreds of customers in their area and establishes relationships with these customers. Thus, its opportunity cost is smaller than large-scale banks and CBC employees function as service centres. In terms of internal auditing, as pointed out in supervisory board minutes and approved investor bulletins, compliance personnel and the Board Auditing Committee generate their reports independently while having to respond to weekly auditing inquiries from the Central Bank of Greece and the Hellenic Capital Market Commission (Marakakis and Zymvragoudakis 2007, 17–20; Department of Cooperative Credit Supervision 2008, 19–24; Nikiforakis 2008, 25). Apart from this documented efficiency, all CBC members have personal day-to-day experience of how the CBC connects with their needs. As Nobel Laureate Ostrom (2009) argues, humans have great capabilities and are more effective than is commonly understood when they are self-organized. That sense of connectedness and satisfaction from their 'own bank' is captured in informal contacts on site as well as through empirical research (Alexopoulos 2004, 180). The CBC's cooperative formula of polycentric

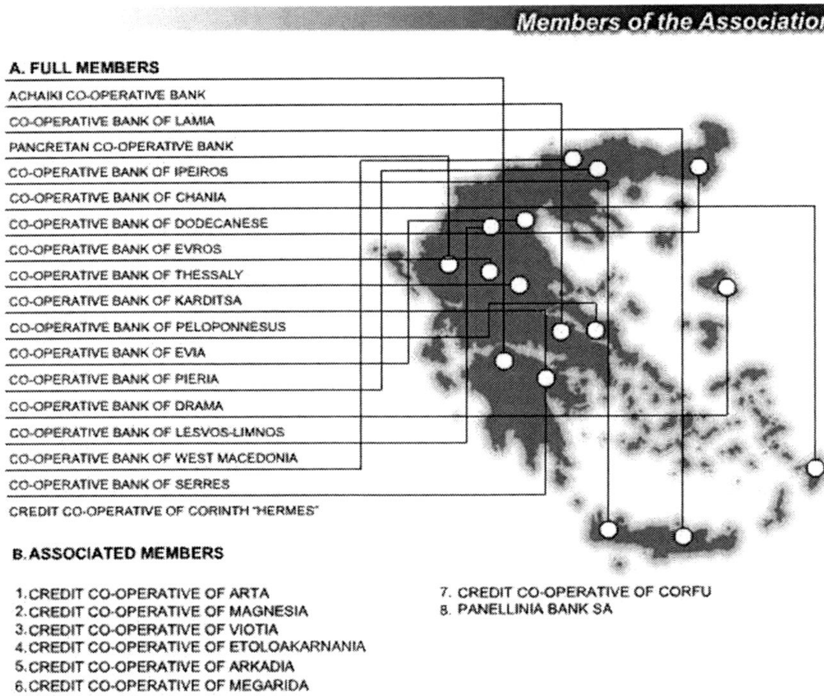

Figure 7.2 The distribution of cooperative banks in the 13 Hellenic regions (source: Association of Co-operative Banks of Greece (2011a); reproduced by permission).

self-organization is quite effective in Hellas and the region of Crete. The CBC is one of the 16 cooperative banks covering the 13 regional authorities of the Hellenic territory (see Figure 7.2) in a growing network that in 2010 consisted of 181 banking branches (Association of Co-operative Banks of Greece 2011c).

A social network representation

The island of Crete consists of four prefectures and is the base of the two largest cooperative banks in Hellas, which have a cumulative network of 84 branches on the island (Pancretan Cooperative Bank 2011, 6). The CBC operates mainly in the western part of the island and is expanding to the east, while the Pancretan Cooperative Bank is more oriented to the eastern part of the island and is expanding to the west. This pattern of expansion is the foundation of competition between the two banks and discloses the dichotomy of choice for 'where to do business' in the local economy. While practicing locality in customs and territory, people in Crete remain connected in wider community-based networks (Hnaraki 2007, 67).

The CBC is a bank that was founded by 60 local individuals and entrepreneurs with societal concern (Bantourakis *et al.* 2007, 55–7) and is governed by an open general assembly of members and their directly elected executives. It operates for their greater good as a whole, consisting of pre-existing ties of homophily that transmute to homopolar[8] bonds among members of the Chania community. There are three primary attributes of social entrepreneurship that provide stability and boost growth for the CBC: deep knowledge of the local environment, people, and their relations; hands-on engagement with the economic and social life of employees and customers; and referral trust and solidarity, crucial for self-employed individuals and small to medium-sized enterprises in Crete. At a community level of affinitive local societies, members of the CBC transform their cultural values to ethical—originally meaning 'daily expected'—traits when they decide to register, pay the obligatory share, and start doing business. Daily practiced ethical behaviour is an Aristotelian ideal that 'we are what we repeatedly do': ethos is a way of life diffused through the fabric of the cooperative network. The core value of *philotimo* safeguards integrity and performance in Cretan society, as an enthymeme of a social value added. Hellenism as an identity, manifested in Crete with *philotimo*, enriches transactional ethos with a social dimension that makes the CBC ethical and a benefit dimension that makes it sustainable.

Following the concepts of social network analysis (Scott 2000), the CBC caters for its members' needs by establishing an intra-network of communication and a community of users of its services. Thus, at an operational level, social network analysis offers an analytical tool for representing the operational network of CBC, using UCINET graphs (Hanneman and Riddle 2005). In Figure 7.3, dots are the nodes connected according to information and report flows from one branch to the other, directed towards managerial authority of dependence; 'who is reporting to whom, which branch seeks supports from which other'. Bank headquarters are represented by node 22, and isolated branches by nodes 10 and 21. Social network analysis provides an explicit representation of the CBC network and can be used to examine intra-bank flow of information and perceived authority for 'employee to supervisor' ties and for 'shareholder to employee' ties. Members of the CBC value closeness that the network provides and the safety net of solidarity that deals with their risks. Their *philotimo*, as mutuality, is reinforced in CBC network-based banking.

Discussion

The Hellenic commercial banking system has generally been considered socially responsible during the past decade, and its robustness has been satisfactory due to prudent risk management, increased provisions, and satisfactory financial results (Arapoglou 2008, 51; Rapanos 2010, 28). Competition and the complementary character of cooperative banks seem to play a decisive role in a bottom-up approach of enriching banking operations with ethical principles. In several cases, Hellenic customers ask for *philotimo* that supersedes guarantees,

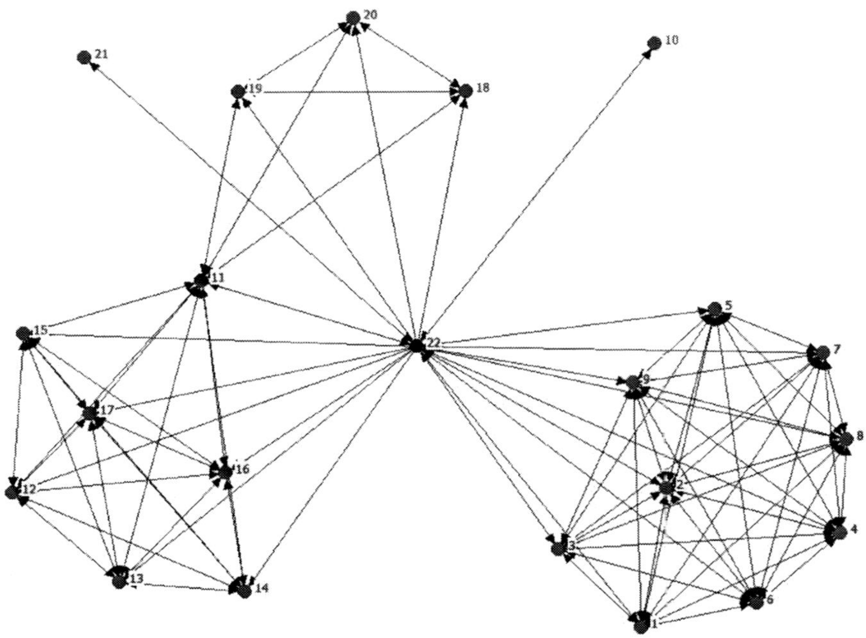

Figure 7.3 Dependency matrix of Co-operative Bank of Chania branches in a network of organizational ties (source: designed by author using UCINET).

tangible collateral, and contractual agreements. The IPA is extending its effect in dealing with cooperative partners (shown in Figure 7.1) of Thomas's realistic philosophy:

> Each partner must be treated in balance—not equally, not in preference but in balance and across time. The skill of management is to ensure that each partner co-operates together to produce the appropriate returns to the shareholder over the short and long term.
>
> (Thomas 1997, 8)

Balance over time is key because it is not expected that each partner will gain equal benefit from each decision made; partners are expected to value common interests. Further research should reveal the formal hierarchical ties that are instrumental in cooperatives' operation in order to achieve social benefits over time. Additional analysis of the dimensions of *philotimo* and their compatibility with cooperative principles may reveal structural connections that connect social relationships with doing cooperative business. Other network-related questions concerning managerial attributes and *philotimo* traits of employees and shareholders include the following:

- With whom do you choose to share important information?
- With whom do you communicate to get your job done?
- Which director is the most likable; which is the most unapproachable, and the most redundant?
- Who is the non-executive that you consult the most?
- Who are you mostly likely to vote for as an executive and what is your motivation?

Responses to such questions are expected to reveal the actual ties (employee–shareholder, employee–supervisor, etc.) that are present in the cooperative organization, as well as the centrality of managerial executives and the mediating roles of betweenness in the function of bank executives.

In the end, the CBC should motivate shareholders, customers, and employees to accomplish 'friendship ties' with all its partners (as shown in Figure 7.1). Cooperative banks are sustainable when people use them because they perceive the bonding as 'similarity'; mutual interests and goals, concern for the local economy and community are connecting the dots; it is a 'homophily' attribution when they value the bank as belonging to their community. As customers, they may have the option to choose to obtain services from any bank they like; but when they make the choice to become customer-members of a cooperative, then bonding and loyalty may be equivalent to friendship with the bank. Further research in social networks should address the issue of network ties and customer preference criteria like those described in Wright's acquaintance description form: utility value, affirmation value, ego-support value, stimulation value, and security value (Wright 1985).

The network setting is responsible for holding local communities tightly together, when the concepts of *value*, *mutual success*, and *philotimo* are among criteria of action for individuals. Thus, a comprehensive social network approach has to determine what *members* think of their cooperative, how *they* value its performance, and in which ways *they* understand that it meets *their* needs. In the end, such an approach has to assess how *central* a cooperative bank is in *their* strategic approach for self-sufficiency and sustainability in *their* local communities. In the case of Hellas, it is important to overcome several historical and political incidents in the rural context, due to which cooperation was undermined and deteriorated into inefficient forms. Moreover, the phenomenon of cooperatives requires a comparative review of the parameters of trust with personality constraints, cultural expectations, learned attitudes, and decision mechanisms that lead to the probability that 'A will connect with B', as members of a cooperative.

This chapter has examined cultural elements of the Hellenic mindset, coupled with socio-economic and legal aspects, to explain the notion of 'what it is to be a member in a cooperative', along with communication-related issues important in economic transactions. Initially, a transactional ethos based on contractual agreements, conditionality, commitments, and reservations contrasts with local cooperatives, but the KYC principle, which is one of the building blocks of international banking and cooperatives, is grounded in personal social ties, and not in impersonal statistics. Thus, cooperatives represent a distinct modern type of social enterprise with customers that are member-patrons.

Cooperative banks' policies favour transactions with liquidity and collaterals and not with intangible derivatives; they are committed to needs-oriented banking. In Hellenic cooperative banks, doing business means implementing social networking bonds: social bonds and ties supersede commodified transactions. Cooperative banks focus on their ability to offer simple and transparent services, customized to meet local needs, and with explicit communication of risks. *Philotimo* provides an ethical foundation for banking customers, employees, and executives—all networked members of cooperatives.

The CBC encapsulates a back-to-basics approach that dictates the motto 'teach your company to feel small again [as when it started]'—a notion that has earned acceptance by the community and inspires personnel. This ethos is what makes people pay attention to detail, work around the clock, stay involved when they are not in office, and put in effort that is worthwhile for their community. Since 2009, it seems that there is a tendency by several commercial or investment banks to return to their 'economization', which fuelled the crisis. Frugality is an attribute of self-sufficiency especially when people are connected by the homopolar bonds of the responsible sourcing and distribution of funds. In the CBC, doing business is another side of the social networking coin; it is a Main Street bank that gives customers a say in how their money is managed—most importantly, by encouraging their input into the ongoing development of the bank's ethical policy. The cooperative bonds of *homo dictyous* override the utilities of *homo oeconomicus* and add to community development.

Notes

1 This chapter uses the root term *Hellenic* instead of *Greek* in accordance with contemporary usage, except for the brand terms *Bank of Greece*, *National Bank of Greece*, and *Association of Co-operative Banks of Greece*. The term *homo oeconomicus*, of Latin origin, emphasizes the ego-interested individual as criticized by Sen (1977, 317 and 332). The term *homo dictyous*, in Hellenic semantics with Latin extension, was coined by Christakis and Fowler (2009) and is utilized here to show the interconnections of cooperation beyond the reciprocity of *homo reciprocans* and the social interaction of *homo communicans*.

2 Cooperative members and their social ties can be considered nodes of a network that supports cooperative business as a spreading phenomenon. Fowler and Christakis (2008) explain such spreading in terms of emotional states and mindsets.

3 It is also a direct response to *rouspheti*—the reciprocal dispensation of favours (Clogg 2002, 4–5)—as practiced and enforced during the post-Byzantine Turkish rule of Hellas, and it remains as a major obstacle to modernization.

4 International Olympic Committee President Jacques Rogge was quoted as saying: 'These Games were unforgettable, dream Games,' in his speech at the Closing Ceremony. He also thanked the 'marvellous volunteers who have charmed us with their confidence and kindness' (Associated Press 2004).

5 Operation of the Hellenic cooperative banks is governed by the law 2076/92, which incorporated into Hellenic Law the European Union's Directive 77/78 that defines the

structure and operation of Credit Institutions, as well as Act No 2258/2.11.1993 introduced by of the Governor of the Bank of Greece.

6 A more flexible legal framework was introduced by Law 3601/2007, following which non-members are accepted as clients under a special license agreement granted by the Central Bank of Greece. Broader flexibility on share ownership was introduced by Law 1667/1986, with L. 3588/2007 and L. 3867/2010.

7 The Central Bank of Greece oversees the cooperative network with the same legal requirements that exist for the commercial sector. Legislation provisions for open capital, non-public traded banks is described in Laws 1667/1986, 3483/2006, 3601/2007, and 3606/2007.

8 McPherson *et al.* (2001) and Kaduchin (2011). The term *homopolar* is taken from chemistry and is contrasted to *ionic* to denote mutually contributed electrons in a covalent bond.

References

Alexopoulos, Y. (2004) *Financial Co-operatives and Rural Development in Greece*. PhD Thesis, University of Leicester, UK.

Alexopoulos, Y. and Goglio, S. (2009) 'Financial deregulation and economic distress: is there a future for financial co-operatives?', Euricse Working Paper no. 001/09. Trento, Italy: European Research Institute on Cooperative and Social Enterprises (Euricse).

Arapoglou, T. (ed.) (2008) *I Symvoli tou Trapezikou Systimatos stin Elliniki Oikonomia* [The contribution of the banking system in the Hellenic economy], Athens: Hellenic Bank Association. Online. Available at: www.hba.gr/main/Ereunes-meletes/Elliniko-TrapezikoSistima2008s.pdf (accessed 30 June 2010).

Associated Press (2004) 'Rogge: Athens "unforgettable, dream Games"', 29 August. Online. Available at: http://sports.espn.go.com/oly/summer04/gen/news/story?id=1870458 (accessed 13 June 2011).

Association of Co-operative Banks of Greece (2010) 'Financial and other data of the group of cooperative banks on 31/3/10', Athens: Association of Co-operative Banks of Greece. Online. Available at: www.este.gr/Docs/f2010en.pdf (accessed 20 November 2011).

Association of Co-operative Banks of Greece (2011a) 'Members of the Association', Athens: Association of Co-operative Banks of Greece. Online. Available at: www.este.gr/en/index.html (accessed 19 September 2011).

Association of Co-operative Banks of Greece (2011b) 'Co-operative Credit in Greece', Athens: Association of Co-operative Banks of Greece. Online. Available at: www.este.gr/en/index.html (accessed 19 September 2011).

Association of Co-operative Banks of Greece (2011c) 'Group of Cooperative Banks', Athens: Association of Co-operative Banks of Greece. Online. Available at: www.este.gr/en/index.html (accessed 19 September 2011).

Baeck, L. (1994) *The Mediterranean Tradition in Economic Thought*, London: Routledge.

Bantourakis, E., Katerinakis, T., and Kalyteraki, S. (2007) 'Katastatiko [Co-operative Bank of Chania constitutional agreement: articles of association]', 3rd ed., Chania, Hellas: CBC Publications.

Basel Committee on Banking Supervision (2004) 'Consolidated KYC risk management', Basel: Bank of International Settlements. Online. Available at: www.bis.org/publ/bcbs110.pdf (accessed 15 June 2010).

Bourantas, D. and Papadakis, V. (1996) 'Hellenic management: diagnosis and prognosis', *International Studies of Management and Organization*, 26(3): 13–32.

Campbell, J.K. (1964) *Honour, Family and Patronage: a study of institutions and moral values in a Hellenic mountain community*, Oxford: Oxford University Press.

Co-operative Bank of Chania (2007) 'Official Communiqué of New Headquarters', Chania, Hellas: CBC Publications. Online. Available at: www.chaniabank.gr/el/the-group/bank/bank-news/press_release/2007/162007.aspx. (accessed on 3 June 2010).

Co-operative Bank of Chania (2009) 'Annual report of 2008', Chania, Hellas: CBC publications. Online. Available at: www.chaniabank.gr/media/26728/apologismos_2008.pdf (accessed 15 June 2010).

Chang, M.L. (2005) 'With a little help from my friends (and my financial planner)', *Social Forces*, 83(4): 1469–97.

Christakis, N.A. and Fowler, J.H. (2009) *Connected: the surprising power of our social networks and how they shape our lives*, New York: Little, Brown.

Clogg, R. (2002) *A Concise History of Greece*, 2nd ed., Cambridge: Cambridge University Press.

Constantelos, D.J. (2005) *Christian Faith and Cultural Heritage: essays from a Greek Orthodox perspective*, Boston: Somerset Hall Press.

Department of Cooperative Credit Supervision (2008) 'Porisma Eleghou [Supervisory paper], unpublished, Athens: Bank of Greece.

DeVito, J.A. (2006) *Human Communication: the basic course*, 10th ed., Boston: Allyn and Bacon.

DiMaggio, P. and Louch, H. (1998) 'Socially embedded consumer transactions: for what kinds of purchases do people most often use networks?', *American Sociological Review* 63(5):619–37.

Donnachie, I. (2000) *Robert Owen: Owen of New Lanark and New Harmony*, East Lothian, Scotland: Tuckwell Press.

Doukas, P. (2007) *Oikonomikes Theories, Arches Dioikisis & Arhaia Elliniki Skepsi* [Economic theories, governance values, and ancient Greek thought], Athens: Livanis Publications.

Fisher, G. (1997) *Mindsets: the role of culture and perception in international relations*, 2nd ed., Boston: Nicholas Brealey.

Fowler, J.H. and Christakis, N.A. (2008) 'Dynamic spread of happiness in a large social network: longitudinal analysis over 20 years in the Framingham Heart Study', *British Medical Journal*, 2008 (337): a2338 doi:10.1136/bmj.a2338.

Gilmore, D.D. (1982) 'Anthropology of the Mediterranean area', *Annual Review of Anthropology*, vol. 11:175–205.

Gortsos, C.V. (1998) *The Greek Banking System*, 2nd ed., Athens: Ant. N. Sakkoulas Publishers.

Granovetter, S.M. (1973) 'The strength of weak ties', *American Journal of Sociology*, 78(6): 1360–80.

Habermas, J. (1996) 'Discourse Ethics, from Moral Consciousness and Communicative Action' in W. Outhwaite (ed.) *The Habermas Reader*, Cambridge: Polity Press, pp. 180–92.

Hall, E.T. (1997) 'Context and meaning', in L.A. Samovar and R.E. Porter (eds) *Intercultural Communication*, 8th ed., Belmont, CA: Wadsworth, pp. 45–54.

Hanneman, R.A. and Riddle, M. (2005) *Introduction to Social Network Methods*, University of California, Riverside. Online. Available at: http://faculty.ucr.edu/~hanneman/nettext/ (accessed 30 June 2010).

Held, D. (1980) *Introduction to Critical Theory: Horkheimer to Habermas*, Berkeley: University of California Press.

Hellenic Deposits and Investment Guarantee Fund (n.d.) *Annual Report 2008*, Athens: Hellenic Deposits and Investment Guarantee Fund Publications. Online. Available at: www.hdgf.gr/binary/en2008.pdf (accessed 30 June 2010).

Herzfeld, M. (1991) *A Place in History: social and monumental time in a cretan town*, Princeton, NJ: Princeton University Press.

Hnaraki, M. (2007) *Cretan Music: unraveling Ariadne's thread*. Athens: Kerkyra Publications.

Hoban, S. and Hoban, G. (2004) 'Self-esteem, self-efficacy and self-directed learning: attempting to undo the confusion', *International Journal of Self-Directed Learning*, 1(2): 7–25.

Hofstede, G. (1997) 'Riding the waves: a rejoinder', *International Journal of Intercultural Relations*, 21(2): 287–90.

Hofstede, G.J. (2009) 'Research on cultures: how to use it in training?', *European Journal of Cross-Cultural Competence and Management*, 1(1): 14–21.

Hofstede, G. and Hofstede, G.J. (2005) *Culture and Organizations: software of the mind*, 2nd ed., New York: McGraw-Hill.

Illouz, E. (2009) 'Emotions, consumption, imagination: a new research agenda', *Journal of Consumer Culture*, 9(3): 377–413.

Ioannou, C.A. (2009) *Managing Employment Relations in Greece: a guide for foreign managers*, Athens: Kerkyra Publications.

Jones, M. (2007) 'Hofstede: culturally questionable?', paper presented at the Oxford Business and Economics Conference. Oxford, 24–26 June.

Kaduchin, C. (2011) *Understanding Social Networks Theories, Concepts, and Findings*, New York: Oxford University Press.

Kengor, P. (2004) *God and Ronald Reagan: A Spiritual Life*, New York: HarperCollins.

Kernaghan, K. (1995) *Public administration in Canada: a text*, 3rd ed., Toronto: Nelson Canada.

Kourvetaris, G.A. (1971) 'Professional self-images and political perspectives in the Greek military', *American Sociological Review*, 36(6): 1043–57.

Koutsantoni, D. (2004) 'Relations of power and solidarity in scientific communities: a cross-cultural comparison of politeness strategies in the writing of native English speaking and Hellenic engineers', *Multilingua* 23(1–2): 111–43.

Lascelles, D. (2011) *The Story of Minos Zombanakis: banking without borders*, Athens: Economia Publishing.

Lin, N. (1999) 'Building a network theory of social capital', *Connections* 22(1): 28–51.

Lyberaki, A. and Paraskevopoulos, C.J. (2002) 'Social Capital Measurement in Greece', paper prepared for the OECD-ONS International Conference on Social capital measurement, London, 25–27 September. Online. Available at: www.oecd.org/dataoecd/22/15/2381649.pdf (accessed 29 September 2011).

Marakakis, M. (2009) 'Se Trohia Anaptiksis I Trapeza Hanion' [Chania Bank in growth trajectory]' interview of Mihalis Marakakis, Chairman of the Board and CEO of Cooperative Bank of Chania, conducted by Giorgos Georgakakis, 4 March. Online. Available at: http://ixnilatontas.blogspot.com/2009/03/blog-post_04.html (accessed 3 June 2010).

Marakakis, M. and Zymvragoudakis, D. (2007) *Enimerotiko Deltio* [Co-operative Bank of Chania Investment Bulletin], Chania, Hellas: CBC publications. Online. Available at: www.chaniabank.gr/media/26379/enimerotiko_deltio_2007.pdf (accessed 15 June 2010).

Mavreas, V., Bebbington, P., and Der, G. (1989) 'The structure and validity of acculturation: analysis of an acculturation scale', *Social Psychiatry and Psychiatric Epidemiology*, 24(5):233–40.

McPherson, M., Smith-Lovin, L., and Cook, J.M. (2001) 'Birds of a feather: homophily in social networks', *Annual Review of Sociology*, vol. 27: 415–44.

Nikiforakis, S. (2008) 'Ekthesi Eleghou kai Leitourgias [External Auditor Report on CBC]', unpublished, Athens: Axon Consulting Reports.

Obama, B. (2010) 'Remarks by the President Honoring Greek Independence Day', White House Archives, 9 March 2010. Online. Available at: www.whitehouse.gov/photos-and-video/video/honoring-greek-independence-day#transcript (accessed 20 August 2011).

Ostrom, E. (2009) Telephone interview of Erlinor Ostrom conducted by Adam Smith, Nobelprize.org, 12 October 2009. Online. Available at: www.nobelprize.org/nobel_prizes/economics/laureates/2009/ostrom-telephone.html (accessed 27 September 2011).

Pancretan Cooperative Bank (2011) 'Corporate Presentation', Heraklion, Hellas: Pancretan Cooperative Bank. Online, Available at: www.pancretabank.gr/cms/uploaded/corporate_eng_may%202011.pdf (accessed 15 June 2010).

Petrochilos, G.A. (1999) 'The Hellenic contribution to economic thought', *Global Business and Economics Review*, 1(2): 215–46.

Psaropoulos, J. (2009) 'From Homer to co-ops' *Business File Quarterly Review* no. 74: 49–50.

Rapanos, V. (ed.) (2010) 'To Elliniko Trapeziko Systima to 2009 [Annual Report of the Hellenic Bank Association for 2009]', Athens: Hellenic Bank Association. Online. Available at: www.hba.gr/main/Ereunes-meletes/EllinikoTrapeziko2010-FullForWeb.pdf (accessed on 15 July 2010).

Salem, P. (2009) *The Complexity of Human Communication*. New York: Hampton Press.

Scott, J. (2000) *Social Networks Analysis: a handbook*, 2nd ed., London: Sage.

Sen, A.K. (1977) 'Rational Fools: a critique of the behavioural foundations of economic theory', *Philosophy and Public Affairs*, 6(4): 317–44.

Shahîd, I. (2009) *Byzantium and the Arabs in the Sixth Century: economic, social, and cultural history*, Vol. 2, Part 2, Cambridge, MA: Harvard University Press.

Shannon, C.E. (1948) 'A mathematical theory of communication', *Bell System Technical Journal*, vol. 27: 379–423 and 623–56.

Social Issues Research Centre (2007) 'Belonging', Oxford: SIRC. Online. Available at: www.sirc.org/publik/Belonging.pdf#search="belonging" (accessed 18 August 2011).

Thomas, T. (1997) 'Inclusive partnership: the key to business success in the 21st Century', *Journal of Co-operative Studies*, 89: 11–21. Online. Available at: www.co-opstudies.org/pdf/Journal%2089%20-%20Vol%2030%20No%201/S3-Thomas-089.pdf (accessed 18 August 2010).

Triandis, H.C. (2000) 'Culture and conflict', *International Journal of Psychology*, 35(2): 145–52.

US Overseas Cooperative Development Council (2007) 'Cooperatives: pathways to economic, democratic and social development in the global economy', Arlington, VA: US Overseas Cooperative Development Council. Online. Available at: www.ocdc.coop/OCDC/CoopPathwaysReport.pdf (accessed 15 June 2010).

Vakalopoulos, A.E. and Vakalopoulos, K.A (eds) (2003) *O Haraktiras ton Ellinon: Anihneyontas tin Ethniki mas Taytotita. Ereyna, Porismata, Didagmata* [The Character of Greeks: tracing our national identity—investigation, lessons, and findings], Thessaloniki, Greece: Ant. Stamoulis Publications.

Van Eck, C. (2003) *Purified by Blood: honour killings amongst Turks in the Netherlands*, Amsterdam: Amsterdam University Press.

Vassiliou, V.G. and Vassiliou, G. (1973) 'The implicative meaning of the Hellenic concept of Philotimo', *Journal of Cross-Cultural Psychology* 4(3): 326–41.

Wellman, B. (1983) 'Network analysis: some basic principles', *Sociological Theory*, 1: 155–200.

Wilkinson, A. and Balmer, J.M.T. (1996) 'Corporate and generic identities: lessons from the Co-operative Bank', *International Journal of Bank Marketing*, 14(4): 22–35.

Wright, P.H. (1985) 'The acquaintance description form', in S. Duck and D. Perlman (eds) *Understanding Personal Relationships: an interdisciplinary approach*. London: Sage, pp. 39–62

Yunus, M. (2006) 'Mohammad Yunus: Nobel Lecture', Oslo, December 10. Online. Available at: www.nobelprize.org/nobel_prizes/peace/laureates/2006/yunus-lecture-en.html (accessed 17 August 2011).

8 Innovative approaches to generating and using cooperative capital

Observations from France and Germany

Amélie Artis and Holger Blisse

Cooperative banks have long fulfilled their role as member-based enterprises satisfying their members' demand for credit. Funding is based on equity capital paid up by members who purchase shares and on savings from both members and other customers. An important innovation of cooperative banks was to provide access to credit for those excluded from the established banking system, and this new approach has provided access to credit at reasonable rates. From their outset, cooperative banks offered low interest credit to farmers and artisans and later, during the second half of the twentieth century, consumer credit for employees. Strongly anchored in the areas in which they operate, these banks are committed and responsible actors who channel savings into investment in the local economy.

Increasingly, cooperative banks have formed complex financial systems (networks) and act in some ways similar to private and savings banks. This convergence of the different types of banking groups is closely connected with the application of new legislation that introduced liberalization and despecialization within cooperative banking (e.g. the reform of the German Cooperative Act 1974 and the French Banking Law of 1984). Since the 1980s, an ongoing process of devolution and despecialization of credit activities, nationally and Europe-wide, has caused a trend of deterritorialization, competition between banks, and increasing rationing in financing.

These institutional changes have affected the supply of, and demand for capital. On the one hand, bank credit has become more limited for (unemployed) people without social networks or sufficient personal capital who want to start new businesses. On the other hand, savers have become more interested in the activities or companies in which they invest. Therefore, new needs for funding that encourages responsible investment have emerged.

In an attempt to fill the institutional gap, civil society decided to promote innovative means of funding in order to support local economies and to encourage direct interaction between savers and borrowers (Artis 2007). In some cases, these activities have been so successful that new institutional solutions have appeared and even new banks have been established, many in the legal form of cooperatives—e.g. the German GLS Gemeinschaftsbank in 1974, the Swiss Freie Gemeinschaftsbank in 1984, the German Ökobank in 1988, and Italian Banca Popolare Etica in 1998—and others as corporations—e.g. the Swiss Alternative Bank Schweiz in 1990, and the German UmweltBank in 1997.

This chapter focuses on institutional solutions in a less regulated, pre-bank stage and aims to identify contributions by established cooperative banks to meeting the new financial needs and developing a responsible attitude to investment. In this chapter, we first analyse and classify innovative examples of solidarity-based finance by focusing on the situation in France. We then ask whether the established cooperative banks in France and Germany are already involved in developing new approaches to solidarity-based finance. Finally, we describe how members and customers of the established cooperative banks contribute to local development by sharing their dividend and interest payments.

New institutions for local financial development in France

Since the 1980s, local financial development in France has been shaped by specific demand and supply transformations. On the one hand, small- and medium-sized enterprises (SMEs), cooperatives, and third-sector organizations have suffered from credit rationing. At the same time, cooperative banks have reduced their commitments to local financial development, and new local financial operators have emerged.

The imbalance in information between insiders and outsiders in the credit market has rendered the provision of external funding to small and atypical firms particularly challenging (Stiglitz and Weiss 1981). Moreover, due to their democratic governance and limited liabilities, cooperative firms and third-sector organizations are facing additional difficulties in finding external financing. For SMEs, their size and lack of equity capital are also barriers to obtaining outside capital.

Solidarity-based finance organizations emerged in France at the beginning of the 1980s to support start-up businesses that had been rejected by commercial banks. Initially, some of these organizations were created by activist savers who wanted to develop direct interaction between savers and borrowers. More recently, these savers have been involved in solidarity-based finance using one of the following four structures.

In *solidarity-based investment clubs*, a direct relationship based on geographical and social proximity—e.g. affinity or shared social network—links groups of savers and sponsors of local projects. Funding is exclusively drawn from private savings and is limited in scale—under €10,000 on average. For example, Club d'Investisseurs pour une Gestion Alternative et Locale de l'Épargne Solidaire (CIGALES, Club of Investors for Alternative and Local Management of Solidary Savings) provides investment funds and solutions for local enterprises or non-profit organizations that respect the club's social, cultural, and ecological criteria and contribute to the development of an alternative solidarity-based economy.

In *associative micro-financing structures*, financial relationships are established between associations and borrowers. Funding comes from donations, which are topped up by banks and local authorities, and credit lines provided by banking networks. Loans range from €3,000 to €10,000. An example is the Association pour le Droit à l'Initiative Économique (ADIE, Association for the Right to Economic Initiative), which is a non-profit organization that assists people excluded from the employment market and, as a consequence, from the traditional banking system. ADIE aims to help its borrowers to create their own economic activity and is designed for those who are either unemployed or receiving minimum benefits. Since its creation in 2010, ADIE has funded over 30,000 micro-companies and generated 36,000 jobs. Another association of this type is the France Initiative Réseau (FIR, France Initiative Network), which organizes collaboration between local authorities, institutional actors, and companies to create an environment that is propitious for the development of economic initiatives and the creation of new jobs. Its remit is to assemble funds for creating companies in the form of interest-free and guarantee-free loans, and to activate local economic potential to sponsor start-ups and accompany entrepreneurs through the creation process.

In *solidarity-based financial cooperatives*, relationships between savers and borrowers are prioritized. The involvement of private savers through their participation in credit commitment committees or coaching for borrowers is important in the daily management of these structures. Some of these organizations offer loans of between €7,500 and €60,000 to firms, while others give priority to loans of up to €100,000.

One example of a solidarity-based financial cooperative is Garrigue, which finances other cooperative firms or firms that promote added social value through stable jobs, democracy, environmental protection, and combating exclusion. Another example is La Nef, which provides responsible, ethical, and transparent management of citizens' savings and focuses on financing responsible and innovative projects such as renewable energy, organic farming, and cultural activities. In 2010, La Nef had over 27,000 members to whom it offered several financial products including long-term savings plans and credit. La Nef is also involved in a project to create the first European and ethical cooperative bank with European partners. A similar initiative in Germany is the cooperative Nord-Hand, Dortmund, which is one example of a solidarity-based finance organization, founded in March 2008 at suggestions of the Economic Promotion Department of Dortmund. Companies that desire to get a loan have to become members of the cooperative and save an amount paid up on the members' shares. Members are evaluated by the cooperative's management and successful requests are forwarded to GLS Bank. The first loan is up to the quarter of the amount saved on members' shares. The solidarity-based finance organization is responsible for the supervision of the loan until it is paid back (Bundesamt für Bauwesen und Raumordnung 2008, 7–9).

In *solidarity-based guarantee funds*, a partnership with local authorities, local banks, and non-profit organization is created; the funds come from private sources such as donations and sponsorships and public sources such as grants. The financial relationship is triangular, involving the borrower, the financial provider, and the non-profit organization. Guarantees can range from €10,000 to €250,000, while costs represent 2.5 per cent of the amount guaranteed and are financed by the borrower.

An example of solidarity-based funding is France Active Garantie, a financial company and subsidiary of the non-profit group France Active. This organization offers guarantees on bank loans to the unemployed and those facing economic marginalization who are seeking to establish their own entrepreneurial activity. It also provides financial support to cooperatives and third-sector organizations recognized as working in the public interest.

Characteristics of solidarity-based finance organizations

Solidarity-based finance relies heavily on relationship-based lending techniques, which make extensive use of qualitative information to reduce uncertainty regarding borrowers (De Young *et al.* 2004; Scott 2004) and use peer monitoring to improve commitment by borrowers and ensure repayments. For example, for SMEs, solidarity-based finance organizations have replaced previous 'family and community' funding practices such as rotating savings and credit groups. These organizations transform 'unofficial' loans into socialized and standardized loans while maintaining inter-personal relationships by using volunteers to give guidance to borrowers. They have been able to put standardized products and services in place and maintain differentiated, interpersonal, and affinity-based relationships. At the same time, they consolidate local partnerships that share their values.

Based on a range of local financing tools and territorial top-up funds, solidarity-based finance draws on geographical proximity to establish close relationships between savers and borrowers. Thus, some organizations maintain their physical presence by setting up 'traveling meetings' with the support of local volunteers or 'mobile banking officers' who are assisted by local authorities to provide financial and logistical resources. Such distinctive approaches that involve geographical, organizational, and institutional proximity provide clearer explanations of local financial development (Gilly and Torre 2000). Organizational proximity helps actors to coordinate their actions and facilitates the construction of local partnerships, while institutional proximity is based on mutual common goals and complementary roles in collective action, and encourages territorial and inter-sectoral partnerships.

The combination of these three kinds of proximity facilitates the development of solidarity-based finance, as is shown by the example of Herrikoa in the French Basque country. Established in 1980 in a hostile environment, this organization remains active in local renewal by financing local companies and plays a leading role in providing local solidarity-based financing networks. During the 1980s, Herrikoa was the only institution in the local financing market actively working in setting up new solidarity-based finance bodies. The development of this diversified, territorialized financing service was based on the existence of inter-personal links based on Basque country-related identity values, which were strengthened through networking and involvement by actors in joint actions (Artis 2007). A study of these partnerships reveals an inner circle of relationships with networks linked to local culture, the cooperative sector, and Basque development and a second circle of wider relationships with social, solidarity-based, and economic development networks (e.g. chambers of commerce and industry) (Itçaina 2010). These interactions strengthened organizational proximity and developed cooperation. The number and frequency of these links promote a level of trust that facilitates exchanges and reduces uncertainty.

In France, solidarity-based finance organizations led to the creation in 1995 of *Finansol*, a professional association that brought together solidarity funding actors. Its aims are to promote solidarity funding through communications, lobbying public authorities, labelling solidarity-based investments according to solidarity and transparency criteria, and to support cooperation between solidarity-based finance organizations and banking and financial establishments committed to a solidarity approach. Finansol publishes periodic surveys on solidarity-based savings and coordinates national campaigns calling for solidarity-based savings; one activity that it organizes is a 'solidarity funding week' to raise the awareness, visibility, and reputation of solidarity funding and increase its institutional recognition. The normalization of these financial practices should broaden the saver base. Finansol has also encouraged established cooperative banks and new financial cooperatives to work together to build savings funds.

Solidarity-based finance organizations and cooperative banks

In spite of their concentration and trend towards universal banking, cooperative banks in France still maintain a local link with their historic centres of activity. These banks broadly cover their geographical areas, with branches in rural areas (the Crédit Agricole network), peri-urban areas (Crédit Mutuel, Banques Populaires), and urban areas (Caisses d'Épargne and Crédit Coopératif): 'Only 12 per cent of cooperative bank sites are in towns with over 100,000 inhabitants (thus 88 per cent are in smaller towns), compared to 35 per cent for commercial banks' (Parpaix 2004, 116). Cooperative banks are currently reviewing their territorial policies and adopting a less costly and more flexible presence. They continue to create local branches, install automatic teller machines in rural areas, diversify their products by creating complementary services such as insurance and real estate brokerage, and create partnerships with local traders to maintain basic bank services.[1] Members contribute to territorial rootedness by helping to detect new local needs and by prompting cooperative banks to pursue solidarity goals by financing local association projects. These new forms of intermediation allow them to maintain banking services that meet the needs of local populations and companies without abandoning financially excluded populations, settlements, and businesses. Moreover, cooperative banks choose to be associated with solidarity-based finance that specifically serves social enterprises and community-oriented projects not satisfactorily financed by the conventional banking sector.

Thus, it seems that the emergence and development of solidarity-based finance organizations are supported by several French cooperative banks. For example, in close collaboration with charities and humanitarian associations, Crédit Coopératif created the first solidarity-based funding pool, with savers agreeing to donate part of the interest on their capital to several third-sector organizations selected by the bank. Based on this initial experience, Crédit Coopératif has developed a broad range of solidarity-based banking products: payment cards (Carte Agir), savings schemes (Livret Agir or Codesol), pooled investments (the Fonds Commun de Placement [FCP] Faim et Développement [Hunger and Development] and Épargne Solidaire [Solidarity Saving]), and ethical investments (the Société d'Investissement à Capital Variable [SICAV] Épargne Éthique Actions). Based on a relationship of trust, these products offer third-sector organizations an appropriate financing relationship and new sources of funding by combining revenues from capital, market resources, and donations. Savers choose which third-sector organizations to support and are informed about the use of their donations and the organizations' activities.

Locally and nationally, solidarity-based finance seeks to go beyond its circle of founders, who are often initiated militants, and become connected with a wider audience. The switch from affinity-based relationships to wider activities is achieved by the creation of common rules and shared values among stakeholders while solidarity-based finance organizations encourage partnerships between stakeholders. Thus, the management of solidarity-based finance (FCPs, honour loans, microcredit, and territorial funds) is organized by intermediate structures combining savers, commercial and cooperative banks, and local firms and authorities. These structures promote collective funding partnerships in which funding decisions are made by a partnership committee. The associative or cooperative format strengthens the collective management of the structures' financial activities, which differ considerably from traditional bilateral banking relationships. The partnership commitment to long-term relationship banking is an innovative approach that creates socialized regulation between private, cooperative, and public stakeholders.

The partnership between cooperative banks and solidarity-based finance leads to the realization of innovative economic and social intermediation (Richez-Battesti and Gianfaldoni 2006, 210). These relationships result in the pooling of information and learning between financial partners, nurture trust-based relationships, and assist the sustainability of locally financed companies.

The alliance between cooperative banks, associative and cooperative structures, and local authorities has been necessary to create social capital for local development. An analysis of these organizations shows the substantial influence of savers' involvement and the role of these structures as mediators in solidarity-based funding relationships. Moreover, it proves that solidarity-based finance has been able to face many of the new challenges in local financial development.

Concurrently, partnerships with cooperative banks have allowed these organizations to renew their commitment to social banking.

Cooperative banks are becoming involved in solidarity-based finance organizations through new structural forms—participation in boards of directors, involvement in organizations' strategic decision-making, and collaboration with credit commitment committees. Moreover, they are increasingly offering specific savings products, solidarity funds, and shareholdings, and making credit lines available or co-financing projects. Cooperative banks are drawing on their history and shared values to rediscover their cooperative specificities—e.g. re-injecting profits into social actions, territorial links, and stakeholder-based governance—through partnerships and the funding of solidarity-based finance. Cooperative banks and their members could also act as initiators of solidarity-based finance organizations and other innovations that contribute to local social and economic development.

How cooperative banks and their members contribute to local development

Generally, the managers of solidarity-based finance organizations and of established cooperative banks are authorized to decide how to invest the savings and funds of its customers and members. It is a matter of practicality whether the owners of the institution—the members themselves—should also be integrated into lending and investing decisions. Members often do not have the expertise to evaluate the business models of borrowers and related risks, and it is difficult to get a fully informed and responsible vote by all members within a short time. A meeting of members, however, could adopt general rules that would act as guidelines for management. In practice, an alternative solution has been adopted by cooperative banks such as the French financial cooperative La Nef, the German GLS Gemeinschaftsbank, and the Swiss Freie Gemeinschaftsbank: they publish information about accepted loan projects in the company's magazine or annual report. As will be discussed in the following section, cooperative banks can exert their influence on local development not only by making decisions on how to invest members' savings and available funds, but also by deciding if and how their annual profits will be distributed.

Dividends as sources of capital for local development

According to Austrian and German national special norms, either in the statutes of banks or in the general law, the members of cooperatives are authorized to decide how the annual profit is shared, although their decisions are based on a proposal by management and generally accepted without variation by meetings of members.[2] For their own economic development, cooperatives would tend to favour retaining their annual profits and strengthening their reserves. Consequently, a decision by a cooperative bank about how to share its annual profits could at worst exclude its members as beneficiaries, and the total amount of the annual profit would be retained by the bank.[3] Some cooperative banks share the annual profit with their members by paying a dividend,[4] although the percentages of the dividend with respect to the total annual profit and the dividend rates differ.

Dividends as sources of capital for local development

New ways of distributing and utilizing dividend payments can be illustrated by examining the activities of two German cooperative banks. While dividends are generally paid directly to the members, in 2007 the meeting of members of the Bavarian VR Bank Kitzingen decided to establish a participation fund. While the proportion of the annual profit committed to the participation fund remains as equity capital in the bank,[5] it is also credited as a virtual account that corresponds to each member's contribution to the fund. As such, it can be paid out to any member with at least five years of seniority in the fund.

As specified in the bank's statute, up to 20 per cent of the annual profit (net income) can be credited to the participation fund (VR Bank Kitzingen 2007, Art. 39b). Under German banking law, the participation fund represents accepted equity capital for the bank (Kreditwesengesetz [Banking Act of the Federal Republic of Germany], Art. 10, 2a, 3). However, the equity capital represented by the participation fund is potentially variable because if a member cancels his or her membership, the individualized part of the participation fund is paid back to the member together with the amount paid up on the members' shares (Blisse and Schäff 2009; VR Bank Kitzingen 2008, 6 and 16).[6]

Another approach to dividends has been taken by the Raiffeisen-Volksbank Aurich. At a meeting in 2009, its members decided to retain 75 basis points of the dividend and channel this money into a fund to benefit activities of public interest in the region of the bank including social projects, projects in arts and culture, and special projects of non-profit-associations. Details are regulated by the Geschäftsordnung für die Regionalfondsbeiräte (rules of internal procedure for the advisory committee of the regional fund).[7] The bank itself donated a matching amount to the fund. The members are entitled to decide on which projects the fund should be spent. If the fund does not spend the entire annual allocation, the rest of the money is transferred to the RVB-community foundation East Frisia (RVB-Bürgerstiftung Ostfriesland).[8] The regional fund will exist as long as the cooperative bank retains a part of the annual profit for the fund every year. The bank intends 'to strengthen with the fund the regional direction of banking services and wants also to activate the co-operative principles and take over responsibility for the community' (Kasten 2009b, 69; Blisse 2010).

While the two banks differ in how they manage their dividends as social investments, there are two important commonalities. First, the members remain beneficiaries of the payment but the amount is not paid directly to them but rather credited to a fund. Cooperative banks are still able to use the amounts invested as equity capital for their banking services, such as making loans. Second, the members agree to separate a part of the annual profit into a fund that coordinates the further investment of the money to promote local social activities. In both ways, members decide how they will allocate their part of the annual profit, which for all members together can be a non-trivial amount. If all cooperative banks established a participation fund or alternatively a regional fund, the total amount provided by members would annually reach some €70 to €80 million. Thus, although the annual contribution of each member is comparatively low, this calculation shows that if many small amounts are united, a remarkably large amount of available funds can be channelled to the benefit of local societies.

Sharing dividend payments for local development

Further examples emphasize the potential of these new forms of investing profits in local development. Two general trends can be identified: first, new members' shares that are not completely paid up should be transferred to the children of members and get completely paid up at their legal age; second, cooperatives can adopt innovations to strengthen solidarity-based finance organizations that aim to improve funding for SMEs, microfinance projects, and renewable energy. Some of the ideas that have been proposed involve broadening membership while others entail forming new cooperatives.

New membership

The idea of so-called young membership is to concentrate on new members' shares that are paid step-by-step with annual contributions. A member of the cooperative bank could subscribe for a new member's share and transfer it later to, for example, his/her child, or, alternatively, children can become members themselves from the beginning while the share will be paid up in subsequent years. This form would strengthen the equity capital of the cooperative bank over the long term.

New cooperatives

A new type of cooperative could support start-ups, which would be local investment cooperatives established by cooperative banks and interested members to provide equity capital to young local companies. The amount paid up on the members' shares would grow with the annual payments from the cooperative bank's annual profit on behalf of each member. The members would be engaged in the development of young companies in the region and take over economic risk. Therefore, they would get a dividend in cases of successful development of these companies that would be credited to their shares as members. These companies might take advantage of this initial cooperation and become credit customers of the cooperative bank.

Another type of new cooperative focuses on supporting microcredit institutions. In Germany, the GLS Gemeinschaftsbank Bochum loans money to the German national microcredit fund and helps to strengthen microfinance institutions. If a member of this cooperative bank wants to become a member of a local microfinance institution, a part of the bank's dividend can be transferred to pay up the members' shares in the microfinance institution. This procedure is particularly helpful for members who plan to apply for a microcredit loan and therefore have to save money on their members' shares.

A third type of cooperative supports the use and development of renewable resources. In addition to its regional fund, the Raiffeisen-Volksbank Aurich has established three photovoltaic cooperatives: RVB Bürgersonnenpark Aurich, RVB Bürgersonnenpark Jümme-Uplemgem-Wiesmoor, and RVB Bürgersonnenpark Friedeburg-Wittmund. These 'solar parks' help to protect the environment and express the regional responsibility of the bank. These parks operate by renting roof areas from local authorities, companies, and private owners to install photovoltaic devices. The profits from the electrical generation are paid to cooperative members, who are citizens of the region. The main partners for renting roof areas are local authorities, so these cooperatives are evidence of a public-private partnership (Kasten 2009a). Similar to these three parks, the Volksbank Niederrhein Alpen established two photovoltaic cooperatives, Alpen-Sonne and Bürger-Solar Rheinberg (Volksbank Niederrhein *n.d.a*, *n.d.b*).

To build up the equity capital of photovoltaic cooperatives or possibly cooperatives in the field of forestry, a part of the annual profit of the cooperative bank could be transferred to members' shares in these cooperatives.

Dimensions of sharing dividend payments

Dividend payment practices differ from cooperative bank to cooperative bank. Payments made directly to members are no longer available to a cooperative bank since the members themselves decide how to spend their (cash) dividends. The examples of German cooperative banks could be extended, but they are sufficient to demonstrate that members have been willing to invest part of their dividend to a new form of disposition. These forms can be distinguished by whether the money belongs to the members as beneficiaries or to a third party such as a regional fund. If the members remain beneficiaries, it can still be distinguished whether the money remains in the cooperative bank and is available for its business or the money leaves the cooperative bank (see Table 8.1).

A meeting of members could decide for all members how to diversify the payment to the members or each member could individually decide which of the available form(s) should benefit. Perhaps the willingness of the members to support new forms of social or economic commitment for the region will also encourage the cooperative bank to do so, as the example of the cooperative bank in Aurich illustrates.

Conclusion

Since the 1980s and in response to the new forms of financial exclusion, solidarity-based and social finance organizations have emerged and offered

Table 8.1 Dimensions of profit sharing

<table>
<tr><td rowspan="3">Beneficiary</td><td colspan="6">Annual profit (net income)</td></tr>
<tr><td rowspan="2">Bank</td><td colspan="5">Dividend</td></tr>
<tr><td colspan="4">Members</td><td>Regional fund</td></tr>
<tr><td>Form</td><td>Reserves</td><td>Participation fund</td><td colspan="2">New Memberships</td><td rowspan="3">(Cash-) Dividend</td><td rowspan="2"></td></tr>
<tr><td></td><td></td><td></td><td>Bank</td><td>New cooperative</td></tr>
<tr><td>Equity capital for…</td><td colspan="3">…bank's business</td><td>…start-ups/
microcredit/solar energy</td><td>…social activities</td></tr>
<tr><td>Direction</td><td colspan="4">Region</td><td>Members</td><td>Region</td></tr>
</table>

Source: Blisse (2010, 104).

financial innovations. As the French example illustrates, solidarity-based finance has been implemented by a range of organizations that share specific characteristics: trust-based relations, coaching, financial partnerships, and anchoring in the local community. These organizations mainly finance SMEs and not-for-profit enterprises such as cooperatives and third-sector organizations.

Solidarity-based finance organizations encourage local solidarity-based funding agreements based on information-acquiring systems, collective commitments, and associations of various stakeholders, not only individuals but also social organizations, cooperative banks, local authorities, and companies. Because of their collaborative nature, solidarity-based finance organizations offer the means to innovatively fund the regeneration of critical parts of local economies. These innovations have also encouraged cooperative banks to renew their relationships with their local areas by enlarging the set of funding options available for local companies and initiating new forms of cooperation.

Initially autonomous and informal, these innovations have progressively been adopted by associations and financial cooperatives. Consequently, the established cooperative banks have participated in developing a range of solidarity-based financial products and services and supported the growth of solidarity-based finance organizations in several regions of France. These partnerships have already contributed to improving the generation and use of capital for local development. At the same time, the established cooperative banks have also started to work on similar initiatives that contribute directly to local social and economic development.

This chapter has highlighted innovative ways of creating institutional solutions to fulfil the new funding needs that have emerged in local societies. Co-operative banks are striving to refresh their historical conditions of origin and develop solutions for those customers and members who are willing to share a part of their banks' financial profits in order to contribute to local social and economic development.

At least two sources of capital have been tapped in France and Germany, where customers and members of cooperative banks have agreed to channel a part of their interest or dividend payments to create solidarity-based organizations through the initiation of regional funds or new cooperatives. Finally, it should be kept in mind that the concept of sharing the dividend as well as suggesting new forms of using it are premised on active participation by members and their voluntary decisions to creatively support meaningful local and cooperative activities.

Notes

1 For example, Crédit Agricole Sud Rhône Alpes has created Points Verts [green points] with businesses in certain rural areas, offering cash withdrawal and cheque deposit services.

2 By statute, some cooperative banks have a fixed percentage in advance that is available for management's decision, such as the Berliner Volksbank (2010, 20, Art. 51(2)).

3 This is normally the case for Austrian Raiffeisenbanks; see Raiffeisenbank Feldkirch (2003, Art 25(1)); Raiffeisenkasse Guntramsdorf (n.d., Art. 27(1)); Raiffeisenbank Halbenrain-Tieschen (2008, Art. 25(1)).

4 This is the case for most Austrian Volksbanks and German cooperative banks.

5 The bank paid €5 to each member whose share was completely paid up for 2007 and 2008, altogether in 2007 €66,315 (9.3 per cent of the annual profit) and in 2008 €70,140 (12.3 per cent of the annual profit). Dividend rates were calculated after the fund for general banking risks was credited €500,000 (VR Bank Kitzingen 2008, 6 and 17).

6 Cooperative banks had implemented a similar fund to care for the evening of life or the death of a member at their beginning in the nineteenth century. The first—Prussian—cooperative societies act in Germany of 1867 provided statutory flexibility for establishing such a fund until 1889, when the act was amended (Hofinger and Blisse 2005). In 1974, the participation fund was included in the Co-operative Societies Act as Art. 73(3).

7 The rules were adopted on 13 May 2009 and came into effect on 9 June 2009.

8 The foundation was established by the bank.

References

Artis, A. (2007) '"La finance solidaire territorialisée": une réponse de proximité en faveur de la construction d'un territoire de référence dans un processus de mondialisation', *Cahier du Ceren*, 19: 20–40. Online. Available at: www.escdijon.com/download/fr/ceren/cahiers_19/4_artis.pdf (accessed 4 September 2011).

Berliner Volksbank (2010) *Satzung und Wahlordnung* [Statute and election regulations], September, Berlin: Berliner Volksbank.

Blisse, H. (2010) 'Der Beitrag einer differenzierten (kredit-)genossenschaftlichen Überschussverwendung zur regionalen sozialen und wirtschaftlichen Entwicklung' in R. Doluschitz (ed.): *Aktuelle theoretische und empirische Beiträge zur Genossenschafts- und Kooperationsforschung*. Stuttgart-Hohenheim: Forschungsstelle für Genossenschaftswesen an der Universität Hohenheim, pp. 91–109.

Blisse, H. and Schäff, J. (2009) 'Zum Beteiligungsfonds bei (Kredit-) Genossenschaften', *Zeitschrift für das gesamte Genossenschaftswesen*, 59(3): 260–4.

Bundesamt für Bauwesen und Raumordnung (2008) 'Quartiers-Impulse—Neue Wege zur Stärkung der lokalen Wirtschaft [New Ways to Strengthen Local Economy]', Ein ExWoSt-Forschungsfeld, ExWoSt-Informationen 31/5, Bonn.

De Young, R., Hunter, W.C., and Udell, G.F. (2004) 'The past, present and probable future of community banks', *Journal of Financial Service Research*, 25(2–3): 85–133.

Gilly, J.-P. and Torre, A., (2000) *Dynamiques de proximité*, Paris: L'Harmattan.

Hofinger, H. and Blisse, H. (2005) 'Reservefonds mit Fürsorgecharakter bei Vorschuss- und Kreditvereinen (Kreditgenossenschaften)', *Bankhistorisches Archiv–Zeitschrift zur Banken–und Finanzgeschichte*, 31(2005): 134–43.

Itçaina, X. (2010) 'Les régimes territoriaux de l'économie sociale et solidaire: le cas du Pays Basque français', *Géographie, économie, société*, 12(2010/1): 71–87.

Kasten, A. (2009a) 'Solargenossenschaften in Ostfriesland: Goldgräberstimmung bei erneuerbaren Energien', posted 14 April. Online. Available at: www.neuegenossenschaften.de/aktuelles/news/2009/04/14/Solargenossenschaften.html (accessed 23 March 2010).

Kasten, A. (2009b) 'Die Region und ihre Stärken stärken', *BankInformation*, 36(10): 68–9.

Parpaix, C. (2004) 'Le rôle des banques coopératives et mutualistes', in D. Demoustier (ed.) *Economie sociale et Développement local*, Les Cahiers de l'Economie Sociale, Paris: Institut de l'économie sociale, pp. 115–20.

Raiffeisenbank Feldkirch (2003) *Satzungen für die Raiffeisenbank Feldkirch registrierte Genossenschaft mit beschränkter Haftung* [Statutes of the Reiffeisen Bank of Feldkirch]', 2 June 2003, Feldkirch, Germany: Raiffeisenbank Feldkirch. Online. Available at: neu.raiffeisen.at/eBusiness/services/resources/media/1022353367898–1022373424822_10 22373820410_1187327841570364 79–1187140846747 34475–1–1-NA.pdf (accessed 25 September 2011).

Raffeisenbank Halbenrain-Tieschen (2008) *Satzung* [Statute], 28 March 2008, Halbenrain, Germany: Raffeisenbank Halbenrain-Tieschen.

Raiffeisenkasse Guntramsdorf (n.d.): *Satzung* [Statute]. Online. Available at: www.raika-guntramsdorf.at/mitglied/satzung.pdf (accessed 22 March 2010).

Richez-Battesti, N. and Gianfaldoni, P. (eds) (2006) *Les banques coopératives en France: le défi de la performance et de la solidarité*, Paris: L'Harmattan.

Scott, J.A. (2004) 'Small businesses and the value of community banks', *Journal of Financial Service Research*, 25(2–3): 207–30.

Stiglitz, J. and Weiss, A. (1981) 'Credit rationing in markets with imperfect information', *American Economic Review*, 71(3): 393–410.

Volksbank Niederrhein (n.d.a) *Die Alpen-Sonne geht auf!* [The sun rises in the Alps!] Online. Available at: www.volksbank-niederrhein.de/Oekologie/alpen_sonne_eg.html (accessed 26 September 2011).

Volksbank Niederrhein (n.d.b) *Bürger-Solar Rheinberg eG gegründet* [Citizen-Solar Rheinberg cooperative founded]. Online. Available at: www.volksbank-niederrhein.de/Oekologie/buerger-solar_rheinberg.html (accessed 26 September 2011).

VR Bank Kitzingen (2007) *Satzung* [Statute] 21 May 2007, Kitzingen, Germany: VR Bank Kitzingen.

VR Bank Kitzingen (2008) *Geschäftsbericht* [Annual Report], *2008*, Kitzingen, Germany: VR Bank Kitzingen. Online. Available at: www.vrbankkitzingen.de/content/bank/Geschaeftsbericht_2008.pdf (accessed 26 September 2011).

Part III

Microfinance and local development

The chapters in this part examine the role and performance of microfinance in different local contexts of the developed and developing world. They build on the extensive experience of credit unions and microfinance providers and present evidence on the observed turn toward introducing and broadening savings mobilization as a stimulus for sustainable local development. Moreover, the authors adopt a critical approach by shedding light on not only the benefits that these institutions provide, but also the shortcomings that arise in addressing poverty and financial inclusion in highly deprived communities.

In Chapter 9, Anita Marchesini and Paul A. Jones address the impact of the transformation within many British credit unions from borrower-oriented into saving-promoting institutions, particularly in low-income areas. In line with the asset-building theory, credit unions foster productive savings behaviour through the adoption of strategies and the introduction of economic and non-economic incentives that assist members to overcome barriers to saving. The authors conclude that the move to become increasingly focused on saving has not only strengthened the institutional and operative viability of credit unions, but also resulted in enabling many people on low incomes to access a safer pathway into financial inclusion.

In Chapter 10, Mokbul Morshed Ahmad analyses the difficulties that microfinance is facing in Bangladesh, despite its many achievements, and provides critical remarks on possible solutions. Some of the issues that he identifies are dropouts affected by the rigidity of the microlending model and the lack of access to savings in times of emergency; exclusion or self-exclusion by many families qualified to be micro-borrowers; delinquencies and defaults that arise when borrowers are unable to repay or do not maintain their affiliations with loan providers; and the risk posed by loans by multiple memberships, even if this practice is forbidden. The underlying concern is the systemic risk resulting from the domination of the market by a few giant microfinance institutions.

In Chapter 11, David Eduardo de la Cerda Garza, Miriam del Rocío Arredondo Barrera, Morayma Lizbeth Martín González, and María de la Luz Bravo Santillán present a field project designed to offer credit opportunities to people in deprived communities of a Mexican municipality. The authors analyse the main factors that hindered the development of microcredit in the rural zones of

Mexico that lack adequate assistance programmes. Eight microfinance organizations are then considered to identify strengths and weaknesses in order to design institutionalized solutions that by easing access to economic opportunities and fostering cooperation at the community level would help eradicate poverty and improve the quality of life in rural Mexico.

9 Re-discovering a paradigm

The promotion of savings by credit unions within the UK policy context of asset-based welfare

Anita Marchesini and Paul A. Jones

The United Kingdom is probably the only European country to have introduced asset-building theory into its national policies by 'encouraging or forcing individuals to hold assets' (Emmerson and Wakefield 2001, 4). In 2000, the publication *Ownership for All* (Kelly and Lissauer 2000) paved the way for a debate about asset building that has characterized much of UK policy development. This debate has focused on the assumption of the benefits of building savings and the urgency of responding to the increasing over-indebtedness of the British population. Since the UK has one of the highest levels of personal debt and recourse to consumer credit in Europe, many British credit unions have had to rethink their purposes and strategic policies, in line with an emerging shift towards a greater focus on saving.

Based on institutional theory (Bowles 1998; Sherraden 1991), this chapter investigates UK credit unions from a new perspective: not solely as providers of affordable credit, but as effective promoters of a thrift mentality and stimulators of saving, in accordance with their statutory objectives. At the same time, these financial cooperatives are seen as playing a key role in educating their members to become *financially capable*—that is, equipped to make decisions about savings and carry them through. These skills are fundamental if members are going to budget and manage their finances, and thereby develop the 'knowledge and skills to understand their own financial circumstances, along with the motivation to take action' (HM Treasury 2007, 19). The promotion of savings is regarded as central to supporting change in the long-term financial behaviour of members.

This chapter is based on a six-month collaborative research study conducted by the Department of Economics, University of Bologna (Forlì Campus) in partnership with the Research Unit for Financial Inclusion at Liverpool John Moores University from October 2009 to March 2010. The aim of the study was to explore how credit unions—individually and through networking—assist people on low incomes to save. There were three main themes underpinning the research: the design and policy guidelines of credit unions' savings products, partnership approaches to service delivery, and membership education and financial capability. The study used a mixed research methodology and collected both quantitative and qualitative data from a sample of 20 credit unions. A questionnaire survey was completed by 15 credit unions (about 15 per cent of a total of 104 England and Wales credit unions contacted).[1] Qualitative methods included second stage, semi-structured face-to-face interviews with ten individual credit union managers and volunteers, and participant observation of the dynamics of interaction between clients, staff, and volunteers.

Economic institutions and the habit of saving

One of the underlying drivers of the current financial crisis has been the expansion of a credit rather than a savings culture. A context of easy access to credit, which was regarded as a stimulus for the economy, was one of the main factors that led to a declining UK savings rate from 1995 to 2007 (Berry *et al.* 2009). As Cooper (2004, 123) observes,

> the UK economy is awash with cheap money. … [F]or the majority of UK citizens credit is now a way of life, and a convenient means of enabling 'us' to buy anything from foreign holidays to this week's supermarket shop.

As of November 2009, UK consumers had £1.46 trillion of outstanding debt and personal borrowing, representing 160 per cent of household annual pre-tax income (National Audit Office 2010).

Inadequate levels of savings often result in the need for expensive credit. It is not surprising that the Family Resources Survey for 2009–10 found that the number of households not having any savings at all is negatively correlated with their total weekly income level (Department for Works and Pensions 2011). Kempson and Finney (2009) stress the substantive distinction between formal and informal savings and find that 38 per cent of lower income families had only informal savings, compared to 21 per cent for the better off.[2] For the period from 2006 to 2008, the Wealth and Assets Survey (Daffin 2009) calculated a Gini coefficient of 0.61 for total household wealth, thus showing a significant level of asset inequality.

This context led to an intensification of the debate about asset building, which has been defined by Thiel and Nissan (2009, 1) as

> a strategy to help people out of poverty [that] differs in its approach to more traditional thinking which seeks to iron out lows in incomes. The emphasis of asset building is on long-term savings, either through savings accounts, wealth creation (e.g. house purchases), but also through investment in education and training.

This definition emphasizes the importance of assets as a *stock* of resources—as juxtaposed to income as a *flow* of resources—for individuals, especially those who live within a context of material insecurity and income vulnerability, when 'without any financial cushion, even a small mishap such as a broken washing machine or fridge can upset the precarious financial equilibrium of making ends meet on a low income' (Sodha and Lister 2006, 8). While virtually all approaches to asset building focus on assets as catalyst for economic development, Prabhakar (2009a) distinguishes a 'citizenship approach' where assets are functional to the establishment of 'social citizenship'. From this perspective, assets have an instrumental value since, by going beyond their market value, 'a wider distribution of assets means greater opportunity, choice, diversity, and self-fulfilment for citizens', thus helping to sustain 'pluralism' (Gamble and Prabhakar 2005, 1).

One of the most important contributions of asset-building theory has been to demonstrate that while the amount of savings is higher among those from wealthier backgrounds, savings rates can be higher among those on low incomes (Durán 2002). Notably, a number of factors explain savings exclusion other than income level (Kempson *et al.* 2005; Finney and Kempson 2009).

Individuals on low to moderate incomes are able to accumulate assets if they are supported by institutions[3] that provide 'purposefully created policies, programs, products, and services that shape opportunities, constraints and consequences' (Sherraden and Schreiner 2007, 30). Similarly, Bowles (1998, 75) argues that 'markets and other economic institutions do more than allocate goods and services: they also influence the evolution of values, tastes, and personalities'. Consequently, 'economic institutions may induce specific behaviours—self-regarding, opportunistic, or cooperative, say—which then become part of the behavioral repertoire of the individual' (Bowles 1998, 79–80).

As institutions affecting saving behaviour, asset builders include multilateral and bilateral agencies, governments, and non-profit and for-profit organizations (OECD 2003). In a broad sense, all actors that operate in the field of microfinance, enterprise support, community building, and financial inclusion provide not only financial assets—such as loans as access to bank accounts—but also non-financial assets—such as promotion of social inclusion and financial literacy—by contributing to the creation, accumulation, and preservation of assets.

Asset building in the UK context

From 1997 to 2010, the Labour government took measures to combat financial exclusion that were initially based on the 'ABC' model: widening access to money *Advice*, increasing the number of *Banked* individuals, and widening access to affordable *Credit*. However, Labour's policies were increasingly influenced by asset-building theory, which proposed 'using the state to distribute assets' (Prabhakar 2009b, 54). On the premise that market goods can also be seen as social goods (Blake and de Jong 2008), Labour decided that intervention was required in order to correct irrational savings decisions, as a kind of a market failure that needed to be addressed (Emmerson and Wakefield 2001). Sherraden (2002, 5) argues that this entailed 'a transition from a Social *Welfare* State to a Social *Investment* State' (emphasis in original). Labour adopted a programme of *asset-based welfare* and subsequently took several public policy initiatives, including cash-match savings accounts for people on low incomes—such as the Child Trust Fund and the Saving Gateway—and tax-free accounts—such as Individual Savings Accounts.[4]

The Conservative-led coalition government elected in 2010 also recognized the need to address the savings and asset crisis from the perspective of a fairer society (Blond and Gruescu 2010), but has not yet specified how these elements will be translated into policy and practice. According to this government, the state should serve as more of a facilitator than an implementer by devolving 'power and responsibility into the hands of families, groups, networks, neighbourhoods and locally-based communities' by encouraging the development of 'volunteers, mutuals, co-operatives, charities, social enterprises and small businesses' (Coote 2010, 2).

This approach implies an even more central role for credit unions. Changes in the legislation and regulation of British credit unions are expected to be enacted early in 2012, and these will significantly enhance their capability to maximize the promotion of savings. These changes will include the opportunity for certain credit unions to offer interest on savings accounts, rather than on the annual dividend as is the case now, and the widening of the definition of the common bond that will enable corporate organizations and groups to make deposits in credit unions.

Credit unions as asset builders

Historically, credit unions originated in the commitment by individuals to come together for mutual benefit and, often, to respond to the needs of the less well off. They 'represent a modern reflection of the long tradition of financial mutual aid within working-class communities' (McArthur *et al.* 1993, 400). As of March 2010, UK credit unions had 870,000 members, including over 100,000 'junior savers' (ABCUL 2010); these figures represent a credit union penetration rate of more than 1 per cent of the British population. Despite the limited size of the credit union sector in the UK, credit unions have grown significantly in the past decade and the trend is on the rise.

The main ethos of credit unions is to provide affordable and accessible financial services, particularly to people who have low incomes or are financially excluded. Credit unions offer access to 'flexible savings accounts, instant and accessible loans, bill payment accounts, affordable home and contents insurance and access to money advice and debt counselling services' (Jones 2006, 43).

They were established predominantly as borrower-oriented, community, volunteer-run organizations, belonging to the 'Traditional Social Development Model' (Jones 2006). Notably a 'philanthropic intent to serve the poor and over-indebted' (Jones 2005, 13) often motivated many credit union staff and volunteers. One of the initial members of Lodge Lane and District Credit Union in Liverpool observed that his credit union

> aims to get people out of the trap of borrowing from high cost lenders. Banks have all closed because this is a deprived area and they did not have

> much business. Many people could not open an account and the banks anyway were not able to serve our members as they struggle to make ends meet from week to week.[5]

Their strong local identity means that credit unions can offer a viable alternative to high-cost credit providers, thus preventing the asset erosion that threatens entire communities. Indeed 'the creation of sources of credit for the benefit of the members at a fair and reasonable rate of interest' is one of the objectives of the Credit Unions Act of 1979.

Nevertheless, given the overlaps between different areas of financial exclusion, a complete anti-poverty strategy cannot rely solely on tackling credit exclusion. Rather, a full financial inclusion policy should consider all the factors that prevent people from accessing financial services.

Aware of these needs, in recent years British credit unions have been transformed through the increasing adoption of a microsavings-led model, identified as one of the key drivers in the development of 'New Model Credit Unions' (Jones 2006). In fact, it is often argued that prioritizing savings was central to building a new organizational culture, similar to the way in which the introduction of current accounts transformed credit union operations (Jones 2008a).

A dual strategy for credit unions and their members

Successful credit unions around the world have been built on the generation of the members' savings and not by raising external capital from external donors or through borrowing on money markets or from banks. For credit unions, there are at least three good reasons to raise funds for on-lending through savings mobilization.

First, attracting savings is central to long-term credit union sustainability, as it frees credit unions from dependence on volatile external funds. In fact, in Britain, dependence on external funds mainly from the public sector arguably compounded the labelling of credit unions as 'social welfare initiatives' (Jones 2006, 39). Internationally, there is strong evidence from empirical credit union research that savings generated from members are not only a more reliable source of funds, but also are less costly to raise and to administer. As noted by Branch and Klaehn (2002, 6–7),

> the market cost of paying individual depositors tends to be lower than the non-subsidized inter-lending rate for loans in financial markets ... internally-generated savings provide an independent and sustainable supply of funds that can be invested in the local community.

Second, mobilizing savings tends to increase the number of new members and of products held by existing clients, thus potentially expanding the outreach of microfinance institutions (Consultative Group to Assist the Poorest, 1998). Moreover promoting savings strengthens a mixed-based and a more economically diverse membership of savers and of borrowers. Not all credit union members want or need to borrow, and many require access to a range of savings products that offer competitive rates of return.

Third, a focus on savings strengthens credit unions as sound and stable financial intermediaries, since '*attracting depositors may instil a stronger demand-orientation and thriftiness in [microfinance institutions'] operations and increase public confidence*' (Consultative Group to Assist the Poorest, 1998 [2]; emphasis in original). Branch and Baker (2000) argue that borrower-dominated boards of directors create internal weaknesses in credit union financial management. They concentrate on the provision of lower-cost loans that tend to reduce the focus on the financial discipline required to generate surplus to pay dividends to depositors. Branch and Baker (2000, 4) maintain:

> [A] major problem of governance is the tendency of borrowers to dominate the boards of directors. To resolve this problem, credit unions should provide balanced and updated services that will attract not only borrowers but also savers. The presence of savers on boards will lead to more effective pressure on credit union management and directors for proper financial management and prudential governance. That will, in turn, protect the interests of savers and help ensure the credit union's long-term sustainability.

This saver-oriented focus on financial discipline accords with requirements by the Financial Services Authority and Financial Services Compensation Scheme (FSCS) for credit unions to protect member savings, a point underlined by Branch and Klaehn (2008, 7–8): 'Directors and managers are forced to operate according to sound principles, including adequate capital reserves, loan loss provisions, and liquidity reserves in order to protect client savings and the existence of the institution'. Ultimately, boards of directors and managers need to prioritize savings promotion and strike a balance between 'net savers [who] demand high deposit rates and strong prudential disciplines' and 'net borrowers [who] tend to demand low loan rates and easy access to credit' (Branch and Klaehn 2008, 7).

Our research survey found that 14 of the 15 credit union managers attached the maximum level of importance to the promotion of savings, and 13 out of the 15 reported that their credit union was equally oriented to both saving and borrowing. When asked about the objectives of their savings policy, most managers identified equally the attraction of new savers and the building of the existing savers' savings balances. In addition, all community-based credit unions within the sample prioritized the maximization of the number of savers with small savings balances; presumably, this objective underlies a savings policy targeting people on low incomes who are likely to save small amounts.

However, it should be noted that nearly a half of all credit union managers, despite their recognition of the importance of savings, neither agreed nor disagreed that they encouraged savings products in the same way as other products. Moreover, just over a quarter of managers reported that they did not consider saving products as the main products that credit unions offer members. These findings indicate a certain ambivalence about promoting savings by some managers. There may be several reasons for this: apart from an inability to pay a dividend on savings, for some credit unions there were issues of high liquidity ratios, high management costs of cash deposits and withdrawals, and marketing costs associated with the promotion of savings. In addition, many credit unions continue to be traditional borrower organizations, and they would require a major change in perspective to adopt a savings-led business model.

Credit unions as a remedy for savings exclusion?

According to Blake and de Jong (2008, 85),

> Not everyone who fails to save is financially excluded. Rather, exclusion describes those who do not have the skills or opportunity to save, as well as people who save in informal or insecure ways, like in a jam jar or under a mattress.

Hence, to evaluate the extent to which credit unions' practices and policies satisfy their members' needs, both the demand side—financial capability—and the supply side—the institutions and product design—of savings exclusion must be examined.

Demand side: linking financial capability and saving

In line with asset-building theory, financial capability is among the institutional factors that incentivize the propensity of individuals to save, for instance, for a pension (Clancy *et al.* 2001; Lusardi and Mitchell 2009). There is strong evidence that financial capability is highly correlated with saving (Atkinson *et al.* 2006) and that it impacts upon economic and psychological well-being (Taylor *et al.* 2009).

Nevertheless not all financial capability education schemes have proved to be effective. Financial decision making seems to be characterized by a chain of paradoxes: although people recognize the importance of a specific financial saving behaviour, they do not always translate this insight into practice. More specifically, behavioural economics has found that when people face savings decisions that are very complex, 'there are ingrained methods of processing information that lead to systematic bias' (de Meza *et al.* 2008, 20). The nub of the problem is to set up policies that may overcome the intrinsic psychological barriers that prevent people from acting productively.

These observations and evidence provide a strong case for investigating whether credit unions implement financial capability schemes in line with two of their statutory objectives: 'the promotion of thrift among the members of the society' and 'the training and education of the members in the wise use of money and in the management of their financial affairs' (Credit Unions Act 1979).

In our survey, a large majority of respondents reported that their credit unions carried out financial education activities, and in an earlier study by Jones (2008b), 91 per cent of his sample reported that financial education is important within their credit unions. One of our informants, the General Manager of Unify Credit Union (Wigan) stressed that,

> Our members have never planned ahead, many have never had a bank account, they had never saved, so it's about educating them and changing the way that they think. This is our main focus, to build up an asset base.[6]

Interestingly, financial capability is not correlated with income (Atkinson *et al.* 2006). In this regard, the Project Manager of Lodge Lane and District Credit Union (Liverpool) observed, 'Lots of our members never had savings in their lives and it does not just apply to low income members'.[7]

One issue is that many credit unions do not have a formal education policy: 'Most of the advice and guidance is given informally on a day to day basis' (Evans and Broome 2005, 233) and it is 'personal and oriented to learning through doing' (Jones 2008b, 39). The findings of our survey show that the vehicles used for financial education are—in order of importance—informal money management advice to members; financial education classes and workshops; financial education leaflets left in community locations; tailored, individual professional money advice; newsletters with money management advice; and financial education in schools. In order to deliver financial education, credit unions sometimes employ a money advice worker, or engage volunteers who are trained in basic financial matters. The credit unions surveyed reported having an average of 30 volunteers, the majority of whom had been involved in at least one financial education session.

Another important point arising from the interviews was that financial education was not delivered in a compulsory manner—such as a condition of membership or obtaining a loan—but rather was embedded in informal interactions with members through loan interviews, the pay-in collection sessions, and to a lesser extent through the joining process.

Notably, three out of four of the credit union managers indicated that they were involved in networks in order to promote members' financial capabilities. These were primarily with other third-sector organizations, such as housing associations, community organizations, and money advice agencies.

In order to introduce children to economic and financial literacy early in the learning process, engagement with schools is widely recognized as important (Grody *et al.* 2008; Jones 2010). Credit unions often run savings clubs in schools, thus enabling children to learn how to deal with money and the value of saving. The manager of Unify Credit Union (Wigan) reported:

> We are now in twenty primary schools across the borough. Children are good little savers. The message does go back to parents from their children but most importantly, the children learn how to save. Financial education is

> also encouraging them to find a way that suits them to save. We have got a member who saves 20 pence pieces and he brought them in with a bag full of copper and by doing that he saved over £100.[8]

Another example was credit unions working in partnership with Citizens Advice Bureaux, a network of charitable UK money and consumer advice organizations, in order to develop projects such as 'Ways to Save' or 'Save Xmas'. In these projects, credit unions deliver training sessions by involving frontline money advice workers and local service users in a deprived area.

For credit unions, the financial capability agenda is a complex commitment. There are substantial costs involved in terms of resources and in the time taken to find partner organizations—both of which are often in short supply especially in volunteer-run credit unions. Perhaps most importantly, there are acknowledged difficulties in engaging members to participate. The manager of South Tyneside Credit Union (South Shields) maintained that:

> Particularly if they are on a low income they think that it is not important because they do not have enough money to manage. I have got this money and all of it has to be spent. It is very difficult to persuade them that there may be some changes they can make to avoid the same situations in the future.[9]

Overall access to savings products and to financial education embody two mutually reinforcing policies since the former is paramount to stimulating a learning process through which financial concepts and understanding can be internalized, while the latter helps instil a long-term saving habit.

Supply side: re-conceptualizing savings products

The shift to a greater focus on saving is to be seen primarily through the wider implementation of flexible and tailored savings products developed either by credit unions themselves or through the adoption of government schemes, such as Child Trust Funds and Individual Savings Accounts.

Our study focuses on credit unions' own products. Drawing on literature on savings exclusion that identifies the saving needs of lower-income consumers and the barriers to saving (Kempson and Finney 2009; Collard *et al.* 2003), three assessment criteria have been adopted: access, features of savings products, and the connection between savings and other financial products.

Access

Four factors are important for assuring access. First, credit unions are well-known 'trusted providers with a local presence [that] can play a role in overcoming both physical and psychological access problems' of low-income members (Kempson and Finney 2009, viii). Trust is connected with safety, which the credit unions in our study emphasized is one of the most important features for encouraging those on low incomes to save. Trust in credit unions is supported by the protection provided by the FSCS, which guarantees the same level of protection for savings as banks and building societies.

Second, credit unions are community-based providers. Consequently, when members invest in their local credit union, they know that the only people drawing benefit are people within their own community, since there are no outside shareholders to pay (Berthoud and Hinton 1989).

Third, credit unions adopt a personal approach, which provides a certain added social value. As the manager of Unify Credit Union (Wigan) observes:

> We are rooted in the community.... We sit down and discuss with the members and we do that at their level.... It is because of the relationships we have with our members that the word spreads out in the community about the credit union.... Our way of encouraging people is just talk to them. If their parents have never saved, most of the time nobody has ever sat down and discussed with them about what they can save.[10]

Fourth, access to savings products can also be widened through partnerships with other organizations. In our survey, 11 out of 15 respondents reported that their credit union belonged to at least one formal or informal network, which included government, private sector, and third-sector organizations. Community venues and housing association offices represent an opportunity for credit unions to extend their outreach and to cross-refer people between agencies.[11]

According to Jones (2008b), 65 per cent of credit unions reported that networking with other organizations is high among the factors contributing to their growth and development. An effective response to the multi-faceted problem of financial exclusion has to be implemented 'in a coordinated and holistic manner' (Jones 2006, 42).

Features of savings products

Credit unions that took part in the survey offer between one and four savings products. All of them offer a standard share account that is linked with the status of being a member and 11 out of 15 offer junior savings accounts. The latter represent 'one model that could be rolled out more widely. The aim is to introduce and normalise particular financial habits in people's lives' (Blake and de Jong 2008, 47).

In terms of targeting, almost half of the survey respondents reported that their credit unions offered savings products—such as Christmas/holiday accounts and general saver accounts—specifically designed for members with low incomes. Notably, these accounts are simple and easy to understand and have transparent terms and conditions—all characteristics relevant to those on low incomes (Collard *et al.* 2003).

Our survey found that almost all volunteer boards of directors and to a lesser extent the credit union managers are involved in the design of savings products that enabled credit unions to respond better to the needs of their members. Often the conceptualization of credit union products mirrors informal savings mechanisms in communities, with members being able to save small amounts with people they trust. This has led Schreiner (2001, 637) to recognize that 'informal finance offers a mine of lessons to inform the design of microfinance'.

Our study also found evidence of convenience in terms of accessibility and flexibility, a characteristic that other studies stress as the most valued feature of savings products (Collard and Smith 2006). Apart from small initial fees and a £1 share to become a member, minimum deposits were not required and minimum account balances above the £1 share did not need to be maintained, thus enabling members to save small amounts.

In terms of delivery mechanisms, credit unions' savings products mirror elements of economic psychology and behavioural economics by offering deposit-side commitment mechanisms, which 'work by helping individuals make regular deposits into a savings account', and withdrawal-side commitment mechanisms, which 'work by deterring withdrawals' (Ashraf *et al.* 2003, 6). The credit union managers we interviewed noted that withdrawal policies should determine the right mix between those who might need the money quickly in case of unexpected events and those who are 'self-aware enough to feel that the money will be safer from their future self' (Ashraf *et al.* 2003, 6).

Some deposit-side features include 'automated transfers from one financial asset to another' (e.g. direct payment by standing order/direct debit, deposits from state benefits), defined as a 'nonbinding commitment device' since the transfers can be stopped at any time (Ashraf *et al.* 2003, 6). Similarly, payroll deductions automatically move money from wages into a savings account, thus eliminating the 'temptations to spend that money…, and the participant no longer has to make, on a monthly or biweekly basis, a conscious decision to postpone consumption' (Beverly and Sherraden 1999, 465).

In addition, all credit unions organize deposit collection sessions at which members can pay their weekly or monthly savings instalments or loan repayments. These are located in convenient local shops or in community centres, churches, or other community locations. There is also growing use of the Paypoint electronic deposit system in which people can pay into a credit union through local shops, garages, and other retail outlets. Collard *et al.* (2003, 22) suggest that 'regular meetings, to which members can bring their savings … provides not only a routine to saving, but also a degree of peer pressure to encourage members to save'.

In terms of withdrawal-side features, credit unions offer labelled or targeted savings accounts, which are characterized by restricted withdrawals during the year. Indeed, the majority of the credit union respondents in our survey reported that they offered savings products for special occasions such as holiday, birthday, and other special events. Underlying these products, there are mental accounting principles that suggest setting a purpose may strengthen individuals' intentions to carry out a virtuous financial behaviour and 'is helpful in overcoming people's impulsiveness or their tendency to neglect the long term' (de Meza *et al.* 2008, 57). The manager of Unify Credit Union (Wigan) noted:

> I have got one member in mind in particular, who once she started to save with us, then never stopped. Once savings begin to build up, people mentally set a target. That person could not even wait to reach £100 in her savings and even though she could have taken the savings out for Christmas shopping, she did not do that. People like to see their savings building up, to keep them intact. That particular woman reached £1000 over a period of years by just putting away only £5 at a time, just gradually. I love the savings part of the credit union.[12]

In line with this observation, research findings show that the majority of saving is undertaken for specific reasons, and consequently people save separately for different needs (Dolphin 2009; Kempson and Finney 2009).

The credit unions surveyed offer savings that can be withdrawn without the payment of withdrawal fees, which can potentially have negative effects since withdrawal fees provide incentives for keeping money in savings accounts and serve as deterrents to making incautious withdrawals (Ashraf *et al.* 2003).

In addition, delayed withdrawals can help individuals to postpone their consumption decisions and 'to avoid the temptation to spend funds on purchases they will later regret' (Ashraf *et al.* 2003, 10). In the case of many credit unions, for example, withdrawals of savings are often prohibited or limited when a member's loan balance is higher than the savings balance. Savings cannot be withdrawn until the loan is repaid, a mechanism regarded by many credit unions as helpful for people who otherwise would not have been able to do so.

Figure 9.1 shows that the savings products offered by credit unions are characterized by more deposit-side than withdrawal-side features. As argued by the manager of Bristol Credit Union, the main incentive that credit unions provide for saving is 'to make it easy'.[13]

The connection between savings and other financial products

Alongside the incentives to save provided by product design, two-thirds of our survey's respondents said that they offered complementary services to support savings. For example, almost half of credit unions offer saving alongside (or following) loan repayment. As Blake and de Jong (2008, 94) observe, 'Credit unions have a strong model here, because they encourage borrowers to save as they repay their loan, and continue saving once the loan is paid off'. Consequently, a strengthening of the saving habit occurs and members are likely to need to borrow less in the future.

In our survey, several credit unions offer additional services at preferential rate for savers, such as good savings records as criteria for assessing borrowing at lower interest rates. Research carried out by Collard and Smith (2006) shows that among the main reasons for saving within a credit union, the ability 'to borrow' was the second most common, mentioned by 39 per cent of the members ($n = 1,473$). Of course, as noted by the Consultative Group to Assist the Poorest (1998, [2]) 'there may be a trade-off between the lower financial

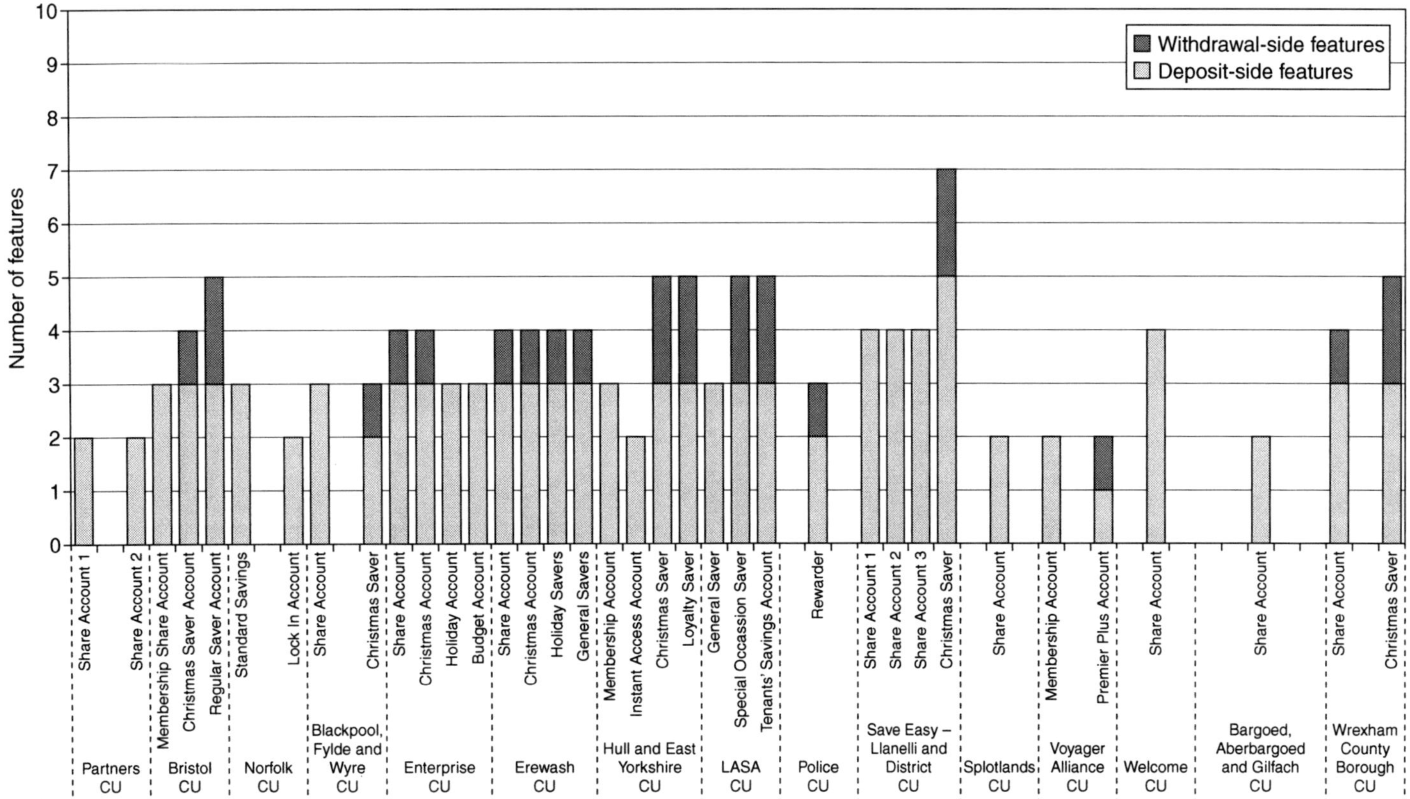

Figure 9.1 Withdrawal-side and deposit-side features of credit unions' savings products (source: authors' survey).

Note

The account types of each credit union (CU) were evaluated in terms of five withdrawal-side and five deposit-side features.

costs and the relatively high costs of mobilizing and administering small deposits'.

Furthermore, findings show that members with high levels of savings tend to take out larger amounts of loans than those with lower savings. There are three main reasons for this: large pools of savings enable credit unions to offer larger loans; those members who have been able to build up savings are regarded as 'loyal members and as good risks'; and 'families with high income ... tend both to build up savings more quickly than their poorer fellow members, and ... also want to borrow in larger amounts' (Berthoud and Hinton 1989, 98–9).

Moreover, the attachment of a savings vehicle to a credit union current account (CUCA) is regarded as an important incentive to save. According to Jones (2008b), access to loans and savings accounts is one of the features of CUCAs that members in his research sample most valued. Specifically, these additional services were felt as important because they enable members to have all their finance services in one place. CUCAs are thus seen as assisting people to save. However, in March 2010 there were only 24 credit unions in total offering CUCAs—about 8 per cent of the members of Association of British Credit Unions Limited (ABCUL) and 5 per cent of all British credit unions (ABCUL 2010). In explaining the value of the CUCA, the manager of South Tyneside Credit Union (South Shields) observed: 'We hoped that it would help people, for instance, transferring money by standing order across into the savings account. Then it would become a regular standing order that would increase the savings habit'.[14]

In addition to savings accounts, all credit unions provide free life savings insurance. ABCUL (2011) claims that, 'On the death of a member savings can be doubled by the insurance and paid to whoever the member chooses', depending on the age of the member at death. This is a product that no other financial intermediary is currently able to offer.

Conclusion

A range of studies have been carried out into various aspects of credit union management and organization, many of which have focused on the delivery of affordable credit, particularly in relation to the eradication of financial exclusion. This chapter has analysed the importance of savings maximization, which is a win-win strategy for credit unions, which benefit from enhanced long-term economic stability, and for their low-income members, who are assisted through saving to progress towards greater financial inclusion (Jones 2004). If traditionally members saved only in order to borrow, this chapter has promoted the idea of saving in order to save.

As a first step in this direction, we have shown that the innovative savings mechanisms employed by credit unions are quite important in promoting saving in low-income communities. In particular, the linking of savings policies and initiatives to financial capability interventions has been central to the way in which credit unions have tackled financial exclusion. Based on our findings, the following recommendations are offered to suggest how credit unions can strengthen the savings aspect of their businesses.

1. Adopt a centralized internal database system uniform to all credit unions that can analyse data relative to the saving behaviour of their members.
2. Implement joint marketing campaigns by underlining the role of credit unions as 'safe and sound' financial intermediaries in order to attract ethical investors who care about the use of their savings.
3. Develop *formal* financial capability initiatives to complement the informal financial education that takes place in credit unions.
4. With the support of the forthcoming credit union legislation and regulation, create savings products with differentiated interest rates, based on the regularity of savings and the length of time that deposits are held.
5. Particularly in the financial industry, foster partnership working in terms of breadth, depth, and quality of outreach, as specified by Andreoni and Pellizza (2009, 261 and 238).

The adoption of these demand-side and supply-side measures would support those community-based organizations belonging to the microfinance sector that are in a good position to rebuild a savings culture at a grass-roots level.

Notes

1. The target was to focus on a core group of motivated credit unions in order to examine the behaviour, characteristics, and attributes of respondents on critical aspects of the research agenda. The sample comprised four different credit union models based on their common bond; moreover, it represented large, medium, and small credit unions. Results coming from the questionnaires were then discussed with experts in the field and compared with qualitative findings coming from consultations and interviews with key stakeholders in the sector.
2. In a study of low-income households, Dolphin (2009, 17) found that informal savings entail 'a range of savings devices, including Christmas clubs, giving the money to a friend or another family member and jars and tins in the kitchen'.
3. Sherraden (2006) identifies seven institutional variables regarded as key elements of the institutional theory of saving: access, information, incentives, facilitation, expectations, restrictions, and security. These drivers emerged from applied research into Individual Development Accounts in the US.
4. The 2010 Conservative-led coalition government decided not to roll out the Savings Gateway nationally and phased out the Child Trust Fund as part of a series of money-saving cuts.
5. Interview conducted by A. Marchesini, 12 December 2009, Lodge Lane and District Credit Union, Head Office, Liverpool. The process of bank branch closures that took place during the late 1980s across the UK has been called 'financial desertification' (Thrift and Leyshon 1997).
6. Interview conducted by A. Marchesini, 26 January 2010, Unify Credit Union, Head Office, Wigan.
7. Interview conducted by A. Marchesini, 12 December 2009, Lodge Lane and District Credit Union, Head Office, Liverpool.

8 Interview conducted by A. Marchesini, 26 January 2010, Unify Credit Union, Head Office, Wigan.
9 Interview conducted by A. Marchesini, 5 February 2010, TEDCO Business Centre, South Shields, Tyne and Wear.
10 Interview conducted by A. Marchesini, 26 January 2010, Unify Credit Union, Head Office, Wigan.
11 Often 'a community outreach worker is employed, whose role is to establish relationships with other organizations in the local area and thus to raise awareness of the credit union in the community'. Interview conducted by A. Marchesini, 14 December 2009, Partners Credit Union, Head Office, Liverpool.
12 Interview conducted by A. Marchesini, 26 January 2010, Unify Credit Union, Head Office, Wigan.
13 Interview conducted by A. Marchesini, 28 January 2010, Bristol Credit Union, Head Office, Bristol.
14 Interview conducted by A. Marchesini, 5 February 2010, TEDCO Business Centre, South Shields, Tyne and Wear.

References

Andreoni, A. and Pellizza, V. (2009) *Microfinanza: dare credito alle relazioni*, Bologna: Il Mulino.

ABCUL (2010) 'Facts and statistics', Manchester, UK: Association of British Credit Unions Limited. Online. Available at: www.abcul.org/media-and-research/facts-statistics (accessed 10 September 2011).

ABCUL (2011) 'Mutual and ethical savings', Manchester, UK: Association of British Credit Unions Limited. Online. Available at: www.abcul.coop/credit-unions/saving-with-a-credit-union (accessed 15 September 2011).

Ashraf, N., Gons, N., Karlan, D.S., and Yin, W. (2003) 'A review of commitment savings products in developing countries', ERD Working no. 45, Economics and Research Department, Asian Development Bank.

Atkinson, A., McKay, S., Kempson, S., and Collard, S. (2006) *Levels of Financial Capability in the UK: results of a baseline survey*, Consumer Research no. 47, London: Financial Services Authority.

Berry, S., Williams, R., and Waldron, M.(2009) 'Household Saving', *Bank of England Quarterly Bulletin* 2009(Q3): 191–201.

Berthoud, R. and Hinton, T. (1989) *Credit Unions in the United Kingdom*, London: Policy Studies Institute, University of Westminster.

Beverly, S.G. and Sherraden, M. (1999) 'Institutional determinants of saving: implications for low-income households and public policy', *Journal of Socio-Economics*, 28(4): 457–73.

Blake, S. and de Jong, E. (2008) *Short Changed: financial exclusion—a guide for donors and funders*, London: New Philanthropy Capital.

Blond, P. and Gruescu, S. (2010) 'Asset building for children: creating a new civic savings platform for young people', Newland: Respublica Policy. Online. Available at: www.respublica.org.uk/documents/cqg_ABC.pdf (accessed 25 September 2011).

Bowles, S. (1998) 'Endogenous preferences: the cultural consequences of markets and other economic institutions', *Journal of Economic Literature*, 36(1): 75–111.

Branch, B. and Baker, C. (2000) 'Overcoming credit union governance problems', in G.D. Wesley and B. Branch (eds) *Safe Money: building effective credit unions in Latin America*, New York: Inter-American Development Bank and World Council of Credit Unions, pp. 203–26.

Branch, B. and Klaehn, J. (2002) 'The keys to striking the balance: an introduction to savings mobilization', in B. Branch and J. Klaehn (eds) *Striking the Balance in Microfinance: a practical guide to mobilizing savings*, Washington, DC: Pact Publications for the World Council of Credit Unions, pp. 1–28. Online. Available at: www.woccu.org/publications/savings (accessed 20 September 2011).

Clancy, M., Grinstein-Weiss, M., and Schreiner, M. (2001) 'Financial Education and Savings Outcomes in Individual Development Accounts', St. Louis: Center for Social Development, Washington University in St. Louis. Online. Available at: http://129.3.20.41/eps/hew/papers/0108/0108001.pdf (accessed 28 August 2011).

Collard, S. and Smith, N. (2006) 'Membership counts: who uses credit unions?', Personal Finance Research Centre, University of Bristol.

Collard, S., Kempson, S., and Dominy, N. (2003) 'Promoting financial inclusion: an assessment of initiatives using a community select committee approach', Bristol: Policy Press.

Consultative Group to Assist the Poorest (1998) 'Saving mobilisation strategies: lessons from four experiences', *Focus* no. 13, August. Online. Available at: www.cgap.org/gm/document-1.9.2558/FN13.pdf (accessed 29 August 2011).

Cooper, N. (2004), 'The myth of easy money: developing financial services that would really help', in D. Darton (ed.) *The Right Use of Money*, Bristol: Policy Press, pp. 123–31.

Coote, A. (2010) 'Ten big questions about the Big Society', London: New Economics Foundation. Online. Available at: www.neweconomics.org/sites/neweconomics.org/files/Ten_Big_Questions_about_the_Big_Society.pdf (accessed 15 September 2011).

de Meza, D., Irlenbusch, B., and Reyniers, D. (2008) *Financial Capability:a behavioral economics perspective*, Consumer Research no. 69, London: Financial Services Authority.

Daffin, C. (ed.) (2009) *Wealth in Great Britain: main results from the wealth and assets survey, 2006/08*, Newport, UK: Office for National Statistics. Online. Available at: www.bristol.ac.uk/geography/research/pfrc/themes/psa/pfrc0914.pdf (accessed 15 September 2011).

Department for Work and Pensions (UK) (2011) *Family Resources Survey: United Kingdom, 2009–10*, London: Department for Work and Pensions. Online. Available at: http://research.dwp.gov.uk/asd/frs/2009_10/frs_2009_10_report.pdf (accessed 25 September 2011).

Dolphin, T. (2009) 'Saving and asset-building in low-income households', London: Institute for Public Policy Research. Online. Available at: www.ippr.org/images/media/files/publication/2011/05/saving_and_asset_building_1746.pdf (accessed 14 September 2011).

Durán, C.R. (2002) 'Saving and asset-building in low income groups in Mexico'. Paper prepared for IDA Learning Conference 'International Perspectives on Asset Building' in Windsor, Ontario, Canada, 4–6 April.

Emmerson, C. and Wakefield, M. (2001) 'The Saving Gateway and the Child Trust Fund: is Asset-based welfare "well fair"?', Commentary no. 85, London: Institute for Fiscal Studies.

Evans, R. and Broome, R. (2005) 'Financial nous and the cycle of deprivation: what role can credit unions play?', *Business Law Review* 26(10): 231–5.

Finney, A. and Kempson, E. (2009) 'Regression analysis of the unbanked using the 2006–07 Family Resources Survey', Bristol: Personal Finance Research Centre, University of Bristol.

Gamble, A. and Prabhakar, R. (2005) 'Assets and poverty'. Online. Available at: www.spckingston.ca/Resources/Assets_and_Poverty_article.pdf (assessed 29 August 2011).
Grody, A.D., Grody, D., Kromann, E., and Sutliff, J. (2008) 'A financial literacy and financial services program for elementary school grades: results of a pilot study', 12 May 2008. Online. Available at: http://ssrn.com/abstract=1132388 (accessed 29 August 2011).
HM Treasury (2007) 'Financial Capability: the Government's long-term approach', January 2007, London: Her Majesty's Stationery Office. Online. Available at: http://webarchive.nationalarchives.gov.uk/+/http:/www.hm-treasury.gov.uk/d/fincap_150107.pdf (accessed 25 September 2011).
Jones, P.A. (2004) 'Changing British credit unions: learning lessons from Latin America', in: S. Karafolas, R. Spear, and Y. Stryjan (eds) *Local Society and Global Economy: the role of cooperatives*, Peristeri, Greece: Editions Hellin, pp. 69–94.
Jones, P.A. (2005) 'Philanthropy and enterprise in the British credit union movement', *Economic Affairs* 25(2): 13–19.
Jones, P.A. (2006) 'Giving credit where it's due: promoting financial inclusion through quality credit unions', *Local Economy*, 21(1): 36–48.
Jones, P.A. (2008a) 'From tackling poverty to achieving financial inclusion: the changing role of British credit unions in low income communities', *Journal of Socio-Economics*, 37(6): 2141–54.
Jones, P.A. (2008b) *Breaking Through to the Future: the strategic development of credit unions in Britain, 1998–2008*, Liverpool: Faculty of Health and Applied Social Sciences, Liverpool John Moores University.
Jones, P.A. (2010) 'Supporting personal finance education in primary schools on Merseyside. An investigation into the impact of a Citizens Advice Bureau project aimed at supporting the development of personal finance education in primary schools in St. Helens and Liverpool', Liverpool John Moores University, Citizens Advice Bureau, J.P. Morgan. Online. Available at: www.ljmu.ac.uk/Faculties/HEA/HEA_docs/CAB_and_Primary_Schools_Report_13_September_2010.pdf (accessed 28 October 2011).
Kelly, G. and Lissauer, R. (2000) 'Ownership for all', London: Institute for Public Policy Research.
Kempson, E., McKay, S., and Collard, S. (2005) 'Incentives to save: encouraging saving among low-income households', Bristol: Personal Finance Research Centre, University of Bristol.
Kempson, E. and Finney, A. (2009) 'Saving in lower-income households: a review of the evidence', Bristol: Personal Finance Research Centre, University of Bristol.
Lusardi, A. and Mitchell, O.S. (2009) 'How ordinary consumers make complex economic decisions: financial literacy and retirement readiness', NBER Working Paper no. 15350, Cambridge, MA:.Mational bureau of Economic Research.
McArthur, A., McGregor, A., and Stewart, R. (1993) 'Credit unions and low-income communities', *Urban Studies*, 30(2): 399–416.
National Audit Office (UK) (2010) 'Helping over-indebted consumers', Report by the Comptroller and Auditor General, Report no. HC 292, Session 2009–10, London: Stationery Office.
OECD (2003) 'Asset building and the escape from poverty: a new welfare policy debate', Organisation for Economic Co-operation and Development. Online. Available at: http://browse.oecdbookshop.org/oecd/pdfs/free/8403051e.pdf (accessed 28 August 2011).
Prabhakar, R. (2009a) 'The Assets Agenda and Social Policy', *Journal of Social Policy & Administration*, 43(1): 54–69.

Prabhakar, R. (2009b) 'What is the future for asset-based welfare?', London: Institute for Public Policy Research.

Schreiner, M. (2001) 'Informal finance and the design of microfinance', *Development in Practice*, 11(5): 637–40.

Sherraden, M.W. (1991) *Assets and the Poor: a new American welfare policy*, Armonk, NY: M.E. Sharpe.

Sherraden, M.W. (2002) 'From a social welfare state to a social investment state', in C. Kober and W. Paxton (eds) *Asset-based Welfare and Poverty: exploring the case for and against asset-based welfare policies*. London: National Children's Bureau Enterprises, pp. 5–8.

Sherraden, M.W. (2006) 'Schemes to boost small savings: lessons and directions', paper presented at conference 'Access to Finance: building inclusive financial systems', World Bank, Washington DC, 30–31 May 2006.

Sherraden, M. and Schreiner, M. (2007) *Can the Poor Save? Saving and asset building in individual development accounts*, Piscataway, NJ: Transaction Publishers.

Sodha, S. and Lister, R. (2006) 'The saving gateway: from principles to practice', London: Institute for Public Policy Research.

Taylor, M., Jenkins, F., and Sacker, A. (2009) *Financial Capability and Wellbeing: evidence from the BHPS*, Occasional Paper Series no. 34, London: Financial Services Authority.

Thiel, V. and Nissan, S. (2009) 'The impact of the economic crisis on asset-building in Europe: using opportunities and creating resilience', London: New Economics Foundation.

Thrift, N. and Leyshon, A. (1997) 'Financial desertification', in J. Rossiter (ed.), 'Financial exclusion; can mutuality fill the gap?' London: New Policy Institute and UK Social Investment Forum, pp. 7–11.

10 Microfinance and poverty reduction in Bangladesh

Challenges and opportunities

Mokbul Morshed Ahmad

Microfinance is the term broadly used to refer to very small-sized, supervised loans, without any collateral. This chapter assesses how microfinance serves the poor in Bangladesh. In the last several decades, there have been many government and non-governmental efforts to reduce poverty. The Bangladesh Rural Development Board as the major government agency has undertaken a series of rural development programmes that aim to reduce poverty through village-based cooperatives, human resource development, expanded irrigation schemes, improvements in physical infrastructure, increases in agricultural production, and creation of employment opportunities for the rural poor. Some of the poverty alleviation programmes implemented by the government have been the establishment of cluster villages, the institutionalization of the Vulnerable Group Development project, implementation of the Upazila/Thana Resource Development and Employment Project, skill development training, and assistance for self-employment.

In addition, there are some traditional but less focused programmes of poverty alleviation in the country. These are Food for Work programme, Food for Education, Pension for Elderly People, Housing for the Poor and Homeless, and a programme of providing insecticides and high-yield varieties of seeds to rural farmers. The government has undertaken development initiatives to expand the area of non-agricultural activities in order to create more employment opportunities. All these programmes have increased to some extent the poor's social and economic awareness and sense of empowerment. Nevertheless, these programmes have contributed little to improving the poverty situation in the country. Consequently, poverty alleviation remains a challenge requiring proper planning and a high level of commitment to implement programmes with skill and integrity.

In 2008, about 50 per cent of the people in Bangladesh were poor according to a US$1.25 a day poverty line, and about 81 per cent of the people lived below US$2.00 a day. The percentage of people who are poor according to the national poverty line is 40 per cent (Alkire and Santos 2010). Islam (2007) found that most Grameen Bank members, especially the extremely poor, could not alleviate their own poverty.

There are probably more non-governmental organizations (NGOs) operating in Bangladesh than in any other country of comparative size. The target-group approach has allowed NGOs in Bangladesh to work successfully with the rural poor and provide inputs to a constituency generally neglected by the state. This approach emphasizes the centrality of landlessness in 'development' strategies, and focuses on the needs of landless women in developing programmes. Another innovation by NGOs in Bangladesh has been the prioritization of non-land-based sources of income generation for the poor, an approach that has been substantially neglected by the state. In particular, these income-generating activities are important for the survival strategies of poor women, whether they are part of male- or female-headed households. This innovation has led to a concentration of efforts in small-scale, home-based income-generating activities such as cattle and poultry rearing, food processing, social forestry, apiculture, and rural handicrafts. The development of these activities has been facilitated by the provision of microcredit, which the landless had previously been denied except by local moneylenders at high interest rates.

Notable among the group-based microfinance and/or non-microfinance programmes are the Bangladeshi NGOs, the Grameen Bank, the Bangladesh Rehabilitation Assistance Committee (BRAC), Association for Social Advancement (ASA), and Proshika. Grameen is the world leader of poverty alleviation through microlending, and the poor borrowers of this bank, who are mostly women, are the main owners of it. In 2010, the borrowers owned 94 per cent of the total equity of the bank, while the Bangladeshi government owned the remaining 6 per cent. Grameen Bank has 7.67 million borrowers and provides services through 2,539 branches, in 83,566 villages, covering about 99 per cent of the total villages in Bangladesh (Microcredit Regulatory Authority 2009).

BRAC was established to help the country overcome the devastation and trauma of the liberation war and initially focused on resettling refugees returning from India. Today, BRAC is an independent, virtually self-financed leader in sustainable human development. It is one of the largest southern NGOs and employs more than 97,000 people, 61 per cent of whom are women, and has 6.37 million borrowers (Microcredit Regulatory Authority 2009). Another large Bangladeshi NGO, Proshika was established in 1976 and currently has two million borrowers spread across 24,139 villages. ASA, which is the largest microfinance institution (MFI) in the world with microlending as its only programme, has 7.13 million clients in 72,204 villages (Islam 2007; Microcredit Regulatory Authority 2009).

The rural credit delivery system in Bangladesh was long dominated by traditional or informal moneylenders, who in the 1990s accounted for about two-thirds of credit delivered in rural areas (Ahmad, 2007). However, increased participation by NGOs and MFIs in the rural credit market has substantially increased the volume of institutional credit in the rural areas of Bangladesh. At present, over 1,000 local and foreign NGOs and MFIs are providing credit to rural people. Despite the fact that the institutional credit has expanded remarkably in the country since the mid-1980s, informal credit continues to remain important in rural areas. Informal credit is easily available, and is therefore more capable of meeting the urgent needs of rural farmers and other poor people.

Informal private credit, however, is exploitative in nature and is often used for unproductive purposes. The dominance of informal credit suppliers continued until institutional sources like loan offices and banks started to evolve in the country. These institutional sources, however, could not eliminate the informal channels since the demand for finance always exceeds the supply from institutional sources. More importantly, most poor borrowers from both rural and urban areas do not have easy access to formal credit sources.

Microfinance in Bangladesh

The amounts of microcredit in Bangladesh vary from Tk.500 to 10,000[1] per client and are provided mainly by MFIs or NGO microfinance programmes but are also supplied by banks and conventional financial institutions. These loans are made to poor people without any assets or with less than half an acre of land on which to undertake employment or other income-generating activities. MFIs develop various tools to provide the poor with financial services so that they can increase their income and productivity. Microcredit programmes aimed at poverty alleviation cover a large number of borrowers with the objective of substantially removing socio-economic imbalances, especially in rural areas.

As of December 2003, 7,207 NGOs and MFIs were involved in microcredit activities in Bangladesh (Credit and Development Forum 2003). There are mainly five different groups involved in the microfinance market: commercial and specialized banks, including four nationalized commercial banks; two private banks; specialized financial institutions such as Bangladesh Krishi Bank, Rajshahi Krishi Unnayan Bank, and Ansar-VDP Unnayan Bank; Grameen Bank; NGOs, government organizations; and cooperative societies. All banks are regulated by the Bangladesh Bank, including the Grameen Bank that the government regulates directly.

The Bangladesh Bank regulates banks according to the Banking Companies Act of 1991. The basic concept of this Act does not fit with the concept of modern day microfinance mainly due to collateral and reserve requirements, capital adequacy, and liquidity provisioning. Therefore, a separate law was enacted to establish and regulate the Grameen Bank. In this sense, the Grameen Bank is a specialized Bank and not an NGO. The success of the group-based financing model of Grameen Bank in Bangladesh has been widely recognized around the world and replicated in more than 45 countries, including the United States. Since its inception and through 2009, the Grameen Bank's cumulative disbursement of microcredit has been about US$8.74 billion. The number of its active members in 2009 was about eight million (Grameen Bank 2011).

NGOs are the major players in the microfinance market in Bangladesh: a rough estimate is that they provide about 60 per cent of the total market (Ahmad 2007). Chahine and Tannir (2010) found that through the transformation of NGOs into MFIs, they reach a wider client base, increase their financial sustainability by enabling cost economies of scale and scope, and improve their capital structure by means of a larger dependence on leveraged financing. However, they also found that the improved financial performance of MFIs comes at a cost of decreased depth in their social outreach. Several reasons have led NGOs to become involved in microfinance.

1 There has been international interest in the Grameen Bank's model of 'development'. The initial success of the model led many donors to accept it as the cure-all for the problem of underdevelopment (Bhatt and Tang 1998; Mosley and Hulme 1998; Montgomery *et al.* 1996; Develtere and Huybrechts 2005; Pitt *et al.* 2006; Hossain and Knight 2008). Nayar and Faisal (1999) found that MFIs demonstrated resilience during the devastating 1998 floods in Bangladesh. However, the replicability of the model has been questioned by some researchers, including Reinke (1998).
2 An important advantage of microcredit programmes is that their 'performance' can easily be measured, which enables NGOs to demonstrate achievements and satisfy their donors. Now that development intervention is driven mainly by 'performance indicators' (McNamara and Morse 1998), this can be a decisive factor.
3 NGOs seek self-reliance and independence from donors. The importance of foreign donations to the NGOs in Bangladesh declined dramatically at the beginning of the 1990s (Microcredit Regulatory Authority 2010). By offering microcredit, NGOs can use the interest paid by their clients to pay some of their staff and other costs. Such charging of clients is one avenue for NGOs to become self-reliant (Edwards 1999; Yaqub 1998; McNamara and Morse 1998; Rutherford 1998; Popham 1998; Abels 1998; Rhyne and Otero 1992). For example, during the 1990s a Bangladeshi quasi-governmental organization lent to NGOs at 4 per cent interest, while NGOs then lent to their clients at interest rates usually ranging from 12 to 16 per cent (Palli Karma-Sahayak Foundation 1998).

Several concerns have been raised about the third tendency. Commercial funding may mean less attention to poor households in microfinance service delivery (Greely 2006). After studying the history of microcredit organizations, Hollis and Sweetman (1998) conclude that depositor-based microcredit organizations tend to last longer and serve many more borrowers than microcredit organizations financed by donations or government loans.

Another option for increased NGO autonomy is to start commercial ventures, such as BRAC's marketing outlet, printing press, and cold storage or Ganoshasthya Kendra's brickfield and pharmaceutical industries. There is growing concern, however, over the involvement of NGOs in such private sector businesses. Many civil society activists believe NGOs are slowly but steadily moving away from their core mission of poverty reduction and into commercial activities. Confusion remains regarding whether an organization is exempt from tax on the surpluses generated by its commercial activities (Sen and Morris 2008).

NGOs can register as non-profit social development organizations under various laws and with several different ministries or departments of the government. Some of these organizations launched microcredit operations from their inception, while others started them sometime later as part of their programmes in, for example, health and education. Thus, there are two types of organizations: those such as ASA that have a clear focus on microcredit operations and those such as BRAC and Proshika that have mixed programmes.

NGOs and MFIs that operate microfinance programmes can be registered under the Societies Registration Act of 1860, the Trust Act of 1882, the Charitable and Religious Trust Act of 1920, the Co-operative Societies Act of 1984, or the Companies Act of 1994. NGOs and MFIs that are interested in receiving donations from foreign sources have to be registered with the NGO Affairs Bureau of Bangladesh under the Foreign Donations (Voluntary Activities) Regulation Ordinance of 1978. However, the government is trying to bring both the microfinancing NGOs and MFIs under the regulation of the Bangladesh Bank, and as part of this effort the Bangladesh Bank created a separate unit to formulate a draft regulatory framework for microfinance NGOs and MFIs.

To understand how NGOs have engaged in microfinance, it is important to know the history of NGOs in Bangladesh. NGOs have operated in Bangladesh since independence was obtained in 1971. BRAC started its operations in 1972 by providing relief and rehabilitation services following the war of liberation. ASA was established in 1978 and started a microcredit programme in 1992. Proshika was founded in 1976 and began its microcredit operations later. Similarly, many NGOs started their microcredit programmes sometime after their other operations.

In Bangladesh, the institutional concentration ratio is highly skewed in favour of large MFIs—only 8 per cent of them dominate 80 per cent of the market. The microcredit industry is growing fast, and as of June 2009 its number of clients surpassed the 30 million mark, of which 24.48 million were borrowers. In December 2004, the number of clients was 14.4 million and the number of borrowers was 11.14 million, indicating that there was more than a 20 per cent average annual increase in outreach in the period up to 2009. Strikingly, about 90 per cent of the current clients and borrowers are women (Microcredit Regulatory Authority 2010). The amount of overdue loans of four large MFIs rose from 4.74 per cent in June 2005 to 5.0 per cent in June 2008. While governance and operational problems in one of the three giant microfinance NGOs—Proshika—have not caused a collapse of the whole microfinance system, a very high share of 63 per cent of the market in microcredit and 54 per cent in micro savings by the other two large microfinance NGOs may pose potential systemic risk. Domination of the market by the big MFIs has increased over the years, which may have created an imperfect market condition. At the end of 2008, the average loan per borrower was at $80, while savings per member stood at $21. MFIs have generated direct employment for over 100,000 people (Microcredit Regulatory Authority 2010).

There are today more than 7,000 NGOs and MFIs that have microfinance operations in Bangladesh. This substantial increase of NGOs and MFIs has attracted the attention of policymakers and triggered increased regulation and supervision of the industry. Savings from the members are built into the system of microcredit operation. At the initial stage, it was compulsory to save and in some cases clients or groups could not borrow until a certain threshold of savings was reached by a group or its members. As they have developed, MFIs have developed new products. Many types of savings and credit programmes, some of which include insurance policies, are now offered by NGOs and MFIs to target groups in this new segment of financial market.

There are several issues concerning the financial product delivered by microfinance NGOs. For example, how is membership defined? According to current practices, members of microfinance NGOs are beneficiaries or clients, and hence they are not members in the same sense as in cooperatives or the Grameen Bank, the members of which own shares in the institutions. Should microfinance NGOs be permitted to collect and provide savings and insurance services? Do they have sufficient organizational arrangements and capacity to manage these services? Should they be permitted to use these savings for purposes other than providing microcredit? How will these savings be protected? Is the system flexible enough to permit savers to use their money when they need it? How will the savers' expected returns be insured? These issues raise questions regarding the regulation and supervision of this industry that have become more urgent since donors started reducing funding and subsidies for the microfinance NGOs.

Initially, microfinance operations in Bangladesh started with the active support of donors, and during that time the lion's share of the Revolving Loan Fund (RLF) came through donors' channels. But this funding has decreased over time. Before 1996, donors contributed more than 50 per cent into the RLF, but this amount dropped to 11.5 per cent in 2006. It is assumed that the direct contribution by the donors to the RLF may vanish in the future. On the other hand, members' savings and service charges are emerging as two important internal sources of funds, which together contribute about 60 per cent to the RLF (Ahmad 2007). Therefore, strategies for tapping local funds are one of the emerging issues for the industry, though it also raises legal issues.

There are other issues involving the regulation and supervision of MFIs that have been highlighted by the emergence of microfinance services as an important financial instrument for poor Bangladeshis that remain outside of the formal financial system:

- minimizing mismanagement of funds by ensuring proper methods of financial disclosure;
- establishing good governance by providing guidelines;
- developing uniform accounting and monitoring systems;
- establishing effective rating systems to identify well-performing institutions;
- linking microfinance NGOs with the formal financial market;
- bringing microfinance NGOs under a single supervisorial authority;
- building a solid legal foundation to operate in the rural financial market.

Another issue for NGOs and MFIs is transaction costs. Identification and selection of target borrowers and the activity of maintaining a high loan recovery rate are costly. Group lending, for example, involves social intermediation, including group formation, training, and other non-credit activities. These activities are necessary to create a sense of responsibility in individual borrowers. Because of such high transaction costs, many microfinance programmes are dependent on subsidized resources.

Supervision of Microfinance Institutions

The Palli Karma-Sahayak ('Rural Employment') Foundation was established by the Bangladeshi government in 1990 to help build and strengthen the institutional capacity of organizations that serve the poor. This foundation plays an important role not only by dispersing funds to partner microfinance organizations, but also by coordinating and helping to implement development programmes around the country.

In 2000, the Bangladesh government created the Microfinance Research and Reference Unit (MRRU) in the Bangladesh Bank to develop a regulatory framework, including uniform policies, monitoring systems, and performance standards. A national steering committee is chaired by the Governor of the Bangladesh Bank and includes members that represent the public sector and private practitioners involved with microfinance. The Terms of Reference for the MRRU were to formulate policy guidelines to regulate microfinance NGOs and MFIs and to set performance standards to ensure their qualitative improvement. It also provides training to the microfinance NGOs on the guidelines, and more than 500 institutions have received training from the MRRU. It also worked to update the list of microfinance NGOs operating in Bangladesh. The Steering Committee of the MRRU prepared a draft law, which needs to be passed by the Parliament. It is expected that after the promulgation of this new law microfinance NGOs will be under a single regulatory system or authority. To get a license to work as an MFI from the MRRU, the NGO must have either outstanding loans of Tk.4 million or a membership of 1,000 clients. In 2006, the MRRU was transformed into the Microcredit Regulatory Authority (2010).

The Bangladesh Bank fully recognizes the importance of microfinance in the overall economy of the country, but it is not yet involved directly with the development of this sector. Its role has been mainly in the regulation, supervision, and orderly development of the formal financial system as well as the promotion of poverty-related lending by specialized agricultural banks and the nationalized commercial banks. The Bangladesh Bank has also supervised Grameen Bank since 1997, although the supervisory arrangement differs from that applicable to commercial banks.

The Bangladesh Bank played a direct role in the development of Grameen Bank. It provided technical support to the Grameen Project at the early stages and supplied soft loans to the Grameen Bank during its initial period. Currently it is channelling support through the banking system by establishing linkages with microfinance NGOs. In addition, the Grameen Bank is currently providing financial and technical support to the Microcredit Regulatory Authority for collecting information, preparing guidelines, providing training to microfinance NGOs, analysing data, and making policies for this sector.

The Bangladesh Bank has given special attention to poverty alleviation programmes. It has instructed all commercial banks to maintain special allocations of loan funds for poverty alleviation programmes. It has also encouraged banks to provide loans to borrowers based on their creditworthiness instead of collateral. Fisheries, livestock, and other small business have been considered special privileged sectors for getting these credit funds. The bank continuously monitors the real disbursement by the banking system for this sector. The bank also acts as an implementing agency for different donors and government supported programmes for poverty alleviation and operates different refinance schemes for small enterprise development, including agro-processing industries and crop production.

Current issues

Although microfinance in Bangladesh has had many successes, some problems have also emerged.[2] The impact of microfinance on poverty has been rather minimal, as discussed above.[3] Bangladesh is also a particular case due to its high population density, the significant outreach achieved by NGOs and MFIs in the country, and the examples set by the Grameen Bank, BRAC, and ASA—organizations considered by many to be flagships of the microfinance industry worldwide.

The foremost problem for all microfinance NGOs and MFIs in Bangladesh is dropouts, due to the cost of recruiting and training new members or clients to replace them. Because of the cost of making the first small loan to new clients, lending usually does not become profitable in many programmes until the third or fourth loan is made to a client. Retention, therefore, is key to profitability and sustainability. Of course, for a client, dropping out may be an advantage if better services are obtained by switching to alternative lender. Little data are available on the rate and causes of dropouts, but the data that do exist suggest that dropout families tend to be smaller, with lower education, and more frequently have participated in other NGO or MFI schemes.

The rigidity of the microlending model, and especially the lack of access to savings in times of emergency, has been identified as an important factor affecting dropouts (Ahmad 2007). The planning and execution of microfinance programmes by NGOs and MFIs have also contributed to the high dropout rate. It is expected that some members will switch to other NGOs or MFIs that have expanded into their areas to escape loan limitations. A sample of dropouts was asked to report their reasons for leaving. The largest number (33 per cent) reported the loan amount was too small, followed by too many meetings (28 per cent), meetings are too long (25 per cent), unwillingness to pay for defaulting members (25 per cent), and loans were too expensive (22 per cent) (Meyer 2002).

Another problem for the microfinance industry in Bangladesh has been exclusion or self-exclusion. Many qualified borrower families in Bangladesh prefer not to participate in microfinance programmes even if they lack access to formal finance. The non-poor account for a larger proportion of the participants. The non-poor also tend to receive larger amounts of credit compared to the poor. Bangladeshi microfinance NGOs and MFIs mostly do not serve the poorest segments of the population, including widows, orphans, the chronically ill, and beggars. These segments of the population are too at risk to participate and sustain debt and members of group lending programmes as well as loan officers discriminate against the very poor due to apprehension that they will not repay on time (Ahmad 2003). The main reason given for not joining was that people felt they did not have enough income to pay back loans and would thus be forced to sell their few belongings in order to repay. Another reason given was that it is hard for some women to leave home to attend obligatory meetings. In a 1997 study, ASA reported on interviews conducted with staff and clients to learn why its programme did not involve many of the poor. The most common responses included a lack of the minimum attire necessary to go to meetings, warnings and intimidation from the local elite, and age requirements that restrict participation. By setting a relatively low maximum age requirement, ASA effectively excluded old people who are often poor (Ahmad 2007).

A further problem is delinquencies and defaults. These arise when borrowers are unable to repay and when borrowers do not value access to additional services to maintain an affiliation with an NGO or MFI. It is difficult to get a clear picture of loan delinquency and default rates in Bangladesh by consulting microfinance reports because some NGOs and MFIs use reporting definitions that are lenient by international standards, such as not classifying loans as overdue until one year after the final instalment falls unpaid.

A final problem is multiple memberships. Most NGOs and MFIs in Bangladesh forbid members from belonging to more than one organization at a time, yet multiple or overlapping memberships clearly exist. There is little data available on this issue for individuals, let alone for households where members may participate in different microfinance schemes. Wright (2000) reports that multiple memberships can be as high as 40 to 50 per cent in areas where many microfinance NGOs and MFIs are operating. One cause of over-borrowing is that members borrow from one microfinance supplier to repay another. Another reason is the inflexibility of some NGOs and MFIs, which forces some clients to work with several organizations simultaneously to meet their credit needs. Moreover, if credit ceilings are low and all group members receive the same size loans, active borrowers may need to borrow from several NGOs and MFIs to get the total sum they need to support their activities. Multiple memberships can also take place when people shop around prior to switching from one NGO or MFI to another to get better services.

Future challenges

Several studies have shown that microborrowers have generally remained tied to rudimentary trading, manufacturing, and other economic activities regardless of the length of time they have been microborrowing. It appears that the repeated use of microcredit often becomes the lifeline for microborrowers to remain in business. Therefore, the overall socio-economic impact of microcredit is marginal (Ahmad 2007). Obviously, some microborrowers have benefited to an extent, but many others have experienced deterioration in certain respects. Regarding the debt burden, the microborrowing process seems to become self-perpetuating for most clients of MFIs. It has been found that while they pay base interest rates between 10 and 15 per cent (in some cases up to 18 per cent), the effective rate of interest and the effective cost of borrowing are as high as 27 and 31 per cent for Grameen Bank, and even higher for microfinance NGOS—between 39 and 41 per cent for Proshika and between 42 and 45 per cent for both BRAC and ASA (Ahmad 2007).

There are still some significant issues concerning microfinance that need to be addressed by the policymakers. One of these is the mode of regulation, which means whether all microfinance NGOs, including very small ones, should be under prudential regulation. The question is whether organizations that do not collect any forms of savings should be under prudential or non-prudential regulation. Another issue is the type of regulation: should all MFIs regardless of their size come under the same system right away or should the large microfinance NGOs be required to go first? Moreover, it has to be determined whether the regulations and procedures for supervising and monitoring banks are suitable for specialized microfinance institutions. Microfinance NGOs mainly serve people in rural areas that are difficult to reach, so the questions is whether these organizations' non-traditional methods can be suitably regulated and monitored with conventional approaches. Moreover, supervision and monitoring involve substantial costs, and the question is who will bear these. Thus, another issue is how to develop cost effective techniques of supervision.

The idea of establishing more microfinance banks like Grameen Bank is one of the major emerging issues in the discussion of microfinance. How are they to be established and managed? What kinds of services are expected from these newly developed institutions from both the supply and demand sides? Last, but not least, who will be the regulator of this sector? All these issues are under discussion by policymakers in Bangladesh. They will not be solved in a day, since solving one question will surely raise others. Analysing the issues, raising questions, and conducting experiments over time should help develop the sector in a sustainable manner.

Policy issues

NGOs and MFIs in Bangladesh must embark on a second phase of microlending with improved financial policies and products to meet client demands and preferences. Indeed, some NGOs and MFIs are already experimenting along these lines. The microfinance industry in Bangladesh also needs to learn from the experiences of countries that are more sophisticated in solving financial issues.

First, flexibility is needed in repayment schedules. The 12-month group loan made to poor women with weekly instalments and little or no grace period is the only microfinancing product offered by most NGOs and MFIs. The benefit of this product is that it is straightforward for clients to understand, for loan officers to issue, and for NGOs and MFIs to control using manual bookkeeping systems. Weekly meetings provide loan officers the opportunity to monitor clients and accumulate loan instalments and savings deposits. However, many clients do not have enterprises that produce a regular steam of income that precisely matches this weekly repayment schedule. They have to make loan instalments out of normal family income derived from other sources when income is not available from investments financed by their loans. For example, those with considerable agricultural income would be better served by seasonal loans. Even borrowers greatly motivated to repay occasionally become delinquent because of emergencies, unforeseen difficulties, and shortfalls in income. Adjustments are needed in their repayment schedules, including extensions for those who lack short-term liquidity to recommence normal payments and formal loan rescheduling for those who are expected to face major long-term repayment problems. Generally speaking, the MFIs that provide emergency grants, rescheduling, or subsidized food maintain rigid repayment structures. Indeed, one study has found that many farmers think that MFIs take advantage of seasonal food shortages between the two annual rice harvests to further drive farmers into indebtedness (Cons and Paprocki 2010). Those who experience major disasters need help and new funds to resume income-generating activities.[4]

Second, flexibility is needed in the sizes of loans; indeed, this is perhaps the single most important change that would be attractive to both existing and potential borrowers. Some potential clients would borrow if they could get smaller loans while some active clients with good repayment capacities would not drop out or incur the costs of multiple memberships if they could borrow larger amounts than permitted in the typical programme. Group meetings would then be used primarily as a method to reduce the cost of collecting savings and loan payments rather than to exert peer pressure on clients, although group leaders would still be involved in assisting with collections from overdue borrowers. Weekly meetings could also be discontinued entirely by some MFI loan officers for their long-term clients who organize informal collectors to assemble payments and passbooks for weekly collection and recording of payments by loan officers. Group meetings may have useful externalities for women borrowers as it gives them opportunities to leave their homes and learn from other entrepreneurs, but meetings represent high transaction costs for many borrowers and there is little evidence that useful training occurs in these meetings after the initial training period.

Third, the Bangladesh microfinance sector needs new product lines. The 1998 flood in Bangladesh revealed the weaknesses of NGO and MFI savings programmes for clients in times of emergency. At the time, most NGOs and MFIs required small amounts of compulsory savings so the accumulated balances were usually too small to cover the losses experienced by clients. Moreover, when Grameen, BRAC, and smaller NGOs and MFIs allowed clients access to their compulsory savings during the emergency, they struggled to meet the demand for funds. Grameen, for example, reported that 95 per cent of the affected clients' compulsory savings were withdrawn in the four months that access was permitted. However, if there was only one simple 'collector' per village, then meaningful and less-costly intermediation might prove to be possible. At the same time, it would minimize social intermediation costs for such types of transactions, it would lower the interest rates charged, it would create synergies and economies of scope, and it would facilitate the launching of innovative products.

Insurance is one such product that may appeal to the poor, and it is now being introduced by NGOs and MFIs. It is still in the early stages of development and is often subsidized. INAFI Bangladesh is now conducting a survey and identified several NGOs and MFIs offering insurance. By making the coverage mandatory, the insurance is cheaper to provide and reduces loan defaults and collection costs. The problem up to now has been that clients perceive that insurance is designed largely to protect the portfolios of the NGOs and MFIs, so it is considered as just another cost of borrowing (Kono and Takahashi 2010).[5]

Developing new products and institutions requires refocusing on clients, listening to their demands and preferences, and learning about their financial strategies. Understanding client behaviour requires an awareness of the economic goals of poor households, of how poor people manage resources and activities, and how they deal with risk. Microfinance needs to be deeply re-examined, and go beyond fine-tuning the existing approaches. The entire industry must rise above its institutional sluggishness of simply replicating existing models.

Conclusion

This chapter has examined the current situation of microfinance in Bangladesh and speculates about the future. In spite of their large number, very few MFIs have solid institutional arrangements. At a minimal level, such arrangements should include the proper delegation of power, a defined set of business rules, and a chart of duties; the institutional capacity to manage their businesses; and appropriate record-keeping systems. Moreover, policymakers are increasingly asking questions about such MFI practices as charging interest rates without having adequate justification, the utilization of surplus money for various commercial ventures, the collection of deposits like banks without legal authority, and a lack of financial transparency. Dropouts, overlaps, and delinquencies appear to be rising, and many of the poor do not take advantage of NGO and MFI products and continue to borrow from exploitative informal sources. These factors point to the need for redesigning microfinance in Bangladesh. The microfinance industry in Bangladesh should develop new products and policies, but this will be difficult to do since the industry benefits from, and hence prefers to maintain, the status quo.

Notes

1 In December 2010, 1 US$ equalled about 70 Bangladeshi taka (Tk.).
2 For a discussion of microfinance in India, see Young (2010).
3 For a similar argument for Indonesia, see Takahashi *et al.* (2010).
4 For a discussion on the consequences of rescheduling after natural disasters in Bangladesh, see Shoji (2010).
5 For a discussion on micro-insurance in Africa, see Cohen and Sebstad 2005; for health insurance in India, see Ito and Kono (2010).

References

Abels, H. (1998) 'Quality standards for micro-finance institutions', paper presented at the Third INAFI Asian Regional Seminar on Scaling up and Sustained Growth in Micro-Finance, Dhaka, Bangladesh, 28 February to 1 March.

Ahmad, M.M. (2003) 'Distant voices: the views of the field workers of NGOs in Bangladesh on microcredit', *Geographical Journal*, 169(1): 65–74.

Ahmad, Q.K. (2007) *Socio-economic and Indebtedness-related Impact of Micro-credit in Bangladesh*, Dhaka: University Press.

Alkire, S. and Santos, M.E. (2010) 'Bangladesh Country Briefing', Oxford Poverty and Human Development Initiative (OPHI) Multidimensional Poverty Index Country Briefing Series, Oxford: Department of International Development, University of Oxford. Online. Available at: www.ophi.org.uk/policy/multidimensional-poverty-index/mpi-country-briefings/ (accessed 4 September 2011).

Bhatt, N. and Tang, S.-Y. (1998) 'The problem of transaction costs in group-based micro-lending: An institutional perspective', *World Development*, 26(4): 623–37.

Chahine, S. and Tannir, L. (2010) 'On the social and financial effects of the transformation of microfinance NGOs', *Voluntas*, 21(3): 440–61.

Cohen, M. and Sebstad, J. (2005) 'Reducing vulnerability: the demand for microinsurance', *Journal of International Development*, 17(3): 397–474.

Cons, J. and Paprocki, K. (2010) 'Contested credit landscapes: microcredit, self-help and self-determination in rural Bangladesh', *Third World Quarterly*, 31(4): 637–54.

Credit and Development Forum (2003) *CDF Microfinance Statistics*, Dhaka: Credit and Development Forum.

Develtere, P. and Huybrechts, A. (2005) 'The impact of microcredit on the poor in Bangladesh', *Alternatives: Global, Local, Political* 30(2): 165–89.

Edwards, M. (1999) 'NGO performance: what breeds success? New evidence from South Asia', *World Development* 27(2): 361–74.

Grameen Bank (2011) 'Grameen Bank at a Glance'. Online. Available at: www.grameen-info.org/index.php?option=com_content&task=view&id=26&Itemid=175 (accessed 11 November 2011).

Greely, M. (2006) 'Microfinance impact and the MDGs: the challenge of scaling-up', IDS Working Paper no. 255, Brighton: Institute of Development Studies.

Hollis, A. and Sweetman, A. (1998) 'Microcredit: what can we learn from the past?', *World Development* 26(10): 1875–91.

Hossain, F. and Knight, T. (2008) 'Can micro-credit improve the livelihoods of the poor

and disadvantaged? Empirical observations from Bangladesh', *International Development Planning Review*, 30(2): 155–75.
Islam, T. (2007) *Microcredit and Poverty Alleviation*, Aldershot: Ashgate.
Ito, S. and Kono, H. (2010) 'Why is the take-up of microinsurance so low? Evidence from health insurance scheme in India', *Developing* Economies, 48(1): 74–101.
Kono, H. and Takahashi, K. (2010) 'Microfinance revolution: its effects, innovations, and challenges', *Developing Economies*, 48(1): 15–73.
McNamara, N. and Morse, S. (1998) 'Donors and sustainability in the provision of financial services in Nigeria', *IDS Bulletin* 29(4): 91–101.
Meyer, R.L. (2002) 'The demand for flexible microfinance products: lessons from Bangladesh', *Journal of International Development*, 14(3): 361–8.
Microcredit Regulatory Authority (2009) *NGO-MFIs in Bangladesh*, vol. 5, June 2008. Dhaka, Bangladesh: Microcredit Regulatory Authority, Bangladesh Bank.
Microcredit Regulatory Authority (2010) 'Microfinance regulations in Bangladesh: development and experiences', paper presented at the conference 'Microfinance Regulations: Who Benefits?' Dhaka, Bangladesh,15–17 March.
Montgomery, R., Bhattacharya, D., and Hulme, D. (1996) 'Credit for the Poor in Bangladesh: the BRAC Rural Development Programme and the Government Thana Resource Development and Employment Programme' in D. Hulme and P. Mosley (eds) *Finance against Poverty*, vol. 2. London: Routledge, pp. 86–158.
Mosley, P. and Hulme, D. (1998) 'Microenterprise finance: Is there a conflict between growth and poverty alleviation?', *World Development* 26(5): 783–90.
Nayar, N. and Faisal, M.E.H. (1999) 'Microfinance Survives Bangladesh floods', *Economic and Political Weekly*, 3–9 April, 34(14): 801–3.
Palli Karma-Sahayak Foundation (1998) *PKSF – A Guideline*, Dhaka, Bangladesh: Palli Karma-Sahayak Foundation.
Pitt, M.M., Khandker, S.R., and Cartwright, J. (2006) 'Empowering women with micro finance: evidence from Bangladesh', Economic Development and Cultural Change 54(4): 791–831.
Popham, P. (1998) 'Financial consultant makes money work for Pakistani slum-dwellers', *The Independent*. 10 October 1998.
Reinke, J. (1998) 'Does solidarity pay? The case of the small enterprise foundation, South Africa', *Development and Change*, 29(3): 553–76.
Rhyne, E. and Otero, M. (1992) 'Financial Services for microenterprises: principles and institutions', *World Development*, 20(11): 1561–71.
Rutherford, S. (1998) 'The savings of the poor: improving financial services in Bangladesh', *Journal of International Development*, 10(1): 1–15.
Sen, K. and Morris, T. (2008) *Civil Society and the War on Terror*, Oxford: INTRAC.
Shoji, M. (2010) 'Does contingent repayment in microfinance help the poor during natural disasters?', *Journal of Development Studies*, 46(2): 191–210.
Takahashi, K., Higashikata, T., and Tsukada, K. (2010) 'The short-term poverty impact of small-scale, collateral-free microcredit in Indonesia: a matching estimator approach', *Developing Economies*, 48(1): 128–55.
Wright, G.A.N. (2000) *Microfinance Systems: designing quality financial services for the poor*, London: Zed.
Yaqub, S. (1998) 'Financial sector liberalization: should the poor applaud?', *IDS Bulletin* 29(4): 102–11.
Young, S. (2010) 'The "moral hazards" of microfinance: restructuring rural credit in India', *Antipode*, 42(1): 201–23.

11 Microcredit

A model for activating poverty zones in Mexico

David Eduardo de la Cerda Garza, Miriam del Rocío Arredondo Barrera, Morayma Lizbeth Martín González, and María de la Luz Bravo Santillán

The worldwide economic crisis has caused financial changes that have increasingly led countries to focus on providing improved opportunities for their impoverished inhabitants. The development of microfinance has been one important response to poverty and has helped millions of people around the world to mitigate their precarious situations by providing financial opportunities that improve the quality of their lives.

In Mexico, however, microcredit has had only a limited impact in relieving poverty. Epstein and Smith (2007) argue that one reason for this is that Mexican banks, such as Banco Azteca, have altered microfinance by extending microcredits as a profit-making venture rather than for its original purpose as a non-profit tool for social development that benefits excluded sectors of the population. This misapplication of the microcredit model averted public attention from the well-known proposition of the Nobel laureate Muhammad Yunus that credit should be granted as a human right based on individuals' potential.

Inspired by the principles of the founder of the Grameen Bank, in May 2009 the Centro para la Solidaridad y Filantropía (CESYF, Centre for Solidarity and Philanthropy) of the University of Monterrey set to create a microfinance model that could be applied in Mexico. The specific aim was to offer credit opportunities for people living in the two small communities of Tepozanes and El Refugio, located in the municipality of General Zaragoza in the state of Nuevo León. The project identified the main factors that have prevented and delayed the development of microcredit in Mexico: the social environment in the so-called 'polygons of poverty' (priority attention municipalities and micro-regions) and assistance programmes.

In order to understand local conditions, field research was carried out in Tepozanes and Refugio Nuevo León, two areas classified as 'polygons of poverty'. Subsequently, eight microfinance organizations were analysed in order to identify their strengths and weaknesses, so that a microfinance model could be elaborated that would offer value added, including a measurement of growth.

This project proposes an adjustable model that can help to improve the quality life of inhabitants in Mexico's polygons of poverty by granting microcredits.

In order to develop the project, the methodology of the Comisión Episcopal de Pastoral Social (2007), also known as the Medellin methodology, was utilized. This methodology consists of an integral process of reflection on reality in order to respond with concrete actions focused on transformations, and it is developed in three important steps to offer concrete solutions to society. The first is 'seeing', which means analysing those structures that cause injustice, inequality, extreme poverty, hunger, and war—that is, the anti-culture of death. The second is 'judging', which entails confronting the analysed reality by generating judgment criteria that foster work towards a more equal and fraternal society. The third is 'taking action', which implies the construction of alternatives that are put into practice in order to change society and translate these alternatives into concrete commitments.

Theoretical framework

According to Lacalle Calderón (2005), traditional banks often deny credit to the poorest, who do not meet the banks' guarantee requirements. For Global Envision (2006), this is why alternative credit and saving institutions, such as financial cooperatives and development institutions, have emerged to provide basic financial services to clients who had previously been rejected by conventional banks. Microfinance is understood as financial services for people with scarce earnings who are unable to satisfy the excessive collateral that mainstream banks require. Currently, microfinance promoters are focusing increasingly on offering broader financial services for the poor and integrating microfinances in the development of financial systems.

Without any doubt, one of the main advocates for microfinancing in granting microcredits is Grameen Bank, founded by Yunus in the 1980s. Grameen Bank is based on the idea that poverty was not created by the actions of the poor, but by the way in which society is structured and economic policies are applied. Thus, according to Yunus (1998), the microcredit idea is to help each individual to tap their full potential, and it is a tool that releases dreams and helps even the poorest to achieve dignity and respect.

As of October 2011, Grameen Bank had 8.3 million borrowers, 97 per cent of whom are women. With 2,565 branches, it provides services to 81,379 villages, covering more than 97 per cent of the total number of villages in Bangladesh (Grameen Bank 2011a). Grameen Bank has a surprisingly low ratio of non-performing loans: in 2010, it was a mere 3 per cent (Grameen Bank 2011b). The Grameen model has been adopted in many countries since the replication of the model has proved capable of improving the quality of life of millions of poor families around the world by providing them with access to affordable financial services.

In Mexico, most of the people who live in rural zones are peasants and indigenous people who, together with their families, strive to improve the development opportunities of rural communities. The acute socio-economic needs within these areas has led to the implementation of the 'polygons of poverty' approach, which responds to the necessity of establishing standard criteria to identify and delimit the existing areas where people with different levels and types of poverty are living, and overcoming the heterogeneity of the various criteria used by governmental agencies. The polygons of poverty present a degree of social and economic backwardness that justifies community development interventions through institutions and programmes to improve the quality of life and, mainly, eradicate poverty (Consejo Nacional de Evaluación de la Política de Desarrollo Social 2009).

In Mexico, several federal government and state organizations provide assistance programmes that focus on promoting the development of the countryside and poverty eradication. These programmes are an important factor in the performance of microcredits since they tend to provide support to those communities that need a stimulus to start a process of development. The Universidad de Monterrey has promoted programmes that support the development of unprotected communities by creating CESYF in 2003. The mission of CESYF is 'to provide the University Community with the opportunity to develop social awareness and accountability with the participation in programmes focused on individuals' dignification and social development, which achieves a feeling of transcendence in serving others' (Centro para la Solidaridad y Filantropía n.d.; authors' translation). CESYF implemented a programme of rural community development in Tepozanes and El Refugio, which were considered candidates for applying the microcredit model.

As part of the research for the development of the proposed model, a visit was carried out on 7 and 8 March 2009 to the two communities. Both are small communities with a few dozen families, where men either do agricultural work or else travel to the city of Monterrey to work in construction; women, on the other hand, face limited employment opportunities and strive with their meagre means to improve the quality of life within their communities. These families have an average of three to four children and the vast majority lives in houses made of wood or adobe. Community public services—such as public lighting, sewage, and drinking water—are available to all families, while most of them lack access to electric power. During this visit, it was also observed that the common lands of Tepozanes and El Refugio are very distant from the municipality, preventing easy access to these communities. Access to credit is very limited, since those families who need some kind of financing turn to the cajas de ahorro (savings banks) in General Zaragoza, where they get loans at a rate of 10 per cent per month. Moreover, if for any reason they cannot repay monthly, a penalty is imposed that makes the amount owed increase and become quite difficult to repay. Having acquired specific knowledge of the specific socio-economic characteristics, an adjusted version of the microcredit model was developed to respond to the poverty problem that these communities experience.

Comparison of microfinance models

Several microcredit institutions were analysed in order to identify the success factors and the elements that limit the performance of such initiatives in the development of rural communities.

Grameen Bank

The Grameen Bank was founded in 1983 in Jobra, Bangladesh, and focused on offering financing opportunities to low-income people to develop their micro-businesses (Yunus 1998). Grameen Bank receives contributions from several institutions such as the Ford Foundation, the Arthur Foundation, the South Shore Bank of Chicago, the International Fund for Agricultural Development, and various commercial banks in Bangladesh along with limited support from government funds.

According to Yunus (1998), the Grameen Bank trains its employees to understand the needs of their communities and insists on promoting the value of each person involved in its projects. Its employees are sent to each of the rural communities in the poorest counties in which the bank operates, enabling them to get to know and understand the local people. Focusing on the poorest people and mainly on women, employees form solidarity groups of five members who, as part of their loan contract, receive training on techniques of mutual support, money management, and self-employment. Each group's representatives attend annual conventions of the bank, where new ideas to encourage the use of microcredits are discussed. The solidarity groups, as well as bank employees, have established 16 resolutions focused on improving the quality of life for the members of Grameen Bank. In each community, the solidarity groups gather in a general assembly and decide to whom credit will be granted.

Individual loans without guarantees are granted from 1,000 to 2,000 Bangladeshi taka, with an annual interest rate of 20 per cent; each group retains 5 per cent of the amount granted for its emergency fund, while group saving is also encouraged on a weekly basis. The first loans are granted to two members of the solidarity group; once these are repaid, then loans are made to the next two members. The individual responsible for the group is the last beneficiary. Loans are made for small businesses that support weekly payments, but borrowers have one week of grace in cases when they have difficulty in making payments. Repayment starts one week after the loan is granted and instalments are fixed at 2 per cent of total loan.

Grameen de la Frontera

This organization was founded by Marshall Saunders in 1999 in Sonora, Mexico. Using the same methodology as Grameen Bank, its objective is to eradicate extreme poverty (BBC Mundo 2006). According to Grameen de la Frontera

(2009), the institution obtains funds from the Grameen Foundation and extends credit mainly to women in order to improve their living conditions. Loans of 1,000, 2,000, and 4,000 Mexican pesos are granted and must be repaid on a weekly basis within six months to a year, while the annual interest rate is 50 per cent.

Alternativa Solidaria Chiapas

This is a non-governmental organization located mainly in the city of San Cristóbal de las Casas, Chiapas, Mexico. Alternativa Solidaria Chiapas is guided by Grameen Bank's methodology and grants credit to solidarity groups (Micro-rate 2006). It obtains funds from various sources including the Gruma Foundation, Ford Foundation, Kiva (until 2009), Iberoamericana University, UNESCO, ProDesarrollo, the Grameen Foundation, and Global Impact (Alternativa Solidaria Chiapas 2009). Alternativa Solidaria Chiapas trains its employees who work in communities in Chiapas, and it operates based on solidarity groups of five people who get together weekly or bi-weekly. This institution offers financial services such as life insurance and microcredits. The loans range from 1,000 to 4,000 Mexican pesos and have to be repaid on a weekly or bi-weekly basis at annual interest rates ranging from 43 per cent to 63 per cent. Alternativa Solidaria Chiapas maintains strategic alliances to promote human rights, health, and gender equality and supports programmes against violence in the communities of Chiapas. The alliances support the non-financial services of the institution by establishing nutrition and literacy programmes.

Industrial Credit and Investment Corporation of India

This organization was established by Indian business executives and the government in 1994, with the objective of creating an organization that could support financial development for small businesses in the country (Prahalad 2005). The Industrial Credit and Investment Corporation of India is organized by a manager, a coordinator, and a promoter who supports the creation of solidarity groups. These groups are created by 20 women who gather monthly to analyse the needs in the community and receive training from the organization's members. Each group has a leader and two 'encouragers' who collect the equivalent of a US dollar from each member during monthly meetings. This money is used to open a savings account in the name of the group. After six months, this self-support fund becomes accessible to the members of the group who can use it for emergencies at an annual interest rate of 24 per cent. Any group member can apply for such a loan provided she has been saving with the group for at least 12 months. Group lending depends on the leader-manager's authorization and if approved consists of an equivalent of US$5,000 divided equally amongst members, thus resulting in US$250 a person. The repayment period lasts 43 months and each group member pays the equivalent of US$8 per month.

BancoSol

In 1984, Banco Solidario was founded in Bolivia by a group of business people who were exploring the possibility of creating a non-profit institution that would support micro-enterprises through working capital loans. Supported by Acción Internacional, this organization is located in eight cities (BancoSol n.d.). BancoSol receives funds for debt securities emission, as well as offering public shares. The employees at BancoSol receive training focused on selling financial services, including individual credit and solidarity credit. In the latter case, credit is granted to groups of three to 20 members for an amount ranging from the equivalent of US$4,000 to US$8,000, which is used for small business start-ups. The participants pay a rate of 22 per cent per year with repayment on a weekly, bi-weekly, or monthly basis.

Banco Compartamos

This organization was founded by José Ávalos in 1990 as the Program Generadora de Ingresos with the aim of helping micro-businesses to grow and contribute to the development of Mexico. In 2006, it was established as a full bank (Banco Compartamos n.d.). Supported by Acción Internacional, Banco Compartamos receives funds by issuing debt securities and offering public shares. Similar to BancoSol, employees in Compartamos are trained to sell financial services. Banco Compartamos offers individual and group credit ranging from 4,000 to 15,900 Mexican pesos. Group size ranges from three to 20 members, and they pay interest rates of 72 per cent per year on a weekly, bi-weekly, or monthly basis. A striking detail that sheds light on the extremely adverse conditions that define access to credit in this case study is that members must turn in an official ID and proof of their address in order to obtain credit. While this prerequisite may sound at least typical in the context of any developed part of the world, it should be kept in mind that in these segments of the Mexican population, a citizen's identity or even permanent residency cannot be taken for granted.

EnComùn de la Frontera

This organization was established by the Catholic Relief Services in 2001 and is currently located in Nogales, Sonora. The programme aims to address poverty and inequality problems of the country (Diocese of Ciudad Juárez 2009). EnComùn de la Frontera forms groups of ten to 25 people in local communities, through which it selects a board that runs the community bank. The community bank grants credit up to 2,000 Mexican pesos, charging interest rates from 42 to 45 per cent per year. The payment frequency is every 14 days in order to repay the loans within four months.

Foundation for International Community Assistance (FINCA) Mexico

This organization is a branch of FINCA located in Washington and was established by John Hatch in 1991. It follows the philosophy of Grameen Bank and develops its services according to people's needs (Microrate 2004; FINCA International n.d.). FINCA Mexico obtains international credit funds from Visa International, the Inter-American Development Bank, and HSBC Bank as well as national credit funds from the Programa Nacional de Financiamiento al Microempresario (PRONAFIM, National Programme for Financing Microbusinesses) and the Fideicomisos Instituidos en Relatión con la Agricultura (FIRA, Trust Funds for Rural Development). FINCA promotes a philosophy among its employees that focuses on training and motivation.

FINCA Mexico offers credit to groups of 20 women, each of which forms a directive board, and 80 per cent of the clients live in rural zones. The minimum loan is 20,000 Mexican pesos for each solidarity group, and the average loan per person is 2,700 Mexican pesos. An interest rate of 72 per cent rate is charged and weekly repayments are required.

After studying and analysing these eight microcredit institutions, 24 variables were identified and used to describe the policy that each institution follows; the results are presented in Table 11.1. These variables were then used to specify the proposed microfinance model.

Proposed model

After analysing the microfinance institutions together with CESYF, a flexible model was produced that is adaptable to the needs of each community according to its culture, habits, and key factors; see Figure 11.1.

The model has six factors: administration, education, and integration are located on the vertical dimension and agents, actions, and scope on the horizontal dimension. The administration factor refers to those elements related with the financial management of the model where the agent responsible is the civil association. The education factor covers training for employees and solidarity groups as well as the critical steps for the integration of all agents in the community gathering points under CESYF responsibility. The process of integration by the community lasts until a satisfactory result is achieved. The agents in the model are the civil associations, CESYF, and the community. Actions refer to the activities necessary to achieve the objectives for each agent. Scope shows the final actions that each agent must carry out for the sustainability of the model.

The civil association is in charge of managing all microcredit financial movements and processes and works with CESYF in the training and integration of the solidarity groups in the communities. CESYF serves as the intermediary between the community and the association and is in charge of motivating the community to conceive new ideas and projects for a better quality of life. CESYF knows these communities well since it has been working with them for

Table 11.1 Comparison of microfinance organizations

	Variable	*Banco Grameen*	*Grameen de la Frontera*	*Alternativa Solidaria Chiapas*	*Industrial Credit and Investment Corporation of India*	*Acción Internacional*		*EnComún de la Frontera*	*FINCA Mexico*
						BancoSol	*Banco Compartamos*		
1	**Legal Figure**	private entity social bank	civil association	civil association	limited public company	multiple banking institution, corporation	corporation, multiple banking institution	civil association	civil association
2	**Funds coming from foundations**	X	X	X				X	
3	**Funds from private capital**				X	X	X		
4	**Issuing shares**				X	X	X		
5	**Issuing debt securities**					X	X		
6	**Employee training (KSF)**	X		X	X	X	X		X
7	**Number of employees per community (KSF)**	2 employees		1 to 3 employees	1 to 3 employees				
8	**Creation of solidarity groups(KSF)**	X		X	X	solidarity groups and individuals	solidarity groups and individuals	X	X
9	**Gender of solidarity group (KSF)**	women		women	women	women/men	women/men	women/men	women
10	**Number of members of solidarity groups (KSF)**	5 people		3 to 7 people	20 people	3 to 20 people	3 to 20 people	10 to 25 people	20 people

continued

	Variable	*Banco Grameen*	*Grameen de la Frontera*	*Alternativa Solidaria Chiapas*	*Industrial Credit and Investment Corporation of India*	*Acción Internacional*		*EnComún de la Frontera*	*FINCA Mexico*
						BancoSol	*Banco Compartamos*		
11	**Representatives of solidarity groups**	2 representatives, 1 president, 1 secretary		1 leader	3 representatives, 1 leader, 2 'encouragers'			1 directive board, common bank	1 directive board
12	**Existence of self-funding among group members**	X			X				
13	**Gathering point (KSF)**	X		X	X				
14	**Type of guarantees (KSF)**	no guarantee	no guarantee	no guarantee 20% deposit	no guarantee	official identification and proof of funding	official identification and proof of address	no guarantee	taxpayer registry, proof of address and business
15	**Credits focused on small businesses**	X	X	X	X	X	X	X	X
16	**Savings promotion (KSF)**	X		X	X				
17	**Percentage of granted loans directed to self-funds**	5%			24%				
18	**Interest rate in solidarity credit**	20% annual	50% annual	43 to 63% annual	18% annual	22% annual		42 to 45% annual	72% annual

19	**Credit amount**	1,000 to 2,000 Bangladeshi taka	1,000 to 4,000 Mexican pesos	1,000 to 4,000 Mexican pesos	US$5,000 per group	US$4,000 to 8,000	4,000 to 15,900 Mexican pesos	2,200 Mexican pesos for each member	20,000 Mexican pesos per group
20	**Credit term**	6 months to 1 year	6 months to 1 year	1 year	3 years and 7 months	1 year or depending on the amount for credit	1 year or depending on the amount of credit	4 months	4 months
21	**Payment frequency (KSF)**	weekly	weekly	weekly and bi-weekly	monthly	weekly, bi-weekly, monthly	weekly, bi-weekly, monthly	14 days	weekly
22	**Offers non-financial services (KSF)**	X	X	X	X	X		X	
23	**Establishes resolutions for quality of life and dignity, amongst others (KSF)**	X	X	X					
24	**Training for self-support group (KSF)**	X	X		X				

Source: Created by the authors from sources indicated in the text.

Note
KSF = key success factors.

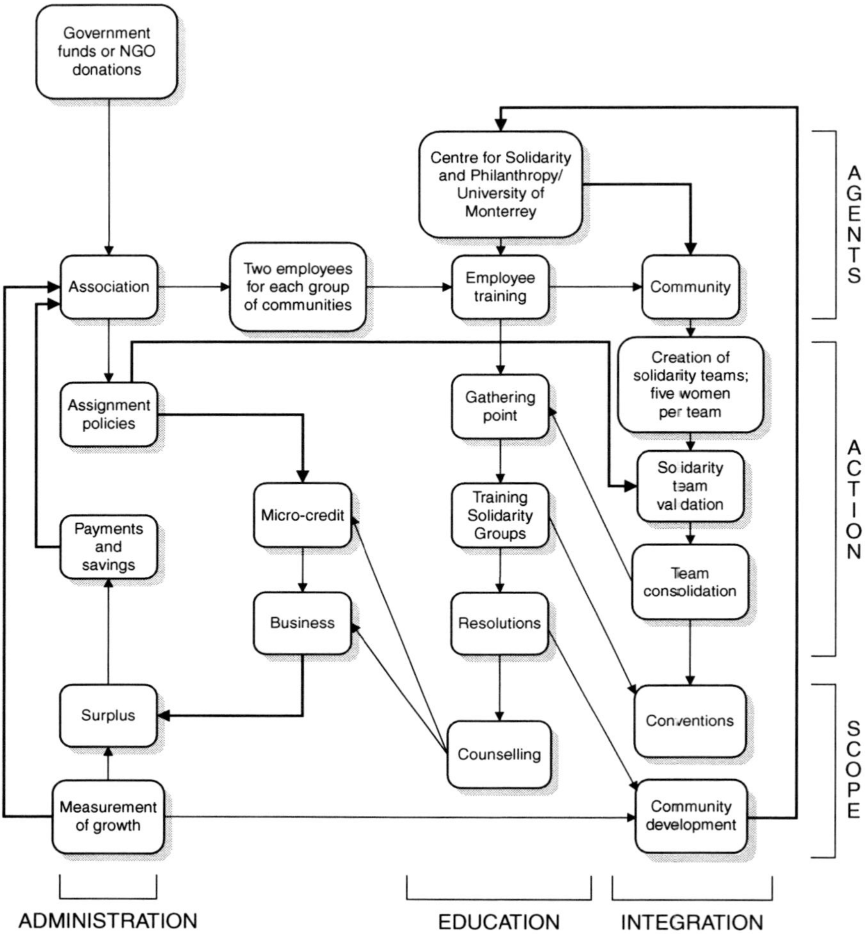

Figure 11.1 Model of sustainable microfinance (source: based on data compiled in Table 11.1).

five years, so it has created the necessary bonds to provide confidence in the model by the residents. The community is the potential user of microcredit to stimulate the economy, but in order to be eligible must satisfy several requirements. The model establishes interrelationships among the agents, so each function is essential for the functioning of the others.

The civil association requests and receives financial support from the government and/or donations from private institutions; these funds support the credit granted and cover operating expenses. The civil association is able to obtain resources from some institutions that support microfinance projects such as ProDesarrollo, Empresas y solidaridad, Global Impact, and the Ford Foundation.

The association designates two employees responsible for a defined small group of communities who work together with CESYF. These employees are trained for such immersion in communities, and this training is one of the factors leading to success since these institutions educate their personnel to be committed to the project and the community being served. After training, CESYF and the association's employees focus on the community to create solidarity groups with five women, who support and exert control over each other. The careful formation of these groups is considered a critical factor for the success of the associations, because if one member fails to make her repayments on time, the remaining members of the group will not have access to loans. The model hinges on women, because as noted in the theoretical framework and verified during the field study, women are most responsible for attaining a better quality of life for their families.

When these groups are formed, they must follow the procedures of the association in order to establish guidelines that enable improved performance and organization for their counselling when obtaining a credit. The procedures consist of establishing groups of five women of the community, attending the community meeting organized by CESYF, and having a minimum of one source of income in each household.

Once a group is formally established, it may receive training from employees in the gathering point in the community. Training is an important factor to educate the solidarity groups in certain cultural aspects that influence their quality of life. As our field visit found, rural communities harbour certain attitudes of complacency and passivity that affect their work. Moreover, in the visit carried out to the community of Tepozanes, a lack of trust was found among people towards banking institutions due to their negative experiences in the past.

As part of follow-up to this training, a series of annual conventions has been carried out to generate new ideas and improvements for the community. When obtaining the training, there have been resolutions by the solidarity groups for changes in the guidelines and policies that may lead to a better quality of life and development of the community.

Since resolutions are a key factor of success in the Grameen Bank, the proposed model establishes seven resolutions for group training:

1 Respect and apply the four principles based on the Grameen bank: discipline, togetherness, courage, and hard work.
2 Clean your house, maintain the environment, and improve existing infrastructure.
3 Participate in organized encounters.
4 Educate your children.
5 Do not commit injustices.
6 Carry out collective investments and be willing to help others.
7 Re-establish discipline in cases where this has lapsed.

These resolutions are based on the Grameen Bank model and the culture we studied in rural communities, where an important factor for achieving social mobility is education. Social solidarity in communities is the result of the support amongst the members in the community. After implementing the resolutions, the solidarity groups receive counselling about how to complete the application forms established by the association to obtain microcredit.

Considering the savings culture, rural communities have not been adequately served by conventional financial institutions since only 6 per cent of the rural population has access to bank accounts. Thus, the model suggested establishes microcredit without collateral since it is necessary to ease access to credit for poor people. There is a limit of 2,000 Mexican pesos for a six-month period that is granted to each member after the group has received training on how to manage small businesses and begun to save. Repayment is weekly at a 20 per cent biannual rate, so following the premises of microcredit, there is a weekly payment of 100 pesos. The model promotes savings as a success factor, so 5 per cent of the biannual payment goes to a mutual fund and 3 per cent to a savings fund.

At the same time, CESYF and the civil association provide counselling for the community in order for group members to manage the businesses supported by microcredit loans. As a new key factor within the model, the business should generate a surplus enabling the members of the group to both meet their payment obligations and improve the quality of their lives.

Another positive aspect of the model is that it establishes guidelines for measurement, where the performance of the model is assessed in terms of how it affects the economy. This function responds to the demand of the civil association to evaluate the performance of the model and generate continuous improvements that promote the local economy. Among quantitative factors evaluated, there is the surplus of each business financed by microcredit, while the qualitative measurement focuses on aspects of community development. This approach recognizes measurement of growth as necessary for evaluating the performance of the model as well as of the community supported.

Development is the final objective of the community, and a better quality of life is part of this objective. Improvements in infrastructure, nourishment, health, and education lead to the improved well-being expected by each member of the groups. These achievements support the measurement of growth and the project evaluation that CESYF uses with these communities.

As part of the proposed model of microfinance, it is necessary to have an organization or legal figure that is in charge of managing the funds and distributing loans to the target population. After having analysed the private and civil welfare associations active in the area, we concluded that this should be a civil association and not a private welfare organization.

Conclusions

This chapter has stressed that the lack of access by the poor to financial services and the high interest rates charged by commercial banks are some of the major causes of poverty in Mexico. The Mexican financial system has not been able to respond to the demand of the population that lives not only in the 'polygons of poverty', but also in many other areas of the country. Consequently, it is important to propose tools that facilitate the poor's access to financial services, so that they can satisfy their basic needs by creating micro-enterprises.

According to Article 5 of the Federal Law for Promotion of the Activities Carried Out by Organizations of Civil Society in Mexico, civil associations may define their social purpose as improving popular nourishment, promoting gender equality, supporting the defence and promotion of human rights, promoting sports, educational, cultural, artistic, and scientific activities, spreading economic activities, cooperating for community development, and supporting the development of indigenous communities.

In the context of this law, the Universidad de Monterrey, through CESYF, tries to build a society with equal opportunities through programmes that focus on communitarian development in the zones of Chihuahua, Coahuila, and Nuevo León. CESYF provides access to the communities of General Zaragoza, since it knows the needs of the people who live there. Having analysed the diverse approaches to microfinance, most models have been based on Grameen Bank, which was a pioneer in the use of microcredit. For this reason, our proposed model is also based on the Grameen model. With the aim of creating an adaptable tool for Mexico's culture and conditions, the proposed model of microfinance offers the poor residents of General Zaragoza opportunities to obtain loans to improve their lives by developing micro-enterprises.

The project has not only helped CESYF to develop and institutionalize microcredit solutions, but also created an important tool for improving conditions in the communities where poverty problems exist. This work has not yet finished, and the proposed model is an initial effort to make economic opportunities more broadly accessible, to eradicate poverty, and to improve the quality of life in Mexico.

References

Alternativa Solidaria Chiapas (2009) 'Alternativa Solidaria Chiapas'. Online. Available at: www.alsolchiapas.org (accessed 5 April 2009).

Banco Compartamos (n.d.) 'Crédito Mujer [Woman Credit]'. Online. Available at: www.compartamos.com/wps/portal/ProductosServicios/Credito/CreditoMujer (accessed 11 February 2011).

BancoSol (n.d.) 'Banco Sol: del microcrédito a las microfinanzas [Banco Sol: from microcredit to macrofinance]'. Online. Available at: www.bancosol.com.bo/archivos/otros/historiamicro.s.pdf (accessed 11 February 2009).

BBC Mundo (2006) 'El secreto es la garantía mutua [Mutual guarantee is the secret]'. Online. Available at: http://news.bbc.co.uk/hi/spanish/business/newsid_6129000/6129580.stm (accessed February 2009).

Catholic Relief Services (n.d.) 'Microfinance'. Online. Available at: http://crs.org/microfinance (accessed 10 February 2009).

Centro para la Solidaridad y Filantropía (n.d.) 'Centro para la Solidaridad y Filantropía [Centre for Solidarity and Philanthropy]'. Online. Available at: www.udem.edu.mx/exaudem_comunidadvirtual/acento/cesyf.html (accessed 10 February 2009).

Comisión Episcopal de Pastoral Social (2007) 'Doctrina Social de la Iglesia [Social Doctrine of the Church]'. Online. Available at: www.pastoralsocial-caritas.or.cr/noticias/comunicado5.htm (accessed 28 January 2009).

Consejo Nacional de Evaluación de la Política de Desarrollo Social (2009) 'Medición de la pobreza [Measurement of poverty]'. Online. Available at: www.coneval.gob.mx/cmsconeval/rw/pages/medicion/index.es.do;jsessionid=9c645ca434628c5c8b05331cfe28107db27fb8695bc645c0bcc28fede8ecfc6c.e34QaN4LaxeOa40Nbx10 (accessed 11 March 2009).

Diocese of Ciudad Juárez (n.d.) 'Catholic Relief Services'. Online. Available at: www.diocesisdeciudadjuarez.org/nota1.html (10 February 2009).

Epstein, K. and Smith, G. (2007) 'The ugly side of microlending: how big Mexican banks profit as many poor borrowers get trapped in a maze of debt', *Business Week*, 13 December. Online. Available at: www.businessweek.com/magazine/content/07_52/b4064038915009.htm (accessed 23 August 2011).

FINCA International (n.d.) 'Microfinance and Village Banking'. Online. Available at: www.villagebanking.org (accessed 11 February 2009).

Global Envision (2006) 'The history of microfinance', posted 14 April. Online. Available at: www.globalenvision.org/library/4/1051/ (accessed 23 August 2011).

Grameen Bank (2011a) 'Introduction'. Online. Available at: www.grameen-info.org/index.php?option=com_content&task=view&id=16&Itemid=112 (accessed 28 December 2011).

Grameen Bank (2011b) 'Grameen Bank: performance indicators and ratio analysis'. Online. Available at: www.grameen-info.org/index.php?option=com_content&task=view&id=632&Itemid=664 (accessed 28 December 2011).

Grameen de la Frontera (n.d.) 'Grameen de la Frontera: misión' [Grameen de la Frontera: a mission]'. Online. Available at: www.grameendelafrontera.org/EsHome.htm (accessed 5 April 2009).

Lacalle Calderón, M. (2005) *Microcréditos: de pobres a microempresarios* [Microcredits: from poor people to small entrepreneurs], Barcelona: Ariel.

Microrate (2004) 'Finca México: non-profit organization'. Online. Available at: www.mixmarket.org/sites/default/files/medialibrary/20501.285/FM_RARATI_1204_FINAL_ENGLISH.pdf (accessed 11 February 2009).

Microrate (2006) 'Alternativa Solidaria Chiapas, A.C. (ALSOL)'. Online. Available at: www.mixmarket.org/sites/default/files/medialibrary/20501.2709/ALSOL_Rating_06.pdf (accessed 11 February 2009).

Prahalad, C.K. (2005) *La oportunidad de negocios en la base de la pirámide: un modelo de negocio rentable, que sirve a las comunidades más pobres* [Business opportunities at the bottom of the pyramid: a profitable business model for the poorest communities], Bogotá: Grupo Editorial Norma.

Results (2006) 'Media call on microcredit and borders'. Online. Available at: www.results.org/website/article.asp?id=2458 (accessed 11 February 2009).

Yunus, M. (1998) *Hacia un mundo sin pobreza* [Toward a world without poverty], Barcelona: Editorial Andrés Bello.

Conclusions

A tale of two models

Yiorgos Alexopoulos and Silvio Goglio

> It was the best of times, it was the worst of times, it was the age of wisdom, it was the age of foolishness, it was the epoch of belief, it was the epoch of incredulity, it was the season of Light, it was the season of Darkness, it was the spring of hope, it was the winter of despair, we had everything before us, we had nothing before us...
>
> Charles Dickens, *A Tale of Two Cities* (1859)

It was the worst of times for cooperative banking

Much of the literature on financial cooperatives has argued that financial cooperatives seem to be 'appropriate technology' for relatively backward economies, and should become less important in the process of economic development as individuals' market opportunities expand. Accordingly, it should be expected that financial cooperatives would fade away or disappear altogether as economic development proceeds. The vast majority of researchers have focused on the performance of the model of cooperative banking that could not *decently* fit into any mainstream banking profitability assessment, let alone a more *complex* institutional or developmental evaluation that, if attempted, would probably be characterized as outdated and ideologically patronizing.

However, recent events have shown that cooperative banks have not faded away with economic development but rather, demonstrating their flexibility, been among the fastest growing groups of financial institutions in some developed countries. Their long history has proven that they are adaptable, innovative, and capable of redefining local potential. Moreover, researchers and authorities have increasingly explored whether the idiosyncrasies of the cooperative banking model can be exploited to rationalize and strengthen the banking market. The advocates of stakeholder models have started seeking evidence in financial cooperatives of a socially accountable and sustainable *modus operandi* in banking, focusing on features that were until recently lost in a *perfect market* logic.

It can be the best of times for cooperative banking

What has the current crisis actually changed? It has provided arguments against the dominant theory of perfect information and the capacities of self-regulating markets. The crisis has also provoked widespread rethinking about the potential contributions of credit in local development. Finally, it has highlighted the pressing need for local societies to work towards exerting control on the global and its self-organized governance.

This book has stressed that in the modern financial arena a chasm was developed between perceived and actual risks, with contradictory repercussions on critical economic variables. The dominant speculative short-sighted mentality of the trader has replaced the prudent far-sighted mentality of the banker, while the function of financial institutions as ephors of capitalism, as envisaged by Schumpeter, has been simply neglected and jeopardized. Along the same lines, we have suggested that the philosophy and performance of stakeholder-oriented banks needs to be further reassessed and compared to that of profit-maximizing banks. Thus, the focal point of this book has been on understanding the qualitatively different components of a model that has an operational character closer to the banker than the trader: in other words, a character resistant to short-term profit making and tenaciously loyal to long-term viable approaches that benefit banks, customers, and societies.

The analyses presented in this volume reveal that even before the outbreak of the crisis that forced a reassessment of the merits of different ownership structures, there was no convincing evidence supporting the claim that joint-stock ownership was superior to stakeholder-ownership in European banking. Therefore, the resilience of the stakeholder model stems from its competitive advantage, rather from alleged regulatory interference. It is tempting to suggest that the limited, sometimes blurred, research focus on cooperative banks did not actually stem from any confirmed inferiority of cooperative banking compared to conventional banking, but was rather based on two questionable assumptions: first, the pretentious superiority of the dominant model and a superficial vision of the consequences that a restricted diversity in the banking field would have on the economy and society; second, a scientific persistence in assessing the performance of cooperative banking on the basis of methods and criteria that were inappropriate to address the model's multiple dimensions. Hence, one of this book's central objectives has been to draw attention to the significant institutional and organizational features of credit cooperatives that call for a careful application of assessment and regulatory procedures. In order to provide a less idealistic and more pragmatic representation of institutions as complicated as financial cooperatives, it was necessary to employ tools, methods, and case studies that would shed light on the distinctive features of these cooperatives.

Since a critical issue for the financial and real world is the scarcity of capital, the volume focuses on the attributes of capital in cooperatives that require a sensitive treatment in order to avoid adverse consequences for their operation and development. It illustrates how capital in cooperative businesses differs from capital in investor-oriented businesses, both conceptually and in terms of behaviour, and considers the implications of 'the cooperative capital difference'. This approach has valuable implications for prudent public policy towards cooperative capital and is particularly interesting given the increasing pursuit of procedures that entailed hybridization and/or de-mutualization during the previous decade. Evaluating how different policies to attract capital have influenced cooperative institutions surpasses the operation of the intermediary itself and shapes the behaviour and needs of its members and society. Thus, while we have shown how cooperatives foster productive saving behaviours in low-income social strata throughout the world, as a further step we have illustrated innovative cooperative approaches that were employed in order to 'create' capital at the disposal of local societies. The value of these case studies is twofold: first they demonstrate that in order to understand the overall impact of cooperative banking, the analysis needs to be extended beyond the limits of the banking outlet and towards the members and customers that use this model to redefine their personal and local potential; second, they confirm that successful cooperative intermediation is actually located in the efficient dialectic procedure between the bank and its members. In essence, we stress that the critical parameters of a meaningful cooperative behaviour should be traced within the requirement to reconcile the financial and socio-economic needs of a given community and the growth strategies of the cooperative bank.

In placing these interactions under evaluation, we have visualized the cooperative banking network as the epicentre of an inclusive social network. Our argument is that reality goes beyond the limits of *homo oeconomicus* and calls for advanced approaches in order to overcome cultural and geographic barriers and promote a spirit of cooperation among local residents—in other words, to carry out the functions necessary to fill structural holes in the community and spread bridging social capital.

The historical and cultural variety of the cooperative banking model suggests that no simple or linear development path can be prescribed for all credit cooperatives since their development varies due to the influence of historical and contemporary economic and social conditions. Cooperative credit is a flexible mechanism, so its organization can and should evolve in conjunction with the development of the territory where it operates. Similarly, the institutional and legal framework should acknowledge different approaches to performing banking activities and not support the evolution of financial cooperatives solely for narrowly commercial and profit-oriented motives.

Nevertheless, the book has insistently argued that local societies support only sound institutions that make a difference to their everyday and long-term sustainability. For financial cooperatives, this support directly draws on

- their ability to apply with clarity an operational excellence at least on par with their competitors while the ability to innovate is considered pivotal;
- their need to preserve a sufficiently distinct and prudential banking behaviour that confirms the essential features of the model in the industry; and

- their capacity to express and communicate with clarity the differences of the cooperative financial institution and provide a consistent and sustainable development pact for the institution itself and the benefit of its membership and local society.

The new context brought on by the crisis and the restructuring of the financial sector certainly challenges financial cooperatives and requires deep reflection about their general and local strategies, their daily activities in relation to both members and customers, and their loyalty to their constitutive social principles. Thus, the key issue is whether cooperative banks possess the characteristics to reconfirm—if not reintroduce—and defend a new and efficient role in local banking markets, if they are to translate their constitutive features into a modern and competitive banking setting. In other words, given the necessary restructuring that these financial institutions must undergo to respond effectively to their local customers' needs, it should be asked how long they can continue to benefit from their locally competitive positions due to their lower information costs in screening and monitoring loans.

An epoch of belief, a season of light, and a spring of hope

While the steam engine of global growth is located in the emerging economies of the developing world, most of the developed world is stalled in an unstable development trend. The financing of local economies in the current circumstances is a critical parameter for sustaining a promising path out of recession and a necessary condition for defending and/or redefining the socio-economic opportunities of local societies. There seems to be a growing consensus that in most cases cooperative banks have outperformed their commercial rivals in channelling funds to local economies, but this trend needs to be confirmed and the contribution and actual performance of cooperative banks needs to be further examined.

This volume has argued that cooperative banks should stress the target of becoming/remaining true local banks; in that sense, we define local banks not only as proximity banks and/or relational banks, but also as financial institutions rooted in the territory, with intensive relationships with the territory, and able to support local economic activities inside a coherent strategy of development. For this purpose, the bank's decisional bodies must be 'in the territory', and have both a good local knowledge of the socio-economic reality in terms of its strengths, weaknesses, and possible developmental paths and privileged relationships with local economic actors. For example, while a *relational* bank might grant credit to small entrepreneurs based on long-term knowledge about repayment prospects, also with minimal financial collateral—i.e. on the basis of moral collateral—a *local* bank would also extend credit in more cases since it would understand the potential of investments specifically for the territory. In this sense, the local bank should be regarded also as an agent of social change and development.

In our opinion, the essential questions for research in cooperative banking are the following: Can cooperative finance, and stakeholder banks in general, perform a more incisive role than they currently do in encouraging and supporting local development? Can cooperative banks become true proactive agents of development? To do so, banks should not only perform the role of screening, monitoring, and enforcing credit on investments and entrepreneurs, developing the Schumpeterian channel, but they should go beyond that by sharing a vision and supporting a model of development of local areas and by activating structures that support other agents of development, using to this end part of their own profits. This approach opens up several questions about the relationship between banks and local authorities and about the level of representation by the population in cooperative banks and the local authorities.

In this regard, it is evident that public authorities, and more specifically the state, cannot represent all social interests, and even if they could this would probably be very costly in terms of monetary and social input and, eventually, efficiency. Thus, support of collective action is needed in order to succeed in finding a middle ground, especially in the field of public goods and values. The role of social capital is crucial in this process for facilitating the reconciliation of different interests toward the common goal of sustainable development. This role is best understood by considering that local systems produce indivisible services, mostly positive external economies, only if these are valorized by public or collective actions through appropriate governance. Social capital is catalytic in creating and evaluating these external economies, whereas when social capital and common values are weak, the production of negative externalities becomes more profitable for local actors, including banks—i.e. it is tempting to externalize part of production costs to local society and the environment. Therefore, in its function of selecting interests and instruments to satisfy them, the state must accept that new social agreements and contracts are subjected to experimentation among private, collective, and public actors. This experimentation can be implemented through new procedures and legitimating processes, or it can even be accomplished by recovering and updating traditional institutional arrangements. It should be underlined that this experimentation does not stem from the state structure or the market system, but rather from civil society or pre-existing grass-root initiatives.

This framework opens up ample opportunities for cooperative banks to translate and implement the constitutive principles of the cooperative movement in a dynamic current context; to demonstrate the strength of a third way of organizing economic activities that is different from, but complementary to, the market and the state; to experiment with new institutions and efficient organization that is consistent with grass-root initiatives and values; and to support competitiveness and quality of life within the territories and local societies. In conclusion, a cooperative bank's internal evaluation should focus not only on its capacity to make profits and surpluses, but also on the effects of its activity on the territory, reconciling business efficiency with regional efficiency. This also means that it is not sufficient to make loans to local entrepreneurs, even if it is considered risky under a strict banking credit scoring approach; it is also necessary to apply a qualitative analysis of the bank's loans and their impact on territorial efficiency and sustainable development. Finally, the focal point of financial cooperatives in local development remains profit, but long-term profit, or some other indicator of the social efficiency of meaningful financial intermediation.

Index

Page numbers in *italics* denote tables, those in **bold** denote figures.